THE MANUAL OF ASTROLOGY

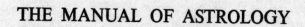

THE MANUAL OF ASTROLOGY

ASTROLOGY

IN FOUR BOOKS

TREATING OF THE LANGUAGE OF THE HEAVENS
THE READING OF A HOROSCOPE, THE
MEASURE OF TIME, AND OF
HINDU ASTROLOGY

INCLUDES THE INFLUENCE OF THE
PLANET PLUTO

BY

"SEPHARIAL"

WITH SET OF TABLES

THE STANDARD WORK

LONDON

W. FOULSHAM & CO. LTD.

NEW YORK · TORONTO · CAPE TOWN · SYDNEY

W. FOULSHAM & CO. LTD.,
Yeovil Road, Slough, Bucks., England

Carefully revised and republished 1962

572-00242-4

CONTENTS

BOOK I.—THE LANGUAGE OF THE HEAVENS

BOOK II.—THE READING OF A HOROSCOPE

BOOK III.—THE MEASURE OF TIME

BOOK IV.—HINDU ASTROLOGY

APPENDIX

SUPPLEMENT TO REVISED EDITION

PREFACE

In an experimental subject like Astrology there is always something fresh to be said, and much that needs to be told anew in the light of a more catholic experience than that enjoyed by astrological authors of the seventeenth and eighteenth centuries. The discovery of the planet Pluto in 1930 has enlarged the field of our researches, and much has been added to what is already known in regard to the nature and dominions of the planets.

The present exposition of the predictive art will find more favour with students of Astrology than with the lay reader, though, in the choice of a guide to the celestial science, the present Manual may recommend itself to the lay reader, as containing the fullest possible information under the several heads of our subject, and being, at the same time, devoid of those abstruse calculations and technicalities which have beclouded some of the most learned and brilliant expositions. The treatment of that portion of our subject which deals with prenatal influences, the intra-uterine period, and the law of sex, has the merit of originality, and truth. The section dealing with Hindu Astrology, after Parâshara, is properly dissociated from the body of the Manual by the difference of zodiacal measurement observed in the East, as well as by the interpretation of planetary influences in relation to the conditions of Oriental life; yet it is deemed of sufficient interest and merit to introduce in these pages. In effect, then, the characteristics of fullness and simplicity have been considered in the preparation of this work, and it is believed that the Manual will give the average student a better grip of the key to celestial science, and a wider view of the ground-plan of Astrology than has hitherto been afforded. The author desires to recognise to the fullest extent the merits of all former writers whose works have opened up and illustrated the subject of planetary influence to many thousands of intelligent minds, Lilly, Coley, Sibley, Ashmand, Simmonite, whose works have been consulted for the purpose of this Manual.

The law of life is a law of progress, and we, who from our temporal standpoint take note of the passage of events, can, if we will, see therein the working out of this law by means of the cyclic recurrence of those events in successive generations and ages.

The astronomer realises this in the return of the planets and comets in their orbits, and the succession of phenomena attaching thereto is found to be continually repeating itself, but always in relation to the experience of new and successive generations. Thus all humanity is taught the same lesson, and the same book is repeatedly studied by each succeeding age. The astronomer, by his science, is able to predict the return of the comets, the conjunctions, occultations, and other phenomena of the planets, together with the eclipses of the Sun and Moon, centuries in advance of their occurrence.

The astrologer, taking note of the cyclic repetition of events in conjunction with concurrent celestial phenomena, is enabled, by similar methods, to predict when such and such events, shall occur again. There is nothing supernatural in this when once we come to know the laws of planetary influence, the impressibility of Nature, and the power of man to read such impressions.

Perhaps the reader will think that in saying this we go too far without appeal to common experience, but as far as Astrology is concerned, we go no further than the reader himself can prove by an application of the rules contained in this Manual to his own life and that of others. It is not to be supposed that a scientific structure, such as Astrology purports to be, can have been in building through the ages upon the basis of a mere conceit of the imagination, or similar insecure foundation which could not stand the test of the plumb-line and level of science. On the contrary, we claim that the predictive art is set firmly in the immovable foundations of Nature, and that the whole plan and superstructure is but a presentation of certain well-defined laws operating in and from the archetypal world. Pythagoras held it as a truth that all things were formed after a type existing in the Universal Mind, and that all forms were but the expression of certain numbers or quantities existing in the soul of things. It is in the imperishable rock of numbers that the fadeless footprint of astral science was first set.

It is because of this mathematical basis in Astrology that the science is rendered so easy of proof, in contradistinction to many other less scientific modes of divination.

SEPHARIAL.

THE MANUAL OF ASTROLOGY

BOOK I

THE LANGUAGE OF THE HEAVENS

CHAPTER I

THE DIVISIONS OF THE ZODIAC

IN Astrology the Ecliptic, or Sun's annual path, is divided into twelve equal parts; and as the entire circle consists of 360°, each twelfth part will contain 30°. These twelve divisions are called Signs of the Zodiac. They are named and symbolised thus:—

Name	Symbol	Name	Symbol
1 Aries—Ram	♈	7 Libra—Balance	♎
2 Taurus—Bull	♉	8 Scorpio—Scorpion	♏
3 Gemini—Twins	♊	9 Sagittarius—Archer	♐
4 Cancer—Crab	♋	10 Capricornus—Goat	♑
5 Leo—Lion	♌	11 Aquarius—Waterman	♒
6 Virgo—Virgin	♍	12 Pisces—Fishes	♓

The Zodiac is a pictorial history of the evolution of the Universe, and a synthetic diagram of human progress through the ages. One cannot but pause to wonder and admire, when considering the wisdom of that man who first conceived the idea of writing this stupendous record of our race in the starry heavens. There the moth and dust of time had no advantage, nor could the busy hand of man reach there to mar the sacred records with excisions and interpolations. A star that originally belonged to the head of the Dragon would remain his vulnerable point for ever, until the time should come when the record was fulfilled, and the wounded heel should bruise the serpent's head. Kristna might change to Hercules and to St. George, and each of the great heroes who are depicted as closing with the dragon or the serpent in the struggle for life, would find his place in the history and mythology of the nations; but the stars would remain unchanged, and all the musings of the poet, the reasonings of the philosopher, and the calculations of the searcher of the skies would not avail to move one star from the bright mosaic of the Zodiac. So the record was set there, and so it has remained to this day. Therefore the zodiacal signs form the ground plan of Astrology, and the specific nature and power of each sign have to be thoroughly known before the modifying influence exerted by the several planets can be estimated with any degree of accuracy.

Astrology attributes to each sign a certain influence over the physical and mental constitution of man, and chief attention is given to that sign which is rising in the East at the moment of birth, such being termed the " ruling sign " of the horoscope.

The signs are subject to a certain classification, due to their observed *elemental* and *constitutional* natures.

THE ELEMENTS

The four " elements," as they are called, in use among astrologers are—1, Fire; 2, Air; 3, Water; 4, Earth. They correspond to the spirit, mind, soul, and body of man, and are symbolical of the spiritual, mental, psychic, and physical processes in him. The signs are thus distributed:—

△ *Fire*	+ *Earth*	= *Air*	▽ *Water*
1 Aries	2 Taurus	3 Gemini	4 Cancer
5 Leo	6 Virgo	7 Libra	8 Scorpio
9 Sagittary	10 Capricorn	11 Aquarius	12 Pisces

The practical significance of this division of the signs into elements will fully appear in subsequent chapters. Each group of three signs is called a " Triplicity."

THE CONSTITUTIONS

The signs have a *threefold* constitutional nature, and each sign is either volatile, fixed, or mutable. The " volatile " signs are active and forceful; the " fixed " are determined and masterful; while the " mutable " are passive and servile. These three constitutions of the signs may again be regarded as *acute*, *grave*, and *flexed*. Their symbols and the signs that correspond to them are here set out.

Movable or Acute ∧	*Fixed or Grave* ⊟	*Common or Flexed* ⌣
1 Aries	2 Taurus	3 Gemini
4 Cancer	5 Leo	6 Virgo
7 Libra	8 Scorpio	9 Sagittary
10 Capricorn	11 Aquarius	12 Pisces

Certain other classifications of the signs are in use among us, and necessary to be known. These are:

The Sex of the Signs.—Every odd sign, ♈, ♊, etc., is *masculine;* every even sign, ♉, ♋, etc., is *feminine.*

The *Human* Signs.—♊, ♍, ♒, and the last half of ♐, which are the only zodiacal signs depicted by human figures on the symbolic globe. The sign ♎ is also called " humane."

Bestial Signs.—♈, ♉, ♌, ♑, and the first half of ♐ ; symbolised by the figures of animals whose names they bear.

Violent Signs.—♈, ♊, ♏, ♑.

Double or *Bicorporeal* Signs.—♊, ♐, and ♓. ♐ is shown by a centaur, half man and half horse; ♊ by two children; and ♓ by two fishes bound together by a cord.

Cardinal Signs.—♈, ♋, ♎, ♑. Already named as " movable or acute," they are the angular points which mark the equinoxes and tropics—*i.e.,* ♈ and ♎ are equinoctial; ♋ and ♑, tropical.

The *Fruitful* Signs are—♉, ♋, ♏, ♐, and ♓; the *Sterile* Signs are—♈, ♊, ♌, and ♍: while ♎, ♑, and ♒ are indifferent in this respect.

The *Mute* Signs are—♋, ♏, and ♓.

The Signs of *Voice* are—♊, ♎, and ♒.

THE DECANATES

Each sign, consisting of 30°, is subdivided into three parts of 10° each, called " decanates " or " decans." These latter are symbolised by a series of figures, which are fully described in the *Brihat Jâtaka* of Varaha Mihira, written in the fifth century, and also in different form by Johannes Angelus, a sixteenth century writer, reprinted by " Raphael."

Each decan is ruled over by one of the planets, which confers upon its subject a certain character corresponding to the nature of the planet and the sign in which the decan is placed. The planets ruling the decans are given in the chapter on " The Relation of the Signs and the Planets."

Many other subdivisions are in use among the astrologers of the East, who subdivide the sign into tenths of a degree, making 300 parts to each sign. But as we have lost the signification of these minute subdivisions, they have no practical value, and are only mentioned here as affording a possible field of research to diligent students.

LUNAR MANSIONS

One subdivision, however, has been handed down to us from the Chaldeans, which has an important function in modern practice. It consists of a division of the cicle of the Zodiac into 28 equal parts of 12⁴⁄₇ degrees each. This 28th part is called a " Mansion " of the Moon, and is the space measured by the Moon in the Zodiac by her daily motion, inasmuch as she returns to any given degree of longitude on the 28th day of her course. A learned friend of the present writer, unacquainted with this ancient division of the Zodiac, suggested a new sevenfold division of the Ecliptic into seven arcs measuring 51³⁄₇ degrees each, and this he applied to the anomalies arising out of the law of the Lunar Epoch, published by the author in 1890. But it is found that this septile aspect or arc of 51³⁄₇ degrees, if measured from the four cardinal points, yields a series of 28 points, exactly corresponding to the above Lunar " Mansions." Thus, rejecting the fractions of degrees produced by this division, the points of the Zodiac, counted from Aries 0 degrees, are as follows:—
♈ 0, ♉ 21, ♋ 13, ♍ 4, ♎ 26, ♐ 17, ♒ 9. Those from Libra: ♎ 0, ♏ 21, ♑ 13, ♓ 4, ♈ 26, ♊ 17, ♌ 9. Those from Cancer: ♋ 0, ♌ 21, ♎ 13, ♐ 4, ♑ 26, ♓ 17, ♉ 9. Those from Capricorn: ♑ 0, ♒ 21, ♈ 13, ♊ 4, ♋ 26, ♍ 17, ♏ 9. If, therefore, we arrange these in the order of their natural sequence, we have the beginnings of the twenty-eight Lunar Mansions.

SIGNS					SENSITIVE OR CRITICAL DEGREES		
♈ ♋ ♎ ♑	..	..	0°	..	13°	..	26°
♉ ♌ ♏ ♒	..	..	9°	..	21°		
♊ ♍ ♐ ♓	..	..	4°	..	17°		

This table shows that the cardinal points, the 13th and 26th degrees of the *Cardinal* signs, the 9th and 21st of the *Fixed* signs, and the 4th and 17th of the *Common* signs, are " sensitive " points of the Zodiac. These degrees should be remembered, as they enter largely into a later portion of this work, and are employed in the correction of uncertain horoscopes, as well as in the prognostications drawn from the lunar motion.

CHAPTER II

THE SIGNATURES OF THE ZODIAC

ARIES.—The *physical peculiarities* of this sign are to be seen in the long neck, bony or angular face, broad temples, narrow chin, grey or greyish-brown eyes, and crisp or wiry hair, sometimes sandy, sometimes very dark. Generally a distinctive mark on the face, such as a scar or mole.

Mental qualities: Ambition, courage, impulse; desire for prominence; enterprise, ingenuity, audacity.

TAURUS.—*Physical marks:* Strong neck and shoulders, oftentimes a stoop; pensive brows, full lips and nostrils, curling or wavy hair, full forehead, dark eyes, heavy jaws.

Mental qualities: Amorous, passionate, determined; laborious, patient; proud, obstinate.

GEMINI.—*Physical qualities:* Tall, slender, elegant; long fingers, straight nose, generally long; wide forehead, long face; often fine expressive eyes.

Mental qualities: Artistic, learned, dexterous in the manual crafts, inventive; curious, subtle; eloquent in speech or writing; much occupied; humane.

CANCER.—*Physical marks:* Broad forehead, wide chest, rounded body; laborious walk, sometimes rolling or swaying; grey eyes, full face, fleshy body, with a tendency to pendulous cheeks and double chin in mature years. The figure is often top-heavy; the hands and feet are small.

Mental qualities: Changeful, roving disposition; ambitious, inclined to public life; prudent, sympathetic; imaginative and romantic.

LEO.—*Physical marks:* Strong, broad shoulders; upright walk, cheerful expression; fearless eyes, generally of a grey tint; wavy hair.

Mental qualities: Faithful, proud, fearless; ambitious, generous, artistic; opposed to cliques and secrecy; oblivious to enmity; rich in life and feeling.

VIRGO.—*Physical qualities:* Full forehead; hair generally swept back and falling about the ears, inclined to baldness on top of the head; grey or blue eyes, straight nose, wide shoulders, active walk, quiet voice.

Mental qualities: Learned, searching after knowledge, methodical; inclined to art and literature; benevolent; fond of the occult; disposed to collecting in some form or other; very critical and precise.

LIBRA.—*Physical marks:* Tall, elegant figure, gaining flesh towards the prime of life; blue eyes, fair skin, which becomes ruddy or

B

pimpled in mature years; brown and fine hair, good teeth and finger nails. Frequently the hair of a man ruled by this sign is parted in the middle or nearer the centre than the side of the head. The nose is long and straight, Grecian type.

Mental qualities: Genial, kind nature, happy disposition; fond of show and of approbation; just, persuasive, imitative; artistic, neat, and orderly; amorous but fickle.

SCORPIO.—*Physical marks:* Dark or dusky complexion; curling dark hair, sometimes crinkled or frizzy, and growing on the temples more thickly than is common; oftentimes some defects in the feet or lower parts of the body; aquiline features, the eagle showing plainly in the profile; prominent brows and sharp facial angles.

Mental qualities: Boldness, confidence in self; fond of contests and strifes, very daring when put to the touch; sarcastic, wilful, impulsive, and determined; of fixed views, subtle mind; not easily imposed upon, but sometimes capable of imposition; frequently a fondness for mystery, or some form of research, occult or chemical, shows itself.

SAGITTARY.—*Physical marks:* Tall, well-made figure, sometimes stooping, however; rather long face; fine, rounded forehead; grey or blue eyes, sometimes brown, but always fine and expressive; good complexion; frequently bald about the temples; fond of athletic exercises.

Mental qualities: Generous, good-tempered, just, frank, a firm friend; inclined to philosophy and religion; eclectic; not much inclined to exact science; fond of travelling.

CAPRICORN.—*Physical marks:* Prominent features; long nose, frequently bent inward at the point; firm lips; strong but narrow chin; thin neck; deficient in the lobes of the ears; dark, thin hair; small beard, if any; sometimes affected at the knees.

Mental qualities: Wilful, strong in purpose; very ambitious, desirous of government; reserved; capricious; quiet and reclusive, but forcible in action; changeful.

AQUARIUS.—*Physical marks:* Tall, full figure; fine, clear complexion, blue eyes, brown or flaxen hair, oval face; defects in teeth. This sign, next to Libra, produces the finest types of beauty.

Mental qualities: Kind, humane, retiring, patient; fond of literature and science; frequently a good singer or musician;

quiet, happy disposition; love for humanising influences, surroundings, and pursuits; very fond of a few people; excellent friends.

PISCES.—*Physical marks:* Short stature; fully-fleshed body, pale complexion, full but watery or weak-looking eyes; small hands and feet, short limbs; dark, sometimes black hair; generally stoop at the shoulders.

Mental qualities: Loquacious, gay, changeful, passionate; secretive in many things; difficult to know; generally disposed to a double life; quick in understanding; good judgment; versatile.

Note.—These descriptions are only given as guides to the detection of peculiarities conferred by the ruling sign, not as complete portraits of any one of them. They are beautified in a female geniture, and softened by the sex influence, and in all cases largely controlled by the prevailing planetary influence. The sign which rises at birth, together with that occupied by its ruling planet, contributes largely to determine the personal appearance.

THE ZODIAC AND THE HUMAN BODY

The signs of the Zodiac have dominion in the human body as follows:—

Aries	The head and face
Taurus .. .. —	Neck, throat, and ears
Gemini	Arms and shoulders
Cancer	Breasts and stomach
Leo	Back and heart
Virgo	Belly and uterus
Libra	Kidneys and loins
Scorpio	Sex organs and anus
Sagittary	Thighs and hips
Capricorn	The knees
Aquarius	Calves and ankles
Pisces	The feet.

The internal government of the signs is distributed thus:—

♈, ♋, ♎, ♑—Head, stomach, ovaries, reins, liver, and skin.

♉, ♌, ♏, ♒—Throat, heart, generative system, kidneys, and blood.

♊, ♍, ♐, ♓—Lungs, bowels, nervous system, and matrix.

Thus, should ♂ (Mars) be in ♊ (Gemini) at the time of birth, the native would be liable to inflammatory action in the lungs, and hurts to the arms. But as Gemini rules *both* arms and *both* lungs, the house in which Mars is found must be taken to determine which member is likely to be affected. The odd signs and houses correspond to the *left* side of the body, and the even to the *right* side, in a male horoscope. In a female horoscope, the reverse of this is the case.

CHAPTER III

THE PLANETS

ASTROLOGY considers the Sun and Moon as " planets " in respect to their functions when taken in relation to the Earth as a centre of action, inasmuch as, in regard to ourselves, they are agents of the sidereal influence, quite apart from their generic status in intracosmic life. Consequently, the geocentric positions of the plantes—*i.e.*, their longitudes in the Zodiac as seen from the Earth—are employed in all astrologic speculations and measurements.

The ten bodies which may be considered as agents of celestial influences are thus named and symbolised:—

Neptune	♆	Jupiter	♃	Venus	♀
Uranus	♅	Mars	♂	Mercury	☿
Saturn	♄	Sun	☉	Moon	☽
		Pluto	♇		

Other symbols are in use for the purpose of indicating certain points in the Zodiac or positions in the horoscope. Thus, the Moon's North, or Ascending Node, is denoted by ☊; its South, or Descending Node, by the same symbol reversed, ☋. These symbols are generally called the Dragon's Head (☊) and the Dragon's Tail (☋).

The *Part of Fortune*, a position we shall deal with later, is thus indicated ⊕. It is an old Egyptian hieroglyph for " land, property, or possession," and stands for the same in the astrologic art.

The planets are classified in the following manner:—

Major Planets—♇, ♆, ♅, ♄, ♃, ♂
Minor Planets— ♀, ☿, ☽
Masculine—♅, ♄, ♃, ♂, ☉
Feminine—♇, ♆, ♀, ☽

Note.—The planet Mercury (☿), in this respect, as in others, to be particularised in due course, is either *male* or *female*, according to the planet to which it is in closest aspect at the time of birth; or if no planet is in aspect at all, the sign Mercury occupies will determine its sex and influence. It is the peculiar function of Mercury among the spheres to reflect the nature and influence of the other planets, and for this reason we find it referred to in mythology as " the Winged Messenger of the Gods," and the " Interpreter," for it translates the language or influence of the planets into terms of human thought and feeling upon this earth.

The *Benefics* are ♃, ♀, ☉, ☽, and ☊ according to tradition.

The *Malefics* are ♇, ♆, ♅, ♄, ♂, and ☋ according to tradition.

The *positive* or *electric* planets are ♃, ♂, ☉.

The *negative* or *magnetic* planets are ♄, ♀, ☽, ♆, ♇.

Uranus is of both natures, combining in itself the magnetic and electric influences, and thus produces cataclysmic and sudden effects.

The electric planets produce heat and expansion in the body of the earth and man, and conduce to a positive, forceful, and confident state of mind corresponding to this warmth and expansion of the physical functions.

The magnetic planets render the mind and body negative and timorous, susceptible to external influences, and thus to a variety of affections.

Mercury and Uranus have a variable nature according to their position and relations in the horoscope.

Planetary Temperament

The *Specific Natures* of the different planets are as follows:—

Pluto is changeful according to mood and desire. Forceful, hard, selfish and destructive yet can also express initiative, self-sacrifice, willing to take risks in service of others.

Neptune is nervous, susceptible, æsthetic, neurotic, inconstant, warm, moist, and fruitful.

Uranus is variable, spasmodic, impulsive, eccentric, cold, and barren.

Saturn is nervous, secretive, defensive, binding, constant, cold, dry, hard, and barren.

Jupiter is generous, expansive, genial, temperate, vital, moderately hot, moist, and fruitful.

Mars is electric, forceful, active, inflammatory, hot, dry and barren.

Sun is electric, fearless, strong, vital, fiery, inflammatory, sanguine, hot, dry, and rather fruitful.

Venus is gentle, pacific, graceful, temperate, passive, warm, moist, and fruitful.

Mercury is active, excitable, changeful, nervous, cold, moist, and moderately fruitful.

Moon is lymphatic, changeful, plastic, wandering, romantic, magnetic, cold, moist, and fruitful.

Planetary Flavours

Pluto rules extremes.   It can give the odour of the skunk and the perfume of the lily.

Mars rules over hot acids, pungent odours, and burning astringents.

Sun is sweet and pungent.

Saturn is cold, astringent, and sour.

Venus: sweet and warm.

Moon: insipid and odourless.

Jupiter: sweet and fragrant.

Neptune: sweet, subtile, and seductive.

Mercury: mildly astringent and cold.

Uranus: cold, astringent, and brackish.

Planetary Forms

Pluto gives squarish type of features and body, but pliable with capacity for contortion.

Saturn gives hard, clear-cut outlines, straight short lines, and cramped forms.

Jupiter gives full, generous curves.

Mars: sharp angles and barbs, and pointed, fine, straight lines.

Sun: regular circles, full curves, and helical scrolls.

Venus: curved lines and rhythmic scrolls.

Mercury: short incisive lines and slender curves.

Moon: irregular curves and crooked lines.

Uranus: broken lines and mixed forms.

Neptune: rhythmic curves and curved lines, nebulous and chaotic forms.

Planetary Colours

Pluto: Smoky cloud formation susceptible to sudden change to almost any colour according to circumstance.

Neptune: mauve or lavender.

Uranus: streaked and mixed colours.

Saturn: black, dark brown, and indigo.

Jupiter: purple, violet, mixtures of red and indigo.

Mars: scarlet, red, and carmine.
Sun: yellow-brown, orange, gold, and the deeper shades of yellow.
Venus: lemon yellow and pale blue, " art tints " in general.
Mercury: slate colour, spotted mixtures.
Moon: white, opal, pearl, green, and iridescent silvery hues.

Planetary Notes

The Notes of the Gamut corresponding to the several planets are as follows:—

$$\hbar = D, \quad \text{♃} = B, \quad \text{♂} = G, \quad \odot = C, \quad \text{♀} = A, \quad \text{☿} = E, \quad \text{☽} = F.$$

It is curiously significant that ♆ and ♅ do not contribute to that " music of the spheres " which delighted the mind of the great Pythagoras, while at the same time their axial rotations are contrary to the order observed by the other planetary bodies, being from east to west.

♇ too does not conform to the musical scale but is associated with a form of sound which can be likened to the boom of distant thunder.

Note.—The late Mr. Mark Knights, who met his death by asphyxiation, on the 20th March, 1897, has traced a reference to five of these planetary notes in Shakespeare's *Taming of the Shrew*, folio edition, 1623.

Planetary Metals

Pluto governs plutonium.

Neptune	„	geranium and strontium.
Uranus	„	uranium.
Saturn	„	lead.
Jupiter	„	tin.
Mars	„	iron.
Sun	„	gold.
Venus	„	copper.
Mercury	„	quicksilver.
Moon	„	silver.

The atomic weights of the different metals ruled over by the planets bear a curious relationship to the order of the planets and the days of the week.   Thus—

♂ rules iron ..	..	..	..	..	atomic weight	56
♀ „ copper	..	..	..	..	„	63
☽ „ silver	..	..	..	..	„	108
♃ „ tin ..	..	..	..	..	„	118
⊙ „ gold ..	..	..	..	..	„	196
☿ „ mercury	..	..	..	..	„	200
♄ „ lead	..	..	..	..	„	207

If these be arranged around a circle, and united by a seven-pointed star, it will be seen (1) that every alternate planet around the circle falls in the order of the days of the week, if counted from right to left: ♄ Saturday, ☉ Sunday, ☽ Monday, ♂ Tuesday, ☿ Wednesday, ♃ Thursday, ♀ Friday; (2) that the seven-pointed star runs from one to another planet in the order of the Chaldean planetary system: ♄, ♃, ♂, ☉, ♀, ☿, ☽. This cannot be the result of either "chance" or "imagination," since the Chaldeans did not make the atomic weights of the metals, though they named the planets as their rulers.

Planetary Parts in the Human Body

Pluto governs that part of the head where the "opening" in a child is situated, together with the umbilical cord and the nerve centres that connect the solar plexus with the sacral plexus and the top of the spinal column with the pineal gland.

Neptune governs the telepathic and psychometric functions, the psycho-physical processes which induce to intuitive perception, etc.

Uranus governs the magnetic and physical aura, and the nerve fluids.

Saturn rules over bones and articulations, liver, spleen, left ear, the calves and knees; the secretive system generally.

Jupiter rules the thighs, hams, and feet, the right ear, and absorptive system.

Mars governs the forehead, nose, sex organ, gall, kidneys, muscles, and sinews; the muscular system generally.

The *Sun* rules over the heart, back, vital principle, the left eye in males and the right eye in females; the arterial system generally.

Venus governs the throat, eustachian tubes, aural ducts, reins, ovaries, chin, and cheeks; it governs the internal generative system, as Mars does the external; the veins generally.

Mercury governs the nerves, brain, bowels, lungs, hands, arms, tongue, and the mouth; the nervous system generally.

The *Moon* rules over the breast and stomach, the right eye in males and the left eye in females, the fluidic system, saliva, lymph, etc., and the glandular processes generally.

Planetary Occupations

Pluto rules nuclear scientists, aeronauts, and spacemen generally, TV engineers and technicians, weather forecasters, archaeologists, all those who work in underground and subterranean spheres.

Neptune denotes æsthetic, artistic, and inspirational pursuits. It has much influence in the expression of artistic and literary genius, and is astrologically responsible for many forms of the higher psychic and spiritual powers exhibited by phenomenal persons. At the same time it is associated with the " watery triplicity," and governs occupations in which the watery element is predominant.

Uranus—Lecturers, public functionaries, government or civic officials, travellers, engineers, inventors, patentees, and all who follow uncommon pursuits, such as astrologers, electricians, mesmerists, phrenologists, spirit mediums, metaphysicians, and psychologists; also those who deal in electrical apparatus, scientific mechanism, etc.

Saturn—Land and property dealers, miners, coal merchants, dealers in lead and other Saturnine commodities, plumbers, jailers, sextons, grave-diggers, undertakers, watchmen, etc.; such as follow laborious employments, and those that work at night or underground.

Jupiter—Senators, judges, councillors, divines, clergymen, physicians, lawyers, bankers, collegians, clothiers, especially woollen merchants, and provision dealers generally.

Mars—Soldiers, surgeons, chemists, gunners, workers in iron and steel, dentists, butchers, smiths, barbers, cooks, and workers who use sharp instruments, iron and steel, or fire.

The *Sun*—Persons in authority, courtiers, noblemen, kings, princes, emperors, and those who hold titled offices under the Crown; also jewellers, goldsmiths, gilders, and those who work with gold.

Venus—Musicians, painters, singers, poets, actors, artists of all kinds; makers of toilet accessories, and those who deal in scents, flowers, and articles of ornament; silk mercers, embroiderers, makers of gloves, bonnets, and women's apparel, linen-drapers, clothiers, fancy dealers, etc.; also pastry-cooks, sweetmakers, confectioners, maid-servants, and butlers.

Mercury—Literary men, writers, accountants, schoolmasters, preceptors, interpreters, secretaries, registrars, orators, messengers, printers, booksellers, clerks, postmen, carriers, etc.

The *Moon*—Sailors, travellers, fishermen, those who manage public conveyances, dealers in fluids, public salesmen, nurses, mid-wives, water-carriers, female officials, etc.

Planets as Significators

A planet is called the " Significator " of a person when holding the ascendant or other important position in the horoscope. The general signification of a planet may be applied to the person under its influence. In a general sense the Sun and Moon are called " Significators," but every planet is such in a particular sense, as our studies will show. Thus, when chief significator,

Pluto indicates an experiencing of extremes of good and bad. It will give the inspiration aiding the arresting of failing conditions of both a private and business nature, the turning of what seem to be lost causes into successful projects.

On the other hand there will be times in the life when objectives will seem to recede just when the point of realisation appears imminent, plans will be frustrated and brought to nought.

Neptune denotes many changes; uncertain fortunes; rise or fall by the influence of women; artistic faculty; secrets in the life; intrigues and covert alliances.

It renders the native, or person born under its influence, æsthetic, artistic, intuitive, unstable, sensitive, mystical, imita-tive, highly emotional, self-deceptive, and enthusiastic.

Uranus gives constructive and mechanical ability, sudden changes, estrangements, sorrows, exiles, enmities, uncertain fortunes, and blind impulses.

It makes its subject erratic, eccentric, impulsive, ingenious, and inventive, firm in opinion, critical, sarcastic, self-centred, romantic, heroic, and in many ways peculiar.

Saturn gives delays, impediments, defects, secrets, fatalities, falls from position, misfortunes, melancholy moods, chronic hurts, sorrows, disease, and hurts to women and children.

It makes the native independent, unhappy, secretive, cautious, jealous, miserly, and governed by habit.

Jupiter confers fortune, happiness, plenty, success, honours, friends, protection, supremacy, and productiveness.

It renders the subject jovial, generous, prudent, courtly, ambitious, sympathetic, and humane.

Mars gives enmities, strifes, wounds by fire and steel, treasons, calumnies, thefts, sudden deaths, glory in battle, burnings and poisonings, enthusiasm and madness, sharp pains and fevers.

It makes the native fearless, brave, easy to anger, demonstrative, impulsive, cynical, expert, witty, independent, given to reforms, and often to destructions.

Sun gives honours, glory, elevation, high patronage, celebrity, public offices, health, and power.

It renders its subjects honest, free, generous, noble, desirous of glory, clever in the arts, judicious, truthful, and of wise counsel.

Venus gives love affairs, attachments, amours, marriage, joy, pleasures, gaiety, favours of women, success, and wealth.

It makes the native gentle, cultured, hopeful, bright, pleasant in manner, loving, poetical, and inclined to sensuous and mental beauty, the fine arts, etc.

Mercury gives relations in family and commerce, industries, journeys, letters, messages, anxieties, worries, many occupations and mental activity.

It inclines to writing and oratory, to the study of science, intellectual conquests; makes the native wary, subtle, talkative, busy, and restless.

Moon gives changes, voyages, travelling, affections of the body according to the sign it is in, mysteries, romances, fancies, popularity, public life.

It makes the subject inconstant, capricious, fanciful, unsettled; capable of securing public honours, but in danger of reversals.

The Relations of Signs and Planets

By empirical art it has been determined that certain signs are ruled by certain planets, and the Ancients have delivered to us a full statement of the dominion of the planets in this respect. The planets Saturn, Jupiter, Mars, Venus, and Mercury have each two houses or signs, over which they rule; the Sun and Moon having one each, as shown in the following diagram. Saturn rules Aquarius and Capricorn, Jupiter rules Pisces and Sagittarius, and so with the rest.

Note.—A planet in the opposite sign to the one it rules is said to be in its detriment or " debility." It is then weak, and disposed to evil.

Houses of Planets

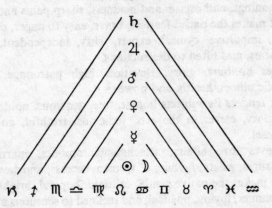

The dominion of Uranus is indefinite, for he has no house of his own, though he is most successfully placed when in the *airy triplicity* —♊, ♎, ♒. In this sense he is the "prodigal son." In mythology he ruled all the spheres, and was the father of Kronos (Saturn). It is worthy of comment that his period of eighty-four years is the product of the number of the signs multiplied by the seven planets over which he rules, *i.e.*, 12 × 7 = 84.

Neptune has affinity with the watery triplicity—♋, ♏, and ♓. It has also some association with the sign Sagittarius. It represents the ocean of space, and is analogous to the *Varuna* of the Hindus.

It has been suggested that both Uranus and Neptune are the spiritual correspondents, or counterparts, of Mercury and Venus— *i.e.*, so far as their influence in human affairs is concerned. This is quite in accord with astrological experience, and may be the reason that Uranus produces eccentrics in the intellectual world, and Neptune eccentrics in the artistic world. They probably are in touch with elements of thought and feeling that are wholly inconceivable to the more mundane types of Venus and Mercury.

Pluto is also a planet having no fixed rulership over any sign but as with Uranus and Neptune it has a spiritual affinity with Mars, for whilst Mars is the planet of war and of partial and spasmodic destruction, Pluto is the planet of annihilation. It has an association with the signs Aries and Scorpio and its influence is very much in accord with the deeper occult and spiritual significance of Scorpio.

Planetary Dignities

Certain signs are found to be in affinity with the natures of the various planets, and when a planet is found in such a sign it is said to be in its " exaltation," and is found to be stronger for good, and less disposed to evil than when otherwise placed. Thus—

Saturn is exalted in ♎
Jupiter   ,,   ,,   ♋
Mars   ,,   ,,   ♑
Sun   ,,   ,,   ♈
Venus   ,,   ,,   ♓
Mercury   ,,   ,,   ♒
Moon   ,,   ,,   ♉

Note.—When the planets are found to occupy the opposite signs to these, they are said to be in their " fall."

The foregoing tables of Houses and Exaltations will show the planets have their friendships and enmities, as follows:—

♄ is opposed to ☉ and ☽
♃   ,,   ,,   ☿
♀   ,,   ,,   ♂

and it will be seen that the signs ruled by these are severally opposed to each other. Similarly, those planets whose houses and exaltations are in the same sign, are friendly. Thus—

♄ is the friend of ♀, being exalted in its sign ♎
♃   ,,   ,,   ☽,   ,,   ,,   ♋
♂   ,,   ,,   ♄,   ,,   ,,   ♑
♀   ,,   ,,   ♃,   ,,   ,,   ♓
☿   ,,   ,,   ♄,   ,,   ,,   ♒

Planetary Dominions

The dominion held by the planets over the affairs of life is due to their correspondence to certain principles of the human constitution, governed by the signs of the Zodiac. Thus—

Pluto rules both the negation and the transforming of conditions. It brings extremes of good and bad luck. A voluntary relinquishing of worldly interests in order to advance spiritual development. A giving up of home, country and fortune to be with one's marital affinity.

Neptune rules ambushes, deceptions, the secrets of the life, sudden death, assassinations, wanderings, exiles, secret societies, impositions, frauds, and disguises.

Uranus rules catastrophes, sudden events, changes, bereavements, suicides, romances, tragedies, and public affairs.

Saturn governs the father, disease, chronic affections, hindrances, falls and bruises, poverty, friendships, long ties, habits, darkness, and decay.

Jupiter governs religion, duties, legal affairs, the clergy, good fortune, the father's relatives, godfathers, guardians, long journeys, devotion, increase, and wealth.

Mars governs fires, fevers, madness, quarrels, ambitions, prowess, energy, adventures, poison, hurts by violence, passions, death, male relations.

Sun rules over honour, fame, occupation, the king or ruler, nobles, advancement, father, constitution of the body, etc.

Venus has dominion over money, adornments, jewels, coins, learning, marriage, pleasures, the arts, and female relations.

Mercury governs the mind, memory, acquaintances, letters, writings, mother's relations, sickness, servants, food, clothing, and journeys by land.

Moon governs the mother, the home, place of residence, voyages, changes, females, marriage affairs, health, worldly condition, native place, the ocean, and the common people.

Note.—In general, the above may be taken as the things signified and ruled by the several planets. But in each case the houses ruled by these planets in the horoscope will determine their particular signification as regards any individual.

CHAPTER IV

THE RELATION OF DECANATES AND PLANETS

EACH sign of the Zodiac is divided into three equal parts of ten degrees each, so that there are thirty-six parts in the entire Zodiac. These divisions are called Decanates. Each of them is ruled over by one of the planets. The thirty-six decans and their rulers are here set forth, together with their general influence on the native when they are on the eastern horizon at birth.

Aries

1st decan, ruled by *Mars*. It confers a warlike and aggressive spirit, a taste for political and public work; disposes to injuries in the head and face; gives success through pioneer work or military service, and renders the life changeful and remarkable in many ways.

2nd decan, ruled by *Sun*. A proud and haughty nature, desiring to bear rule; ambitious and aspiring; loving the practical arts; extravagant and generous nature; impulsive, critical, despising mean or underhand actions; free, but courteous in manner; gives success in governmental positions and military life, and secures the favour of men.

3rd decan, ruled by *Venus*. Gives strong passions, love of pleasures; bright and sparkling nature, love of art and poetry; renders the nature kind and loving, but very impulsive and over-ardent. The decan is not a very fortunate one, but it confers a generous, warm disposition which attracts friends.

Taurus

1st decan, ruled by *Mercury*. It gives a highly-endowed mind, poetical and creative fancy, amiable disposition, steadfast affections, intuitive faculty, fondness for the artistic and beautiful in form and colour; a sensuous love of life, desire for comfort, ease, and luxury, but capable of sustained efforts of a mental nature. It gives success in drama, music, fine arts, and secures the patronage of women.

2nd decan, ruled by *Moon*. This decan gives a changeful and romantic disposition, strong imagination, fine feelings, love of pleasure, fondness for dainty foods and good living generally; it confers the favour of women of position, and renders the native successful in travelling; disposes to artistic and poetical pursuits. It conduces to wealth and the acquisition of property.

3rd decan, ruled by *Saturn*. Dependence and servitude, poverty or extreme difficulty in the attainment of wealth are the fruits of this decan. It renders the nature sensitive and languishing; leads to disappointment in love affairs; overthrows the ambitions, and destroys the pleasures of domestic and married life. It produces enemies, and renders the life generally very unfortunate. It gives, however, much depth of feeling and fidelity in attachments.

Gemini

1st decan, ruled by *Jupiter*. Confers a humane and generous disposition, but unfortunate. Makes a man his own enemy; gives too much self-confidence, and leads to self-hurt. The subject of this decan becomes his own enemy in many ways. He is capable of rising by his own merits. The mind is generous and the intellect strong, but the judgment is perverted, and misfortunes through enemies are less to be feared than through the wrong use of one's own faculties. It gives oratorical powers and taste for judicial and legal pursuits, as well as for literature; but it is not a fortunate decan.

2nd decan, ruled by *Mars*. This decan gives a quarrelsome and violent nature, predisposed to acts of ingratitude and wantonness. The life is filled with useless strife and unprofitable discussion, and the interests are apt to be misplaced, and the faculties, which are very acute, misapplied. It gives hurts and dangers in travelling; confers favours from martial persons, and gives sickness and fevers through acts of indiscretion.

3rd decan, ruled by *Sun*. It confers success in the study of literature and science; gives brillance of intellect, fame, but small fortune; many journeys; helpful relations; an anxious, restless life, but eventual success in literary or artistic pursuits.

Cancer

1st decan, ruled by *Venus*. A sociable and amiable disposition, generous character, kind and attractive nature; many friends; supporters among women of position; good social standing, and success in the artistic world. A fondness for pleasure and for personal decoration mark this decan of Cancer.

2nd decan, ruled by *Mercury*. Gives a strong imaginative intellect; makes a clever writer, a lover of travel and learning; renders the native loquacious and sometimes a tattler, and confers wealth or fame by the use of the pen, but the native makes enemies by too free use of the tongue.

3rd decan, ruled by *Moon*. Love of romance, travelling, adventure, and mystical subjects. Gives public recognition and a certain popularity, honourable or otherwise, according to the position of the Moon at birth; gives many sea voyages and constant changes in life, patronage of women, and acquisition of property.

Leo

1st decan, ruled by *Saturn*. Gives a strong, forcible nature, difficult to control; poverty and trouble in life; domestic infelicity, loss of children; hazardous speculations; lack of sympathy in the nature; austere character, spoiled by false pride. Self-imposition and deception will mar the life. The native is distrustful of others, and lacking in self-confidence also, but is apt to assert his independence at inopportune moments. Much sickness, and a wasting of the vital powers; a careful, watchful nature, seldom achieving any great work, but always laborious.

2nd decan, ruled by *Jupiter*. A fortunate and profitable nature; kind, humane disposition; warm sympathies; fortunate speculations; dutiful family; plenty of *confiance-en-soi;* artistic faculty; inclination to form rather than colour; gain by legacy, and success through marriage.

3rd decan, ruled by *Mars*. Strong, forcible nature, capable of, and desiring command; frank, open, and generous disposition; many journeys; success in foreign countries; inheritance and acquisition of property at the close of life; adventurous spirit, inclined to exploits and hazardous feats. The native bears rule with a high hand, and is successful over his enemies.

Virgo

1st decan, ruled by *Sun*. A patient nature, likely to suffer affliction and privation, and sometimes restraint or imprisonment; it confers a long life, and disposes to the study of analytical and mechanical science, theoretical and practical. The nature is secretive, and the subject of this decan often lives a very retired life.

2nd decan, ruled by *Venus*. An artistic and literary person is denoted, with a love for philosophy and *belles-lettres;* kind disposition, genial and vivacious nature, full of pleasant allusions and bright dialogue; fortunate in the acquisition of property and artistic pursuits. Long voyages are shown; much familiarity with the stage or the artistic world; some falling-off of family fortunes, and an inclination to domestic disputes.

3rd decan, ruled by *Mercury*. The nature is quick and alert, apt in the sciences and dexterous arts; inclined to literature; loquacious and restless; a person of much business, and very versatile disposition; gains honours and position by his own merits, and acquires property; disposed to the study of medicine and hygiene; very particular in the matters of diet and clothing; many changes of residence.

Libra

1st decan, ruled by *Moon*. A genial but weak nature, easily influenced by women, and disposed to extravagance and unsteady habits; clever in general business matters, frequently changing his pursuits or position; a changeful and restless mind, halting between two courses; gains honour and position by public business, and has a chance of acquiring some property in land or houses.

2nd decan, ruled by *Saturn*. Griefs and troubles are shown, but success in the end of life. The native falls and rises in life from his own fault or merit. Fondness for the home life and steadfastness in the affections are characteristics of this decan. In most cases the native is poor, and has some trouble in the marriage state.

3rd decan, ruled by *Jupiter*. A generous, kind, and amiable nature; well-balanced and fruitful mind; happy marriage and much wealth; many journeys; faithful friend and generous enemy. The native is beloved for his justice and probity.

Scorpio

1st decan, ruled by *Mars*. The nature is a strong, forceful, energetic one, capable of immense feats of prowess, of endurance and courage. In strife, the native is implacable and dauntless, scorning defeat and danger of reversal. The ambitions are high; the spirit of conquest strong; the will is not less exalted and powerful. Strange and impulsive love affairs, sickness, caused through indiscretion or excess, are the fruits of this decan; but the native has faithful servants, and is born, in most cases, to command.

2nd decan, ruled by *Sun*. Honours and dignities await the native of this decan. It is replete with masterful and governing qualities. Proud and haughty of spirit, the native bears high rule, and may become tyrannical. The nature is capable of extreme cruelty, unless a strong guiding hand is over it when young. Fame, or a less honourable reputation, is sure to fall to the native of this decan.

3rd decan, ruled by *Venus*. The nature is prone to excess and folly in love affairs. The passions need to be bridled. Many enemies arise against the native, and secret enmity from females may be expected. In marriage there will be trouble. The passions are quick and volatile, and the nature is capable of great passional devotion, which, however, is liable to bring disastrous results.

Sagittarius

1st decan, ruled by *Mercury*. This decan gives much versatility and capacity for general work. More particularly it gives a good judgment, a sober mind, a quick intellect; but powers running into profusion and disorder through richness of intellect and lack of method. Troubles and bickerings in marital life may be looked for; many enemies and many conquests. The native rises in life through the exercise of his faculties, and favours the more humane studies, natural science and philosophy.

2nd decan, ruled by *Moon*. This decan confers much romance and strong imaginative faculty, love of travelling and life in foreign lands. Not infrequently it conduces to high renown, and gives wealth and good fortune. Death in a foreign land is to be feared, and in some way the native is responsible for his own demise. Inheritance or legacy falls to the native. The patronage of ladies in high life may assist in forwarding the fortunes. A certain restless activity of mind, together with a rich creative power, characterises the subject of this decan.

3rd decan, ruled by *Saturn*. The mind is of a philosophical and sober temperament; the passions are strong, but well controlled. Riches are difficult to acquire, but are yet certain to the native of this decan. Philosophical and literary pursuits, a taste for lofty speculations and deep researches, preferably of a scientific nature, are the chief characteristics of those under this decan. Success in literature is promised to those born under it. Friendships are few, but very steadfast.

Capricorn

1st decan, ruled by *Jupiter*. The mind is masterful and ambitious, but often beset with doubts. The sympathies are narrow, and the native is usually a strong sectarian, or disposed to religious austerities, and at times to self-immolation. Sometimes a fatalist, or yet a believer in the occult, the native is ever fearful of his destiny, yet nevertheless carried onward by a prevailing self-confidence and high ambition. Relatives assist, and again obstruct, the progress of the native. Some secret evil mars the life and threatens the fame of a fair destiny. The decan gives very strong religious feeling, capable of arousing a high and worthy ideal.

2nd decan, ruled by *Mars*. The acme of forceful self-assertion, of intense ambition, and of red-hot enthusiasm is reached in this decan of Capricorn. The native may easily achieve high military honours, but is always in danger of overstepping the limits of prudence, and suffering a speedy downfall. Yet friends are numerous and powerful, and favours fall in full measure to the native. The nature is capable of extreme energy, and may become cruel and despotic unless tempered by prevailing influences of a softer and more humane nature. There are many and constant rivals who threaten the fame and position of the native. With moderation and proper feeling, the native will secure very high honours and a wide fame. The keynote of the decan is conquest, and again conquest.

3rd decan, ruled by *Sun*. The disposition is proud, cold, reserved, and austere, wanting in sympathy and grace. The native suffers through his children, and also runs risk of financial ruin by speculations. The spirit is melancholy, and disposed to look gloomily upon life's problems. Not infrequently there is danger of premature death. The struggle of life will be hard, because the nature is too self-centred, and devoid of the wider sympathies.

Aquarius

1st decan, ruled by *Venus*. Bright, cheerful, artistic, and humane in disposition, the native of this decan gathers friends around him. He excels in the lighter sciences and the fine arts, and especially in decorative art and industrial science. He figures in reunions and social gatherings. He is sober and placid in temperament, devoid of unruly passion or excess. He has success in foreign lands, and also in the pursuit of science and literature. He gains property, and has a taste for construction. His life is marked by an even and temperate course.

2nd decan, ruled by *Mercury*. The mind is bent on scientific and philosophical pursuits. Great depth of thought and extreme patience are characteristics of this person. Inventive faculty applied to medicine and hygiene is productive of success. Mathematical science, astronomy, and occult research are indicated; independent spirit, penetrating mind, power of assimilation. A lover of solitude and of learned society. Fortune by science or art. Slow but sure success. The native enjoys a fair name and good reputation.

3rd decan, ruled by *Moon*. A melancholy individual, disposed to solitude and nocturnal life. Changeful in fancy; inclined to the lugubrious, to strange terrors and weird experiences, visions, and hallucinations. Women are likely to cause evil in the life. The native wanders from place to place. Danger of feeble or afflicted vision; long voyages; peculiar and fantastic appetites.

Pisces

1st decan, ruled by *Saturn*. Loss of position; false friends; many secret enemies; morbid enthusiasm and corrupt sympathies; religious spirit, inclining to fanaticism; trouble through love affairs and children; danger of drowning; quarrels and disputes with powerful enemies; early death or affliction of a parent.

2nd decan, ruled by *Jupiter*. High position and much success; two marriages, or inconstancy in the marriage state; eminent friends; certain elevation and honours; a kind, warm disposition and genial nature, very sympathetic, but lacking in constancy. The inherent merits of the native will raise him to a good position, and will confer wealth by good fortune.

3rd decan, ruled by *Mars*. Loss by strifes and enmities, and by unknown and secret means; success in foreign lands, but a menace of danger; troubles in the marriage state; separation from wife and children; female influence strong, but detrimental; danger of severe reversals, but assistance from friends in high position. At times timid, and anon very audacious, the native is not reliable, and will lose many an opportunity of advancement. A certain religious or fanatical enthusiasm inspires the mind from time to time, but it is not constant, and falls short of end. Passionate nature, infected with an utter disregard of the consequences of action. Fanciful projects make a plaything of the native, and lead him from one to another disappointment.

Note.—These readings of the decanates are frequently useful in determining the part of a sign under which a person is born, thus considerably reducing the limits of error in the construction of a horoscope. The characteristics, and also the points of probable destiny, referred to under each *decan*, are capable of considerable modification when the planetary influences so dispose. The decans designate a type of person, whereas the disposition of the planets bring out the individual characteristics and destiny. Thus Nature continually refines and specialises, from sign to decanate, from decanate to degree. The planets Pluto, Neptune and Uranus do not exercise specific rule over any of the decanates as they do not come within the normal septenary scale, but allowing for the octave expression of each planet, Pluto will accentuate the vibration of Mars in the first decan of Aries and the first decan of Scorpio, Neptune will enhance the vibration of Venus in the first decan of Cancer and the second decan of Virgo, while Uranus strengthens the vibration of Mercury in the first decan of Taurus and the second decan of Aquarius.

CHAPTER V

THE HOUSES

THERE are twelve celestial " Houses " in Astrology. They are derived from an equal division of the circle of observation into twelve parts. What is this circle of observation? It is an imaginary line passing from the eastern horizon, through the point immediately overhead, through the western horizon, the point immediately beneath our feet, round to the eastern horizon again. In astronomy it is the " vertical of latitude " belonging to the place of birth. This circle is called a vertical because it is always vertical to the circle of horizon. One twelfth part of the circle of observation constitutes an astrological " House." The following diagram shows how the houses are numbered.

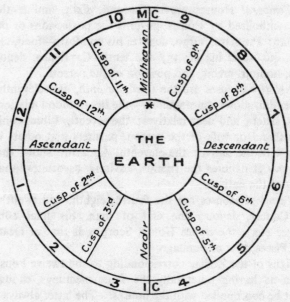

SCHEME OF HOUSES

The star on the Earth shows the place of birth. Above it is the mid-heaven, the line joining them being the cusp or edge of the tenth House. The Nadir is beneath, the Ascendant on the left, the Descendant on the right of the figure. The outside circle is the circle of latitude. The first House is that immediately beneath the eastern horizon. From this house the others are counted in the order shown in the figure. The cusp of each house precedes the space of the house. When a planet occupies a position within five degrees of the beginning of a house, it is taken as being *in* that house, as its influence is actually there. Thus, if Saturn (♄) were bodily in the third House, but within five degrees of the cusp of the fourth, it would be read as *in* the fourth House.

All the affairs of life are distributed among the twelve houses. For purposes of classification the following division has been introduced by the author.

Houses are either *Individual, Temporal, Relative,* or *Terminal.*

The *Individual* Houses are the first, fifth, and ninth, and relate to the body, soul, and spirit of man. The first House, corresponding to Aries, governs the body; the fifth House, symbolised by Leo, governs the soul; the ninth, corresponding to Sagittarius, relates to the spirit.

The *Temporal* Houses are the second, sixth, and tenth. The second, symbolised by Taurus, governs the possessions or property of the man; the sixth, Virgo, denotes his comforts—food, clothing, servants, etc.—and his health; the tenth, Capricorn, denotes the business, honour, credit, and position of the person.

The *Relative* Houses are the third, seventh, and eleventh. The third, Gemini, shows consanguinity—the ties of blood relationship— brothers, sisters, and near relatives; the seventh, Libra, conjugality —the husband or wife of the person, partners and others in legal contract with the native; the eleventh, Aquarius, shows the tie of friendship. It denotes the friends, advisers, associates, and social relations of the native.

The *Terminal* Houses are the fourth, eighth, and twelfth. The fourth, Cancer, denotes the end of man, his final condition, the grave, etc.; the eighth House, Scorpio, is that of Death; the twelfth, Pisces, that of bondage.

The signs of the Zodiac corresponding to the twelve houses may be taken as having potentially the same meanings, though they must not be confounded with the houses. The latter always remain in the same position, and hold the same meanings. The signs, on the contrary, are continually moving through the houses by their diurnal rising and setting, and hence the same sign will be successively in the twelfth, eleventh, tenth, and the other houses, till it comes to rise again in the first house.

The following significations are attached to the several houses. It is absolutely necessary, for the practice of Astrology, that they should be completely mastered:—

The First House denotes the body of the native, his physical
    condition and appearance.

Second House—Money; possessions of value; trade; gain or loss.

Third House—Letters, papers, writings, journeys by land or short
    water journeys; all means of communication, vehicles, railways,
    etc.; brothers and sisters, near relations, neighbours.

Fourth House—The residence, the place of birth; houses, landed
    property, grounds, mines, places under the earth, the grave;
    the mother in a man's horoscope, the father in a woman's
    horoscope; the mother-in-law in a man's horoscope, and the
    father-in-law in a woman's.

Fifth House—Pleasures, love affairs, sex ties outside wedlock; child-
    ren, theatres, schools and educational influences; places of amuse-

ment, bathing, the bedroom, and all sensuous enjoyments.

Sixth House—Health, servants, food, clothing, physical comforts, persons employed, small animals and domestic creatures, climatic and other conditions bearing on health; the father's brothers and sisters in a female horoscope; the mother's brothers and sisters in a male horoscope.

Seventh House—The husband in a female horoscope, the wife in a male horoscope; partners, contracts, agreements; persons opposed to the native in contests, litigation, etc.; open enemies, rivals; the grandparent—according to sex of horoscope (vide Fourth House).

Eighth House—Death, dissolution, losses; the wife's or husband's wealth and possessions; the partner's property; legacies, bequests; the property of the dead; wills.

Ninth House—Religion and philosophy; publications; voyages; foreign countries; long distances from the birthplace; dreams, spiritual occurrences; lawsuits, lawyers; the clergy, church affairs; legal arbitrations, money in chancery; marriage relatives.

Tenth House—The occupation, credit, honour and rank; the father or mother—according to sex of horoscope; the employer, superior, master; business affairs generally, and the government of the country.

Eleventh House—Friends, councillors, companions, associates; society in which the person will move; wishes and hopes; financial affairs of employers and those in command over the native.

Twelfth House—Confinement, restraint, prison, bondage, exile; secret enemies, ambushes, and plots; large animals, horses, etc.; the mother's relatives in a female horoscope, and the father's relatives in a male horoscope.

These are the chief significations of each of the houses. If it should be asked whether a person would have any voyages, then the ninth house would be referred to as governing the subject in question, and the sign and planets occupying that house, or ruling it, would determine whether voyages were likely, and whether they would be good or bad for the person to whom the horoscope refers.

The *Cardinal* Houses are called " *the Angles.*" They are the first, fourth, tenth, and seventh. The second, fifth, eighth, and eleventh are *Succedent* Houses. The third, sixth, ninth, and twelfth are *Cadent* Houses.

The *Angular* Houses are the strongest in the figure, and of these the first and tenth are the more important. Planets placed therein are said to have dignity, and they exert a powerful influence over the life and character of the native.

The *Cadent* Houses are the weakest, and many planets therein considerably lessen the force and mastery of the horoscope, so that not infrequently the native sinks into obscurity, even though it may be that of retired luxury. Forceful and epoch-making horoscopes have the majority of planets in cardinal signs and angular houses.

CHAPTER VI

THE PLANETS AND HOUSES

WHERE a planet occupies a certain house at the time of birth, it stamps its own nature on the affairs of life governed by that house, as detailed in the previous chapter. It is essential to notice whether a planet is in aspect to others or not, whether it is in a congenial sign or the reverse, and what dignities and debilities it may receive therefrom; for these considerations will determine what effect will result from the presence of that planet in any particular house.

The following results will follow from the position of the planets in the several houses, in either a male or female horoscope, providing always that the planets are unaspected. For an explanation of the aspects the reader is referred to the next chapter.

In the First House

Pluto—Will give a unique outlook upon life with an expressing of the principle " I am a law unto myself." A sense of domination will be felt and the potentialities of action, for good or ill will be immense. The capacity to rise in life will be marked and this can be brought about by the expressing of the power of attraction from the good standpoint or by ruthless action which liquidates competitors or opponents from the adverse standpoint.

Neptune—Gives inconstancy, taste for maritime life, a wandering disposition; it endangers the life by plots and enmities, and causes the native to be fearful. It often causes a wasting disease, and a visionary mind.

Uranus—Makes the native erratic, wayward, stubborn. Danger of falls, and hurts by machinery to the head and that part of the body ruled by the sign occupied by Uranus. It causes estrangement from the parents and kindred.

Saturn—Melancholy mind, solitary habits; shy, nervous manners; subjects the native to colds; causes bruises to the head; an uphill struggle; patient disposition.

Jupiter—Good health, fortunate nature, generous disposition, love of justice and equity. It increases the chances of success in life, and brings the efforts of the native to successful issues.

Mars—Causes a mark or scar on the head or face; gives danger of cuts, burns, scalds, and abrasions. Makes the native bold, free and independent, fond of competition and strife, haughty, scorning defeat, and reckless of danger.

Sun—Gives honour and success. A proud disposition; frank, outspoken, generous; despising cliques and coteries; independent and firm. It also gives a love of display and publicity, accompanied by high motives.

Venus—Amiable and docile nature; fondness for poetry, music, singing, dancing, the drama, and fine arts, with every kind of sparkle and glitter. Jewels, scents, and personal ornamentations are favoured by the native of Venus. It confers a sociable spirit, much inclined to brilliant company, pageants, and festivities; and generally conduces to domestic and social success.

Mercury—A restless spirit, given to ceaseless inquiry and concern. Many journeys, much writing; quick, nervous speech; taste for literature of some sort; an inquisitive mind, always on the alert for new information.

Moon—Inconstancy, timidity, changefulness, publicity; liability to many changes of residence and reversals of fortune; if in a movable sign, constant changes in life and a roving disposition; tendency to sleep-walking at some time in life; fruitful imagination; sensitive and intuitive nature.

In the Second House

Pluto—Money will be a focal point in the life. There will be a passionate desire to have money and the power of concentration and magnetic attraction will be used to draw money to the person either through contact with people who have plenty of

money or through contact with financial activities which give
scope for the extraction of personal financial benefit from them.
It can however show a danger of fluctuations and unexpected
losses which occur just when financial hopes and wishes seem
about to be realised.

Neptune—Loss by fraud; financial affairs much involved.

Uranus—Sudden changes in fortune; many ups and downs in life;
financial affairs very uncertain.

Saturn—Business losses; a thrifty nature; hard work for little gain;
sometimes poverty.

Jupiter—The best position for wealth; increase of property; gain
and general prosperity.

Mars—Good earning powers, but extravagant nature. Money runs
quickly through the hands, and the native seldom continues
rich for any length of time.

Sun—Gain by superiors and association with persons of rank and
title. The native is inclined to extravagance and luxury.
Gains by high offices and affairs of government.

Venus—Money comes readily, and is frequently gained by artistic
pursuits or the drama. In a man's horoscope, it denotes that
much is spent on pleasure and the opposite sex; and in a
woman's horoscope, that a good deal goes in dress and finery.
But in spite of everything, money is always ready at hand.

Mercury—Gain by letters and writings, by help of clericals and
professionals, and by common industries. There will, however,
be some chance of loss by theft or sharp practice.

Moon—Changeful fortunes. Gain or loss by females, more particularly married women, and public affairs. The native gains by
travelling in foreign lands, and by fulfilling some public function.

In the Third House

Pluto—Creates a condition of "War in the mind," and shows a
fighting mental tendency with much ingenuity, penetration and
forcefulness in the expressing of views and opinions. Very
good for studies to do with atomic interests and nuclear science
and for play and scenario writing. In personal relationships
and where near relatives are concerned it can have a banishing
influence in that relatives and neighbours move far away and
are lost touch with or the person themselves moves away and
loses contact.

Neptune—Occult sympathies; change of name by deed or *alias;* psychological faculties; curious beliefs; inventive mind, fruitful imagination; dangerous journeys, and imposition or fraud among relatives; power of astral projection, or spiritual vision; high intuitive perceptions.

Uranus—Wayward mind, curious and inventive; estrangement from kindred; troubles in letters, and short journeys; many telegrams; eccentric method of travelling; unpopular ideas, which, if published, only incur severe and adverse criticism.

Saturn—Troubles and losses through journeys and writings; the native does not agree with his relatives; letters are delayed and lost; publications fail; the native's health is endangered by wet journeys and exposure in travelling; the mind is melancholy and unfertile.

Jupiter—Gain by all those things governed by the third house.

Mars—Quarrels and losses through letter-writing; litigation; disputes with relatives; accidents on short journeys.

Sun—Possible fame by writings. Some honours fall to the relatives of the native. The name becomes famous in good or ill association.

Venus—Strong inclination to the fine arts; pleasant travelling; success in letters and writings; peaceful relations among the members of the family; amiable disposition, and bright, fruitful intellect. Poetry, music, singing, and painting are among the pursuits of those under this influence.

Mercury—Much activity; many short journeys; much writing; a busy mind, given to the pursuit of various knowledges, especially literature and science.

Moon—Constant journeys; publicity of some sort; many changes of pursuit and occupation; curious and capricious fancies; unstable mind.

In the Fourth House

Pluto—Often signifies condition of orphanage or shows a destruction of early home life through the parents parting or dying. Many peculiar incidents will occur in connection with domestic arrangements causing loss and strain. It is not a good influence for matters to do with property showing a danger of distraint for debt or a loss of the property through the ruthless methods of other people. There will be loneliness at the end of life.

Neptune—Afflicts the parent involved; threatens danger to the native by plots in his own house; losses through deceitful landlords, and by dealing in property. The native ends his life in seclusion and frequently in an asylum.

Uranus—Unsettled residence, many changes of house; misfortune in the place of birth; trouble through the parents; danger of paralysis or other incurable infirmity in old age; a sudden end to life.

Saturn—Losses and troubles in all matters connected with the fourth house. The native is frequently tied down to a place to his great detriment.

Jupiter—Gain by inheritance, and through all matters of the fourth house; favours from the parents; much success in the place and country of birth.

Mars—Loss by fire and theft at the house of residence; quarrels with parents; loss by speculation in property, buildings, mines, etc.

Sun—Small chance of honours or dignities till the very end of life; attachment to the father (or mother); pride in house and property; inclined to secrecy and occult things.

Venus—Gain and prosperity in all fourth house affairs; a peaceful end to the life; love of home and country.

Mercury—Inconstancy in affairs generally; change of residence through matters connected with business. The native seldom has a fixed residence, but is " here to-day and gone to-morrow."

Moon—Uncertainty of position; some chance of inheritance; changes of residence are frequent; some popularity at the end of life; favours from women.

In the Fifth House

Pluto—Signifies possibilities of abortion or the incitement thereto if it falls in a male horoscope. In a female horoscope it brings a liability to rape or to attack by a sex maniac if badly afflicted. From a constructive standpoint shows capacity for invention, gives creative ability in art, is very good for theatrical acting. Is however very problematical regarding speculation and investment for although it can bring extraordinary benefits it can also wipe out fortunes through terrestrial, industrial or national calamity.

Neptune—Illicit amours; absorbing love of pleasures of a sensuous nature. Unless other indications modify this position, the native will be disposed to chaotic and unnatural acts; will have depraved desires, fantastic appetites, and licentious habits. In either sex it is a dangerous position, and leads to trouble in love affairs and all the evils of erotic mania, seduction, etc.

Uranus—Troubles in domestic life; loss of first child; inconstancy in love affairs; crosses and annoyances in youth; some romantic and impulsive attachments; danger in the pursuit of pleasure.

Saturn—Disappointment in early love affairs; grief; loss of a child; losses through speculations and games of chance; danger of heart affections and drowning.

Jupiter—Good, successful, and dutiful children; gain by speculations; well-regulated appetites and pleasures; chance of a rich inheritance.

Mars—Quarrels and strife in the home-life; rash and impetuous love affairs; loss by speculation. The native wastes his energies in pleasure-seeking. Danger of accident to the first-born. A woman with this position will have difficult and dangerous child-birth, and some tendency to puerperal fever.

Sun—Generally good, giving success in relation to children, schools, and theatres, all sorts of amusements and love affairs.

Venus—One of the best positions for this planet. It gives success and gain through the drama, opera, or comedy, and generally through artistic pleasures and education; good and successful children; domestic peace; much success in love affairs. The first child will be endowed with some artistic faculty, and will be of beautiful appearance.

Mercury—Many little worries and concerns with speculative affairs; inconstancy in love.

Moon—Public success in connection with theatres and places of amusement; fruitful nature, happy disposition, fond of pleasures; much in the company of women or children. An illustrious birth will proceed from this position of the Moon—a child will become famous.

In the Sixth House

Pluto—Emphasises the liability to industrial forms of sickness caused by the work that is carried out and would make one very vulnerable to invisible rays and radiation, especially if connected with atomic work or nuclear processes. Can also show contact with industrial interests to do with mining, explosives, demolition and also re-building. If the work carried out does not appeal it can cause one to suddenly give up the work and to leave the job without saying anything to anyone.

Neptune—Gives a wasting sickness; treachery among servants and employees; peculiar tastes in food and clothing; loss of physical comforts.

Uranus—Nervous diseases; losses and anxieties through servants; changes which interfere with health and comfort.

Saturn—Illness through exposure and want of proper nourishment; general debility; frequently fastidious in tastes; deceitful servants; losses by their deception.

Jupiter—Improves the health; gives many comforts and faithful servants. The chief illnesses arise from excesses and over-indulgence in diet.

Mars—Quarrels and thefts among servants; inflammatory complaints in the bowels and the part ruled by the sign Mars is in; extravagance in food and dress.

Sun—Enfeebles the health, and gives some taste for the study of hygiene and medicine.

Venus—Faithful and good servants; love of fine dress; delicate appetite; very careful in diet; fondness for dainty and pretty adornments; improves the health after marriage.

Mercury—Study of medicine, hygiene, and kindred subjects; many small vexations through servants; journeys on account of health; dyspeptic action arising from excessive mental or nervous action.

Moon—Many changes among servants; uncertain health; variable condition of life. The native generally makes a good servant but a poor master. Much sickness in infancy.

In the Seventh House

Pluto—Signifies that marriage can mean a leaving of familiar surroundings or even one's own country in order to go with the marriage partner to his or her locality which can often be at a very great distance from one's normal location. Does not necessarily mean an unhappy marriage but shows that the trend of affairs after marriage can bring a complete altering of personal activities. If badly aspected, shows a danger of the disappearance of the marriage partner which could be either intentional or unintentional.

Neptune—Causes illicit attachments after marriage; ruins the marriage life by neglect of duties; causes jealousies and scandal. The native may outrage the laws of society, or suffer dishonour by immoral practices with others of the same sex. It is an insidious and sure source of evil in any horoscope, and affects the married life. A wasting disease of a neurotic type afflicts the marriage partner.

Uranus—Impulsive attachments; hasty marriage, frequently followed by estrangement, separation, divorce, or death of the partner; many open enemies and public contests, caused by wilful and stubborn opposition on the part of the native.

Saturn—Ruin by partnerships; death, or enduring coldness of the marriage partner, who will be of a saturnine disposition and habit; many treacherous enemies.

Jupiter—A faithful and well-disposed partner; happy associations; gain by marriage. Enemies become friends, or friendships and benefits arise out of strifes.

Mars—Quarrels and dangers in the married state. In a male horoscope, the wife is frequently a virago, bearing a high hand in domestic affairs, industrious but dictatorial; in Cancer or Pisces, oftentimes a drunkard. In a female horoscope, sudden death of husband, or some serious accident to him. The native is constantly exciting opposition and strife. Violence often results.

Sun—Honours through marriage; successful litigation; honourable opponents.

Venus—A felicitous position for this planet. It confers a happy marriage; gives successful partnerships, peaceful termination to all strifes, and success in public relations.

Mercury—Unsettled married life; troubles through writings and litigation; many small strifes; numerous but insignificant opponents; many worries and vexations.

Moon—Changeful relations with the opposite sex; public opposition; unpopularity; female enmity. In a woman's horoscope it frequently shows that the husband will lead a roving and unsettled life.

c

In the Eighth House

Pluto—Usually shows an unnatural kind of death such as through being involved in a local or national disaster. Suffocation through being trapped in a submarine, coalmine disaster or similar occurrence, or by explosion or disaster where identification becomes impossible. It can also signify a personal disappearance either by choice or through the actions of others where death occurs in strange ways with the body never being found and death having to be presumed.

Neptune—Gives troubles in money matters after marriage—the partner is indifferent and careless and disposed to luxury; a curious, perhaps a lingering death. The native may fall into trances which simulate death, thereby incurring danger of premature burial.

Uranus—Difficulties in financial affairs after marriage—sudden losses through the partner; danger of sudden and extraordinary death from violence, or, if natural, from some nervous affliction such as epilepsy or paralysis.

Saturn—A poor partner, without shadow of a dowry or marriage settlement; difficulties after marriage; lingering death; loss of legacy or other expectation arising from decease.

Jupiter—Marriage brings prosperity—the partner is or will be rich; gain by legacy; a happy death.

Mars—The marriage partner spends the substance of the native; strife concerning the property of deceased persons; danger of a violent death; losses by fire and theft.

Sun—The partner becomes rich by the exercise of his or her talents; steady fortunes after marriage; chance of fame or honours at death. The skeleton may place the laurels on the native's brow. Danger of death in middle life.

Venus—Gain by marriage; chance of favours from deceased women. The partner will be fond of pleasures, jewels, and pretty things, and will spend money thereon; but success in finance comes after marriage.

Mercury—Inconstant fortunes; troubles of a minor character in financial affairs after marriage.

Moon—Unsettled fortunes after marriage; gain in public affairs by the partner. The death is more or less public, and may take place in a public resort or in the open streets, or through a voyage.

In the Ninth House

Pluto—Will give an interest in unorthodox forms of religion and a refusal to adhere to orthodoxy. In extreme cases when Pluto is afflicted can show atheism. Will give a strong desire for travel but much will depend upon individual circumstances. Sometimes shows conditions of exile from native land if part is taken in political and kindred affairs, as a result of unwise personal action or through enmity of others. It is a position associated with space travel interests as well as space travel itself.

Neptune—Gives clairvoyant or other psychic faculties—a visionary nature; strange dreams, curious forebodings; a highly impressionable and simulative nature; danger of mental troubles, legal suits, fraud by trustees or lawyers, difficulties in foreign lands; a chaotic religious mania.

Uranus—Misadventure in foreign lands; troubles through marriage relatives; legal difficulties; taste for occult and eccentric knowledge; antiquarian pursuits; prophetic faculty.

Saturn—Taste for philosophy; religious spirit; troubles in foreign lands; dangerous voyages; loss through legal suits; deceit among relatives by marriage; studious and thoughtful nature.

Jupiter—Clerical honours; success in religious and philosophical pursuits, legal matters, and foreign affairs; gain in foreign lands.

Mars—Freedom of religious beliefs, frequently atheistical, bigoted, or madly fanatical; many strifes; losses in legal suits; danger of violence in distant countries; strife among the partner's relatives; turbulent fancies and distressful dreams.

Sun—Honours through clerical or legal affairs; dignities of some sort in foreign lands; constancy in religious beliefs; proud and confident mind, ambitious spirit; taste for fine arts and science.

Venus—Love of music and the drama, the fine arts, and artistic pursuits. A patron of all that tends to beautify and enliven life; a supporter of peaceful measures and projects; a kind, gentle disposition and cultured intellect.

Mercury—Taste for science and letters, literary pursuits, and every form of knowledge, apart from its uses. A busy, active mind; sometimes meddlesome. Danger of legal worries; a desire for life in foreign countries, and knowledge of distant places; a constant reader and note-maker; a person of many beliefs and opinions.

Moon—Voyages; life in foreign lands; legal or clerical persuasions. The native frequently penetrates into unknown and distant lands, and may gain honours as an explorer in some domain or other. The mind is romantic, fanciful, changeful, and ever in search of novelty.

In the Tenth House

Pluto—Shows insecurity of position. Trouble through prejudice or jealousy of co-workers or employers. Better if possible to work on one's own but even then to be alert for strange twists of circumstances. A part will be played in public and social life but it will not be easy to obtain favours or recognition and services rendered can be very quickly forgotten.

Neptune—Gives a strange and eventful career; chance of honours in some artistic field; a highly inspirational nature capable of attaining honours through some unique achievement. The native does so, however, under curious circumstances, either using an assumed name or some covert means. It endangers the life of one of the parents—according to the sex of the horoscope.

Uranus—Difficulties with employers; a strange and chequered career; many sudden changes of position and credit. Originality will be a marked feature. The native favours eccentric pursuits. Estrangement from parents and kindred; a romantic and changeful life; opposition from public functionaries and governmental bodies; change of occupation; if in Pisces, Sagittarius, or Gemini, two simultaneous occupations.

Saturn—Rise in life, followed by a downfall. Patience and firmness of purpose mark the life of the native. In business, financial ruin is shown; in professional life, dishonour and failure; in government, defeat. A fatality hangs over the native from his birth; danger of the ruin or loss of a parent in early life; public affairs fail or bring loss and discredit.

Jupiter—High honours, wealth, and success. The native rises in his sphere of life, and gains credit and emoluments. It is one of the best auguries of a prosperous and happy life.

Mars—In military life, success; in other fields of work, danger of discredit. The native suffers from slander, and his life is filled with turmoil and strife. Desire for conquest and a spirit of freedom spur the native to outstrip his powers and exhaust his energies. The native is often quarrelsome, but quite as often the subject of constant fault-finding and criticism.

Sun—Honours and success in life; high patronage and success in governmental circles, embassies, etc. The credit of the native is fairly secure, his success steady and generally productive of honours in middle life. A servant with this position will secure service in high circles.

Venus—Frequently confers a gift of prophecy and taste for divinatory arts; artistic pursuits; success in poetry, music, or the drama; high patronage among ladies; success in love affairs, and general prosperity. A peaceful and secure position. Honours, according to the sphere of life occupied by the native.

Mercury—Many occupations; restless spirit; uncertain position; taste for literature; success in trading and in general agencies and commissions; vexations and worries; literary or scholastic profession.

Moon—Desire for public life; many changes and voyages. Women influence the position for good or evil. Unstable position. Changes in occupation; a rise in life, often followed by a reversal. Much occupied with public business, and generally in close association with women. Popularity.

In the Eleventh House

Pluto—Peculiar friendships will be made but it will not be easy to make lasting friendships. Circumstances will again play a strange part, at times bringing unexpected benefit through friends but at other times showing that erstwhile friends can become enemies. Hence there will be periods of loneliness and this will be more noticeable when there has been a strong friendship with someone of the opposite sex.

Neptune—Gives seductive friends and alliances, unreliable advisers; treachery among supposed friends; losses and troubles thereby. The wife or husband is liable to moral delinquency, sometimes making havoc among the native's friends. Strange and unaccountable attractions and associations.

Uranus—Eccentric and unreliable friends; danger of estrangements among them; impulsive attachments which end in hatred. The partner is in danger of indulging in romantic love affairs.

Saturn—False and deceitful friends. The native is frequently ruined by them; hopes are deceived, ambitions frustrated. The death of a child is to be feared; danger of losing the children. The wife may be unfruitful, or the husband disposed to be an anchorite.

Jupiter—Many benefits from friends; association with persons of noble birth. The native's hopes are brought to successful issues; the ambitions are attained. Success will be due to the instrumentality of friends. The wife will be fruitful, and will benefit by child-birth. In a male horoscope, success often comes with the birth of a child.

Mars—Contentions among friends; unsatisfactory relations with others in social life. Friends lead the native into extravagance or some form of dissipation. Danger to the wife in child-birth. In a woman's horoscope, the husband is often profligate.

Sun—Constant and honourable friends; honours through them; association of men in good position; successful ambitions, well-regulated hopes.

Venus—Gain and happiness through friends; fondness for society; favours from females; fruitful marriage; happy associations.

Mercury—Many acquaintances, but few constant friends; some association with literary or scientific men. The associations of the native produce many little worries and anxieties.

Moon—Unreliable friends; patronage of women; many acquaintances, but few lasting attachments. If the Moon is in a fruitful sign, it shows the birth of several children.

In the Twelfth House

Pluto—Has a very peculiar influence in that it can destroy enemies, and so prevent possible personal loss, unhappiness and strain. The banishing influence will operate very markedly when the actions of enemies or unfair competitors becomes too marked for in a very subtle manner circumstances will arise that will seem to banish the enemy or competitor from the person's environment and remove them to such a distance from the person that their power to do harm will be negatived.

Neptune—Ambushes, deceptions, frauds; many secret enemies, plots against the native, and nefarious schemes. The native is beset with dangers, and lives in vague dread of some unknown danger.

Uranus—Strange and unexpected enmities; danger of estrangement or exile from one's kin and country. Eccentric people perplex and harass the native by their underhand actions; danger of falls from horses; accidents causing detention in out-of-the-way places or foreign lands.

Saturn—Secret enemies, who work steadily for the native's downfall; danger of contusions and bruises through animals. The partner suffers from some lingering illness. A secluded life.

Jupiter—Secret enemies over which the native prevails. Enemies become friends; success with large animals and in remote places.

Mars—Danger of violence from enemies in ambush; effusion of blood caused by kicks or thrusts from animals; escape from bondage or restraint; pains in the extremities. Sickness of an inflammatory nature occurs to the partner.

Sun—Danger of exile, or life apart from kindred; enmity of great men or those in office above the native; life in far-off lands. The native vanquishes his enemies.

Venus—Secret love affairs, leading to enmity of women; jealousy; love of horses and large animals; peaceful seclusion to one's own taste.

Mercury—Many small enmities, frequently caused by writings and scandalous reports; the mind is self-absorbed, and narrow in its sympathies; taste for occult science and secret schemes, plots, and intrigues.

Moon—Female enemies; many secrets touching the native; danger of restraint or enforced retirement; love of mystery; fanciful fears; success in isolated positions and remote corners; voyages.

N.B.—The above delineations are subject to wide modification by the aspects of any other planet to the significator. Thus if Saturn should be in second house well aspected by Jupiter and other planets, wealth would be amassed at some time in life, and old age would be comfortable and prosperous.

But the prognostics previously given are for the planets' positions only, when not in aspect to any other, and irrespective of the signs occupied by them. The Sun, Moon, and Mercury are capable of a more exact interpretation when referred to the signs they occupy, and so in a less degree are the other bodies.

When, therefore, a planet, without aspect, is found in any house of the horoscope, the above interpretations will hold good; but consideration should be made of the sign that planet is in—whether a dignity or debility, a congenial or adverse sign, and whether it be movable, fixed, or common, and the element which it signifies. Thus if Uranus were in the third house, it would show eccentric methods of travelling, eccentric and strange messages and means of communication, etc. If it occupied a *watery* sign, such things would occur in connection with the water, electrical launches, and such like inventions. If in an *airy* sign, flying machines, motorcars, electric tramways, etc.

Fixed signs do much to establish and preserve the good or evil signified, and to make it endure.

Retrograde planets show a falling off of such persons, associations, and things as are signified by the house occupied by those planets.

To give a detailed reading of planetary action in regard both to sign and house would require a large volume, and even then the effects of mutual aspects between the planets would be left out of consideration.

The above readings apply to both sexes unless otherwise stated.

CHAPTER VII
THE ASPECTS

An " aspect " in Astrology is a certain distance between any two planetary bodies or between any two zodiacal positions. The chief aspects are:—

The Opposition	..	..	☍, 6 signs or 180° apart
The Sesquiquadrate	..	..	⬛, 4½ „ 135° „
The Trine	..	..	△, 4 „ 120° „
The Square	..	..	□, 3 „ 90° „
The Sextile	..	..	✶, 2 „ 60° „
The Semisquare	..	..	∠, 1½ „ 45° „
The Conjunction	..	..	☌ 0 „ 0 „

The Parallel of Declination (Par.) occurs when two planets hold the same degree of declination, whether above or below the Equator, or on opposite sides of it, *i.e.*, one above and one below.

The last two are, more correctly speaking, *positions*, and not aspects. Those aspects which are formed from the △ are *good*, and produce benefic results, viz., △ and ✶, and in a very minor degree, the ⩒ of 30°, called semisextile.

The aspects formed from the □ are *evil*, and produce results of an evil nature. They are, the ☍, ⊡, □, and ∠.

The *conjunction* and *parallel* of good planets (♃, ♀, ☉) are *good*, and of evil planets (♇, ♆, ♅, ♄, ♂), *evil*.

Mercury is variable in this respect, and always takes the nature of that planet to which it is in closest aspect at the birth; or, if in no aspect, then it takes the nature of the lord or ruler of the sign it occupies.

Good aspects are productive of benefits, even from so-called " evil " planets, the fact being that no planet is wholly good or evil in itself, but it becomes so by its aspect.

The ready measurement of zodiacal aspects is a matter of practical importance in Astrology, and the following rules may serve to facilitate the process.

1. Signs of the *same element* are in trine (△) to one another.

2. Signs of the *same constitution* are in square (□) to one another, or in opposition (☍).

Thus ♈, ♌, ♐, being of the same element (fire), are in trine; while ♉ and ♌ are in square, both being fixed signs and, therefore, of the same constitution. So also, ♉ and ♏, ♌ and ♒ are in opposition for the same reason.

Planets are called " in aspect " to one another when, at birth, they are found to be within 5° of any of the distances indicated in the list of aspects. The Parallel, however, is limited to a distance of 1°.

The lesser of two planets that may be in aspect is said to *apply to* or *separate from* the other. " Application " is when the aspect is not exact, but afterwards becomes so by the motion of the swifter body of the two gaining upon the other in its progress.   Thus, if the Sun were in ♈ 15°, and the Moon in ♐ 10°, the Moon would be *applying* to the △ aspect of the Sun, because the Moon is swifter in motion than the Sun, and would soon gain the 5° necessary to complete the exact △ aspect.

" Separation " is when, at birth or other epoch, the aspect has already been completed, in which case the swifter planet is said to separate from the other. Thus, if the Sun in ♈ 15° had the △ aspect of the Moon in ♐ 17°, the Moon would be *separating* from the △ of the Sun.

N.B.—The larger and slower bodies may apply to the lesser and swifter by *direction*, but not by ephemeral motion. (See Book iii, chaps. ii and iii).

Mutual application happens when two planets are *forming* an aspect, and *the one applied to is retrograde* in motion. Thus, if Jupiter were in ♑ 12°, and Uranus in ♎ 15°, Jupiter would be applying to the square (□) of Uranus. But if Uranus were retrograde (℞), it would be progressing from ♎ 15° towards ♎ 12°, and therefore itself applying to the square of Jupiter. Therefore, ♃ in ♑ 12° □ ♅ in ♎ 15° ℞, would be a *mutual application*.

Aspects, whether good or evil, are of two natures, *dexter* and *sinister*.

Dexter aspects are those thrown to any point from a preceding sign. Thus, if the mid-heaven were ♑ 5° and Jupiter were in ♏ 5°, Jupiter would be in *dexter* sextile to the M.C. (*medium cæli*); but in ♓ 5° it would throw a *sinister* sextile to the meridian. Again, with the Sun in ♐ 10° and Saturn in ♍ 10°, the Sun would be in *sinister* square to Saturn, and Saturn in *dexter* square to the Sun.

Sinister aspects to the Sun, Moon, mid-heaven, ascendant, or other important significator, are stronger for good or evil than the corresponding dexter aspects.

The ☊ and ☋ are only considered when in conjunction with any of the planets at birth. The ⊕ is considered when in aspect and conjunction.

As already explained, the ☊ (Dragon's Head) is considered to be good, and the ☋ (Dragon's Tail) evil, in conjunction with any of the significators. The ⊕ (Part of Fortune) has no qualities of its own, and is merely a significator of the personal property of the native, particularly land, houses, and such like possessions.

CHAPTER VIII

CALCULATION OF THE HOROSCOPE

THE requisites for the calculation of a horoscope, or figure of the heavens for the time of birth, are—(1) An *Ephemeris* for the year of birth, which gives the places of the planets for each day at noon, their declinations, and other necessary material; and (2) a Table of Houses for the latitude of birth.

These can be obtained of the almanac publishers. The cost of an Ephemeris, and a Table of Houses for various latitudes can be ascertained from the publishers, Messrs. W. Foulsham & Co. Ltd., Standbrook House, 2-5 Old Bond Street, London, W.1.

The data required for the calculation are as follows:—

1. The year, month, date, and hour of birth. It is important to have the time of birth very accurately noted, for a few minutes, one way or the other, may throw the horoscope out of all relation to the events of life. It is advisable to make enquiry in all doubtful cases. It will often assist the memory of the parents by asking whether the birth took place at " breakfast, lunch, tea, or dinner time," whether " before or after the church bells were ringing," and so forth. By this means a fairly accurate estimate may be obtained, when a mere question of the " exact time " would yield no satisfaction. A photograph of the native, if of mature years, will also assist the student, by referring it to the rising sign.

2. The latitude and longitude of the place of birth.

3. The sex of the native.

These facts having been duly noted, the calculation may proceed.

Take the following instance:—Male, born 10th April 1940, at 2 a.m. in latitude 52° 28′ N., and longitude 2° W.

The Ephemeris, it must be understood, is calculated for Greenwich, so that a correction is due for all places east or west of that place.

Turning to the Ephemeris for the month of April, 1940, the planets' places for each day at noon will be found tabulated. The birth took place in the morning, ten hours before noon of the 10th. Therefore, the calculation is made from the previous noon. In the column marked " Sidereal Time," the longitude of the Sun will be found expressed in hours, minutes, and seconds of time. Then, to the sidereal time, 10th April, 1940, *add* the time elapsed since noon, *viz.*: fourteen hours, and correction for fourteen hours at the rate of ten seconds per hour. This will give the meridian of the horoscope in hours, minutes, and seconds of sidereal time. Thus—

	H.	M.	S.
Sidereal time, noon, 9th April	1	10	19
Add, time of birth since noon	14	0	0
	15	10	19
Deduct for summer time	1	0	0
	14	0	0
Correction for 13 hrs. at 10 secs. per hour ..	0	2	10
	14	2	10
Deduct for 2° West longitude at 4 min. per degree		8	0
	13	54	10
Correction for 2° West longitude (add)			2
Mid-heaven at birth	13	54	12

Had the birth taken place at 2 *p.m.* instead of a.m., the sidereal time for the noon of the 10th would be the basis of the calculation, and two hours would have been added to it, together with twenty seconds for correction. Again, had the birthplace been 2° *East*, instead of *West*, the two seconds would have been subtracted.

In Great Britain and Ireland the clock time now used is Greenwich Mean Time, therefore allowance must be made for the longitudinal difference of time which is 4 minutes for one degree or four seconds for one minute of longitude. If the longitude is *West* the longitudinal difference must be subtracted (as shown in above calculation) but if it should be *East*, then the longitudinal difference must be added. This longitudinal difference of time must not be confused with the correction for longitudinal differences which is given in the paragraph headed *Note*. For foreign horoscopes there is again a difference of calculation but this is fully explained in Chapter IX.

Note.—For every 3° West longitude two seconds must be *added* to the sidereal time of noon at Greenwich, and the same amount must be *subtracted* for East longitude. Thus, if the birthplace were 15° east of Greenwich, ten seconds would be subtracted from the sidereal time at Greenwich at noon to get the true sidereal time for noon at the birthplace.

Now, having obtained the meridian or mid-heaven of the Horoscope of Birth, draw a circle to represent the earth (a small one will do), and one larger to represent the heavens as given in Book i, chap. iv, the circles being equally divided into twelve parts, and joined by the cusps of the houses.

Turn to the Tables of Houses for the latitude of birthplace. In the column marked " Sidereal Time " the reader will find the 13 hrs. 55 mins. 27 secs., very nearly as above. In the columns on a line with this sidereal time will be found the longitudes of the cusps of the tenth, eleventh, twelfth, first, second, and third houses respectively, viz., ♏ 1, ♏ 23, ♐ 9, ♐ 25.2, ♒ 10, ♓ 28. These longitudes must be placed in their respective cusps, and the remaining six cusps will hold the equivalent longitudes in the opposite signs to them. The figure when completed is thus shown—

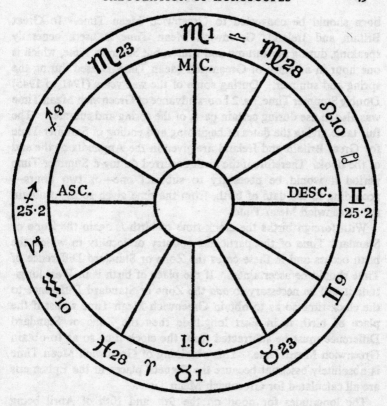

It will be observed that the signs ♎, ♈, ♑, and ♋ are intercepted, and are placed between the cusps of the houses according to their positions in the Zodiac. On the equator, and in places near the equator, the zodiacal and equatorial circles so nearly correspond that a sign is never intercepted, and the signs are almost evenly distributed through the houses. As we proceed north and south, however, the circle of latitude becomes farther removed from the plane of the zodiacal circle, and the distribution of the signs in the houses becomes uneven.

The next process is to place the planets in the figure of the horoscope. These are calculated for the Greenwich Mean Time of birth. Therefore it is essential that the time of birth, which is invariably the *clock* time in force in the country or locality where the person is born should be converted to Greenwich Mean Time. In Great Britain and Ireland, Greenwich Mean Time is used, generally speaking, during the autumn and winter, but Summer Time, which is one hour in advance of Greenwich Mean Time, is used during the spring and summer. During some of the war years (1941 to 1945) Double Summer Time, *i.e.* 2 hours advance of Greenwich Mean Time was also in use during certain parts of the spring and summer. The full table giving the dates of beginning and ending of Summer Time for Great Britain and Ireland are given in the Appendix at the end of the book. Therefore if the birth occurred during a Summer Time period it would be necessary to subtract one—or two hours—according to the date of birth, from the time given so as to obtain the Greenwich Mean Time.

With foreign births the clock time of birth is again the Zone or Standard Time of the particular country or locality in which the birth occurs and in these cases the Zone or Standard Difference of Time should be ascertained. If the place of birth is in *West* longitude it will be necessary to *add* the Zone or Standard Difference to the clock time so as to obtain Greenwich Mean Time whilst if the place of birth is in *East* longitude then the Zone or Standard Difference must be subtracted from the clock time so as to obtain Greenwich Mean Time. This obtaining of Greenwich Mean Time is absolutely essential because the Planets' places in the Ephemeris are all calculated for Greenwich Mean Time.

The longitudes for noon on the 9th and 10th of April being known, the motion in twenty-four hours is obtained by subtracting one from the other; then, by proportion the motion for 1 a.m. (time before noon on the 10th) can be known.

Moon's longitude 10th	..	...	..	..	19° 56'
Moon's longitude 9th	..	..	..	..	7° 44'
Moon's motion in one day		..	..	..	12° 12'
To 12° 12'—logarithm	..	..	..	2938	
Add 11 hrs.—logarithm	..	..	—	3388	
Motion required—logarithm	..	..	6326	=	5° 36'

This, subtracted from the Moon's longitude at noon on the 10th, 19° 56', leaves 14° 20', which is the Moon's longitude at birth.

(*Note.*—The Greenwich Mean Time at birth in the example horoscope was 1 a.m. which is 11 hours before noon.)

The longitudes of Pluto, Neptune, Uranus, Saturn, and Jupiter require only a mental calculation, as their motions are very slow, and frequently will not need to be altered from what is stated in the Ephemeris.

The longitudes of the planets having been found for the time of birth, they need only to be placed in the figure together with the Part of Fortune and the Moon's nodes, and the horoscope is finished, as shown in the following figure:—

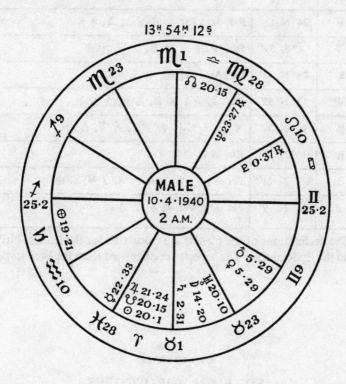

Aspects.—☉ ∨ ☿. ∠ ♀ ∠ ♂ ☌ ♃ ∨ ♅ ☌ ☋ — ☽ ☌ ♅ △ ⊕ — ☿ ∨ ♃ ⁎ ♅ 8 ♆ ⁎ ⊕ — ♀ ☌ ♂ ∠ ♃ ⁎ ⓟ — Asc. △ ☉ □ ☿ △ ♃ □ ♆ — M.C. 8 ♄ □ ⓟ.

The aspects and parallels existing between the chief significators—☉, ☽, Asc., M.C., ♀, and ☿—are set out in the space beneath the horoscope. A more convenient form is here shown.

PLANET	DECLIN.	ASPECTS
☉	7° N. 50′	Par. ♃, ⋁ ☿, ∠ ♀, ∠ ♂, ⋁ ♅, ☌ ♃, ☌ ☋
☽	13° N. 58′	☌ ♅. △ ⊕
Asc.	23° S. 27′	Par. ♀, Par. ♇, Par. ♂, △ ☉, □ ☿, △ ♃, □ ♆
M.C.	11° S. 27′	Par. ♄, ☍ ♄, □ ♇
♀	24° N. 13′	Par. Asc., Par. ♇, ☌ ♂, ∠ ♃, ✳ ♇
☿	4° S. 39′	Par. ♆, ⋁ ♃, ✳ ♅, ☍ ♆, ✳ ⊕
♇	23° N. 48′	Par. Asc., Par. ♂, ✳ ♀, ✳ ♂
♆	3° N. 45′	Par. ☿, ☍ ☿, ⊼ ♃, △ ♅, △ ⊕
♅	17° N. 31′	⋁ ☉, ☌ ☽, ✳ ☿, ⋁ ♃, △ ♆, △ ⊕
♄	10° N. 17′	Par. M.C. □ ♇
♃	7° N. 21′	Par. ☉, ⋁ ☿, ∠ ♀, ∠ ♂, ⋁ ♅, □ ⊕
♂	22° N. 9′	Par. Asc., Par. ♇, ☌ ♀, ∠ ♃

The declinations of the planets are calculated for the time of birth from the Ephemeris.   The aspects are calculated from the horoscope.

CHAPTER IX

FOREIGN HOROSCOPES

East or West Longitude

THESE are of two kinds.   They may be distant from Greenwich by longitude or latitude, or both.   Let us suppose a person born at 2 a.m., New York time, on the 10th April, 1940, in the city of New York, longitude 74° West.   The calculation would then be as follows:—

Convert 74° West into time at the rate of 4 mins. for every degree of longitude. This amounts to 4 hrs. 56 mins.

	H.	M.	S.
M.C. noon (Greenwich), 9th April ..	1	14	16
Add for 74° West at 10 secs. per hour ..	0	0	50
M.C. noon (New York), 9th April ..	1	15	6
Time elapsed	13	0	0
Add for 13 hours at 10 secs. per hour ..		2	10
M.C. at birth	14	17	16

This M.C., or mid-heaven, is referred to in the Tables of Houses for Latitude of New York, 40° 43′ North, and the cusps of the houses are placed in the figure of the horoscope, as previously explained.

The next step is to place the planets in the figure. This involves a correction, as " Raphael's " Ephemeris is made out for Greenwich. The longitude of New York is 4 hrs. 56 mins. West. When it is 2 a.m. at New York it is past 2 a.m. at Greenwich by 4 hrs. 56 mins. Therefore *add* that amount to the time of birth. The result is the corresponding Greenwich time, *viz.*: 6 hrs. 56 mins. a.m. Calculate the planets' places from the Ephemeris for this time, and place them in the figure as before. The horoscope is then complete.

North or South Latitude

Let us now suppose that the birth took place at 4 p.m. in Melbourne, longitude 145° East, and latitude 37° 50′ South, 10th April, 1940. The calculation is as follows:—

	H.	M.	S.
Equation 145° = 9 hrs. 40 mins			
Greenwich M.C., noon, 10th April, 1940 ...	1	14	16
Less for 9 hrs. 40 mins. at 10 secs. per hour ..	0	1	37
Melbourne M.C., noon 10th April, 1940	1	12	39
Time p.m.	4	0	0
Correction for 4 hrs. at 10 secs.	0	0	40
Mid-heaven at birth	5	13	19

We now have to remember that the latitude is South and not North, as in the cases preceding. Take a table of houses for North latitude 37° 50′ (or as near that as possible), and proceed as follows:—

Find the mid-heaven corresponding to 5 hrs. 13 mins. 19 secs. in the table of houses, and add six signs to it—*i.e.*, take the exactly opposite sign and degree. Thus we find the above longitude of the meridian to correspond to ♊ 19° 15′. Therefore we turn to ♐ 19° 15′ in the tables for 37° North, and take out the cusps of the houses in a line with it, but always remembering to *change the signs to the opposite ones*. This simple method saves a somewhat complex mathematical process, and also makes a single set of tables for *North* latitudes of universal utility.

The planets' places are calculated for Greenwich time, 6.20 a.m., which corresponds to 4 p.m. at Melbourne. The longitude being East, the corresponding time is subtracted from the birth time in order to get the Greenwich time. In the case of New York it was added.

The horoscope having been properly calculated for time and place of birth, it is fit to be judged. The rules for this process will be found in subsequent chapters.

CHAPTER X

SUMMARY

THE foregoing chapters have dealt somewhat fully with the alphabet and language of the heavens. If the simple natures of the planets, signs, and houses are thoroughly learned and understood, it will not be a difficult matter for the student to arrive at their compounded natures, when sign, planet, and house are taken together, or when two or more planets shall mingle their influences by aspect or conjunction from any part of the heavens.

The symbols of signs, planets, and aspects should be thoroughly learned, for they are the letters of the celestial book of secrets. Without a knowledge of them the language of the heavens cannot be properly mastered. Afterwards it is necessary to acquire the meanings of those symbols, and the significations attached to the several houses. The symbols should be frequently written out and thought over. The several houses, too, should be thought of in succession, until all their significations are familiar. Some practice will also be needed in the calculation of aspects. A point in the Zodiac should be selected, and from that all the aspects should be set down with the signs and degrees in which they fall. The process should then be done mentally, till practice makes the student perfect.

The method of calculating the horoscope has been given for a.m. and p.m. time, for East and West longitudes, and for North and South latitudes. Nothing now remains save to judge the horoscope, and to indicate the times when events will take place. The remaining sections of this work will be found to embody all that is requisite for a complete understanding and practice of the art of foreknowledge and prediction.

APPENDIX TO BOOK I

Description of Persons according as the Significator may be found in each of the Twelve Signs.—Revised from Lilly's " Astrology."
The Reader is referred to Notes at the end of this Appendix.

PLUTO IN THE TWELVE SIGNS

♇ in ♈

Shows a person somewhat above middle height, oval face but spare in build. Always ready to express new ideas, inventive tendencies but will need to develop practicality if ideas are to be accepted by others and progress made. Much personal courage, would make good headway in connection with military matters.

♇ in ♉

Gives a beautiful figure during first part of life. With women, almost an ethereal beauty with the curves of the body being most marked, but in later life there can be a loss of beauty if the diet is not watched. The artistic side of the nature is drawn out particularly where music and singing are concerned, The tenor voice in men and soprano in women being accentuated.

♇ in ♊

Sometimes increases the height disproportionately showing very tall or even above very tall people, yet size of body will be in accord with height. Thoughts and ideas will be of a futuristic nature, very subtle in their implications, much associated with spiritual and evolutionary matters but averse to orthodox religion.

♇ in ♋

Gives a shorter, more thick-set type of body, during second part of life skin can become somewhat flabby. Has a reaction upon the eyes causing myopia and sometimes cataract. The emotional intensity will react upon home and family interests, causing unpleasantness at times that can either drive other members of the family away or alternatively cause the person to leave home without giving warning or any indication as to his future whereabouts.

♇ in ♌

The artistic appearance will be accentuated, the mannerisms and expression being after the style of the old Shakespearean actor with a fairly full build of body giving a courtly and dignified appearance, with a partially florid complexion and with men, the wearing of a moustache. The temperament will be good natured and there will be a particular understanding of children.

♇ in ♍

Tends to slim the physical body, gives a squarish type of shoulder, darkish hair with sideboards down the face sometimes extending into a thin beard round the face and chin but not extending down the throat. Usually gives an exalted view of self-importance and in certain instances a bullying and cruel tendency with no hesitation in hurting people who disagree with the personal views and attitude towards life.

♇ in ♎

Signifies a medium to tall type of physical body, blond hair in women, fair hair and blue eyes in men.   It accentuates the graceful poise and sense of balance and deportment.   The willingness to co-operate with others and to exercise the function of arbitration is marked and they usually take a prominent part in public and social life so long as they have the support of the marriage partner.

♇ in ♏

Gives a swarthy appearance.   Very sensuous nose and lips whilst the muscular development in both men and women is very marked.   They are the strong people and with physical strength will go voluptuousness.   Sometimes they will express brutality but the women can be very good at nursing and with childbirth whilst the men can excel in boxing.

♇ in ♐

Shows a well proportioned body with inclination towards tallness, but considerable litheness of movement.   The physical activity will be very marked during early and first part of middle life but then tends to deteriorate particularly if sporting interests have been prominent.   A thinning of the hair becomes apparent from the early 30's, but more particularly in men.   A considerable interest in philosophy is shown.

♇ in ♑

Represents a cadaverous type of feature and body with a scrawny neck. Lowers the height and thins the body.   The bony structure is weakened, the knees and legs can be deformed or weak in some way.   They are often avaricious, sometimes miserly and with the latter can deny themselves proper food and sustenance.   Can be hard and unscrupulous in business deals and a hard and tough employer.   At the other extreme a cringing employee.

♇ in ♒

Shows a rather large head with flowing hair, turning grey or white before middle age.   The eyes are also large, fairly wide apart with a roundish type of face but somewhat short neck.   After age 40 they become breathless after a little exertion.   Make very good friends, always willing to proffer advice which is invariably sound.   They seldom criticise or argue.

♇ in ♓

Indicates a fleshy type of body with watery eyes.   Limbs will be big but soft and in women the legs will often be very big.   Yet the physical strength will not be great and there will be a susceptibility to divers ailments, sometimes to drunkenness leading to imprisonment.

N.B.—♇ invariably has an influence over the size of the physical body increasing or decreasing the height according to sign, Gemini and Sagittarius increasing the height, Cancer, Scorpio and Pisces increasing the width or girth, Leo and Scorpio giving considerable physical strength.

NEPTUNE IN THE TWELVE SIGNS

♆ in ♈

Gives protruding eyes with a smallish nose and smallish, pear type shape of face. Ears sometimes seem to stand out sideways. They have a degree of garrulity, are purveyors of gossip, sometimes insinuating in their overtures to others and can be deadly in the art of procrastination.

♆ in ♉

Shows a mixture between a round and squarish type of face, very thick and short neck, medium height of body, spare in early life, women can be extremely beautiful, but turning to corpulency later in life. The ears will be very sensitive to sound hence they make good singers or musicians, whilst the eyes are keen on form and they can make good artists and portrait painters. They are very good eaters and drinkers.

♆ in ♊

Signifies a thin type of physical body but with considerable physical wiriness. They can be very nervy at times, very impressionable and responsive to the gossip and suggestions of other people. A susceptibility to respiratory disorders is shown. Carelessness in dress occurs but they are invariably courteous and well-behaved. Physical and mental restlessness very marked.

♆ in ♋

Indicates a lymphatic or bovine type of physical body. Eyes usually brown and somewhat liquid. Medium height and in women a very full bust. They make good parents, home and family life being very important. There is often an interest in psychic matters, they make very good mediums, are often interested in magic and so can become witches or wizards.

♆ in ♌

Gives a fairly full build of physical body. The physical structure is strong and the health invariably good providing correct habits are maintained. The eyes are sometimes bulbous, never deep set but can be penetrating in their gaze. This is another position giving extremely good artistic capacity especially for the theatre.

♆ in ♍

Signifies a kind of foxy appearance, slims the body, gives flexible limbs but a nervy kind of walk. Fastidious regarding diet and food. Inclined to criticise and find fault, quick to perceive dishonesty. Ingenious in covering up personal faults and failings. Does not make friends very easily although usually desirous of company and of being with other people.

♆ in ♎

Shows a more refined type of physical body. Pleasing features, a magnetic blue eye, but friendly not cold. Usually just above medium height. Women have wavy hair and a good deal of natural charm whilst men are courteous in their approach. Both however have a hearty dislike of anything of an unclean nature and do not take too kindly to domestic life.

♆ in ♏

Tends to coarsen the physical form. Sometimes gives a gypsy appearance but with women a capacity for fascination as well. The sensuous side of the nature is intensified and in certain types there will be a marked jealousy with a nasty temper. In more developed types the psychic capacity is once more accentuated and there will be remarkable ability in divining and in foretelling the future with cards and other paraphernalia.

♆ in ♐

Represents a person of more than middle height but not unduly tall. Fresh complexion, sandy type of hair, rather prominent nose, fairly long legs. Will be a very good companion and very generous but will not condone anything of a deceptive, tricky or unfair nature and will usually be able to discern these traits very quickly when anyone tries to take an unfair advantage. Will be a very prolific traveller.

♆ in ♑

Describes an ill-proportioned form of physical body, the head tending to be smaller than normal, the trunk somewhat more developed with the legs rather thin. Sometimes the men sport a full beard often to cover up a weak chin and pale complexion. They can be somewhat avaricious, not averse to making a sharp deal, and in consequence find it difficult to make true friends or a happy marriage.

♆ in ♒

Gives a very broad forehead, large head, nose inclined to be flatter than normal, eyes somewhat more deep-set, bluey-grey or in women of a green tinge. Musically inclined with very good capacity for piano or stringed instruments, especially the violin. They can make very good composers or conductors and are usually very good company as they will always have a fund of anecdotes at their command.

♆ in ♓

Shows a full stature, fairly powerfully built, but the full strength potential seldom developed with the result that from age 40 onwards a tendency to fatness occurs. In some cases a tendency to drink or drugs will become marked and then the character will deteriorate. On the other hand religious tendencies can also become strong and then many personal sacrifices will be made for others.

N.B.—Neptune invariably has some influence over the eyes showing a susceptibility to weak eyes, short-sightedness, cataract and other forms of eye disease. When in Taurus, Scorpio, Sagittarius can bring blindness.

URANUS IN THE TWELVE SIGNS

♅ in ♈

Indicates a very prominent forehead, thinness of hair. The walk will be of a somewhat jerky, uneven nature, sometimes slow, sometimes quick as if in keeping with the flow of thought that is taking place. They will be somewhat nervy, eccentric people, having unusual but also original ideas. They can be either cranks or geniuses but will invariably do something unpredictable.

♅ in ♉

Denotes a somewhat ungainly type of body, very large and thick set with short legs but longer arms as if to compensate. Thick neck and full throat with roundish type of head. The impression given will be of very great strength. In some instances the men will be wrestlers. Temper will be somewhat uneven, it will not take much to provoke outbursts with accompanying belligerency. With women the lower emotions will often be greatly intensified.

♅ in ♊

Signifies only medium height in apparent contradiction to the general indication of Gemini. Hair will be darker, in women sometimes almost black. Eyes will be smaller, rather piercing in appearance. They will be intellectuals with an obstinate mental trend, desirous of changing the existing order of things but not very practical or clear as to what should take the place of the existing order. Will be quarrelsome with relatives and neighbours.

♅ in ♋

Shows shortness and broadness of stature, particularly with women. Hair will be thick and curly, sometimes of a reddish hue. Feet will be large with a tendency towards flatfootedness. There will be an appreciation of home life but sudden breaks, changes and disappearances can be made without any reasons being given. A somewhat difficult person to live with in the home as they will want to have everything their own way and will be a law unto themselves.

♅ in ♌

Usually shows normal height and body in reasonable proportion. Gives a dignified appearance, with a proud but not necessarily haughty bearing. The physical strength is again marked but if over-exertion occurs there can be a reaction upon the heart. A considerable degree of ambition, with delight in acting and kindred artistic matters as well as in education and science. Invariably makes good friends and will have a marked understanding of children.

♅ in ♍

Gives a smaller type of physical body, mousy coloured hair which goes white rather quickly. There can be a twitching of the eyes or a habit of running the fingers through the hair especially when worried or upset. Will not get on too well with co-workers as they will be too independent wanting to do things on their own or in their own way and refusing to adhere to instructions and routine.

♅ in ♎

Tends to increase size of body and height but in reasonably good proportions. Hair will be unruly and inclined to grow long at the back. Slight slope to forehead. There will be more balance between thought and action but a very strong desire for romance. Ties and associations can be quickly made and yet as quickly broken. Nevertheless the personal factor of attraction will be very marked and they will have many good friends and acquaintances.

♅ in ♏

Represents an unruly individual, swarthy complexion, broad in build, not over tall, sometimes very hairy. Can be slovenly in dress and careless as to cleanliness. Alternatively can go to the other extreme and be very fastidious whilst women can become very good models so long as they keep their figures neat. Will have many strange love experiences but with no sense or appreciation of the orthodox in life.

♅ in ♐

Gives considerable physical strength, increases the height, very strong arms and hands and supple lower limbs. They will be very good horsemen and horse-women, usually fond of hunting, racing and various outdoor sports. In certain instances whilst decreasing the overall size of body will still give considerable natural strength with, in men, capacity for becoming a jockey. In other directions have capacity for missionary work and exploration.

♅ in ♑

Darkens the complexion and skin, sometimes gives a kind of shambling gait as there can be a weakness of the knees. Hair will be lank and dark. Eyes brown and slightly protruding. Sometimes gives a semitic type of face and body. They are very shrewd in business and can become prominent in political or municipal life but do not make friends very easily even though within themselves they may wish to do so.

♅ in ♒

Shows a stocky kind of body, rather prominent eyebrows, fairly large eyes but there can be a weakness of the ankles. As a rule they are very intuitive, interested in the arts and sciences, in astrology and phrenology. Make very good psychiatrists but there is a danger of sudden collapse through undue mental strain.

♅ in ♓

Indicates a degree of physical weakness, short stature, sometimes deformed feet, sickly complexion. Nerve tension very marked, in certain instances can signify a liability to epilepsy or petit mal. Unconventional in their habits they can do things which lead to restraint, hospital treatment or even imprisonment. Not a very easy person to live with.

N.B.—Uranus generally shows a degree of nerve tension which will react very strongly upon the part of the body ruled by the sign in which it is placed. It brings a susceptibility to sudden collapse and in later years of life to a stroke.

The three planets Pluto, Neptune and Uranus are not rulers of signs in the same way as the other planets and therefore are not normally classed as significators. The indications given will therefore be more apparent when the planet concerned is in a rising position and the sign in which it is placed is upon the Ascendant.

SATURN IN THE TWELVE SIGNS

♄ in ♈

Gives a ruddy complexion, a spare, raw-boned person, full-faced, dark hair, not much beard, addicted to boasting; resolute, excitable, and very petulant.

♄ in ♉

Gives a person in no wise comely, but a heavy, lumpish, awkward appearance, dark hair, middle stature, not well made, rough in carriage, sordid, and of a worldly disposition.

♄ in ♊

Represents a person of rather tall stature, dark, sanguine complexion, oval visage, dark brown or black hair, ingenious but unpolished, perverse, and frequently unfortunate in his undertakings.

♄ in ♋

Denotes a person of middle stature, rather short than tall, sickly and feeble, meagre face, dark hair, languid eyes; the body sometimes crooked; jealous, calculating, and suspicious in his dealings.

♄ in ♌

Gives a person of moderate large stature, broad, round shoulders, wide chest, lightish hair, large boned, surly aspect, eyes sunk, apt to stoop. Qualities tolerably good, generous but passionate; not over valiant or courageous when put to the test.

♄ in ♍

Represents a person of a tall, spare body, swarthy, dark or black hair, and it plentiful; a long head, solid countenance; generally unfortunate; inclined to melancholy, retaining anger; a projector of many curious matters to little purpose; studious, subtle, reserved; inclined to servile and shuffling habits.

♄ in ♎

Describes a person above the middle stature, comely brown hair, oval face, large nose and forehead, clear complexion; one opinionated of himself, prodigal of expense. They are given to debate and controversy, and seldom leave any wealth at their death.

♄ in ♏

Represents a person of middle stature, squat, thick, trussed body, broad shoulders, black or dark hair, which is usually short and thick; quarrelsome, adventurous; one who may perform some violent and dangerous actions, though to his own detriment.

♄ in ♐

Gives a large body, brown hair, good make, tolerable complexion; obliging disposition, not covetous, moderately frugal, rarely profuse, but somewhat choleric. One who will not bear an affront, yet willing to do good to all; a lover of his friends, and merciful to an enemy.

♄ in ♑

Personates a lean, raw-boned body, dark or black hair, middle stature, dark complexion, small leering eyes, long visage, and a stooping awkward posture in walking. One who is peevish, discontented, melancholy, covetous, of few words, fearful, retains anger, and is of great gravity.

♄ in ♒

Gives a reasonable full-bodied person, a large head and face, rather inclined to corpulency, middle stature, sad-brown hair, a clear complexion, a sober, graceful deportment. Affable, courteous disposition; of an excellent, searching fancy, and generally very proficient in what he undertakes in arts or sciences; a person of a pregnant genius, yet disposed to be conceited.

♄ in ♓

Describes a middle-statured person, pale complexion, sad or dark black hair, a large head and full eye; sometimes the teeth are distorted. A person not very comely. Active in others' affairs, and given to contention and dissimulation. An uncertain, fickle person in everything; though often presenting a good exterior, yet proving unsatisfactory in the end. They are not loquacious, but deliberative, and do all things circumspectly. They are said to improve as they grow old.

N.B.— ♄ always gives bad teeth; and in this sign they are generally discoloured and rotten.

JUPITER IN THE TWELVE SIGNS

♃ in ♈

Describes a middle stature, but not stout, rather lean than corpulent, a quick and penetrating eye, a high nose, oval visage, with generally pimples or a peculiar redness in the face. They are of a free, noble, and generous disposition; very obliging, polite, and complaisant, especially to their friends.

♃ in ♉

Gives a middle stature, stout, well-set body, but, though compact, not handsome; hair brown, rough, and curling. Complexion swarthy; and frequently the skin looks shining or oily. The disposition reasonably good, judgment sound, deportment good, behaviour free and charitable; kind to women, and very humane and compassionate to the distressed.

♃ in ♊

Represents a well-made, compact body, plump, yet above the middle stature; sanguine complexion, though rather dusky; brown hair, and full, expressive eyes. The deportment graceful, affable, courteous, gentle, mild, obliging, and good-natured. An admirer of the other sex, and a lover of learning.

♃ in ♋

Gives a person of middle stature, a pale, sickly, and unwholesome complexion; oval face; hair, dark brown; body, rather plump, but disproportioned. A busy, loquacious character, very confident, and apt to intermeddle with other people's concerns. A friend of women. Fond of the water, whereon he is usually fortunate. Unless ♂ throw a good aspect to ♃, he is not courageous.

♃ in ♌

Represents a strong and well-proportioned tall body; the hair is a light or yellowish brown, and curling; complexion, ruddy; eye, full and fiery; person, rather handsome. The disposition is noble-minded, courageous, and magnanimous, but lofty, proud, and ambitious; one who delights in warlike actions, is a terror to his enemies, and who scorns to bend to them; fond of contending for honours, etc., and full of daring and enterprise.

♃ in ♍

Gives a person of a reasonably full stature, well built, and what may be termed handsome; sad-brown or black hair, ruddy complexion, but not clear or fair. One who is choleric, and too impulsive; studious, yet worldly, and by his rashness often meeting serious losses; he is not easily imposed or wrought upon by any person.

♃ in ♎

Renders the body complete and elegant, a handsome form, and inviting face; upright, tall stature, rather slender; clear complexion, a full eye, oval face, light brown hair, subject to have pimples or a rash in the face. Disposition and temper mild; behaviour, winning and obliging to all; partial to exercise and recreation; much esteemed and honoured.

♃ in ♏

Gives a middle stature, stout, compact body; dark, coarse hair, fleshy and full face; muddy, dull complexion. Manners, proud and lofty; one who is ambitious, and apt to be overbearing, resolute, confident, improvident, yet quick to take an advantage, therefore to be very warily dealt with.

♃ in ♐

Gives a fine, tall, upright body, good form and make, oval face, ruddy complexion, brown chestnut-coloured hair, full beard; but the hair falls off early in life, especially about the temples; a good eye, and much expression in the face. The mind is just and noble; disposition courteous, humane, affable, and agreeable; manners, polite and accomplished. One fond of horses and hunting.

♃ in ♑

Describes a small stature, pale complexion, thin face, little head, not much beard, weakly person, dark brown hair, said to be darker than the beard. The mind is ingenious, but narrow, wanting in sympathy, and exacting.

♃ in ♒

Personates a middle stature, well set, brown hair, clear complexion, rather corpulent, compact make; and one of a cheerful, obliging disposition, hurtful to none; well conducted, and moderate in recreations; just and merciful, good-humoured, industrious, communicative, inclined to be scientific, and but little given to extravagance.

♃ in ♓

Describes a person of middle stature, obscure complexion, plump, fleshy body, lightish-brown hair. Disposition harmless, studious, and possessed of excellent talents and good acquirements; friendly, kind, and inoffensive. They delight in good company, and to be upon the water, where if ☽ throw not an evil aspect to ♃, they are found to be fortunate.

N.B.—♃ usually gives good teeth, and frequently an apparent mark in the fore-teeth. In an airy sign, he gives broad fore-teeth; in a fiery sign, crooked; in earthy they are discoloured; and in a watery sign the teeth decay suddenly, and grow black and rotten, especially if he be in ☌ with ☋, or in any evil aspect of ♄ or ♂. If he be in a watery sign, in □ or ☍ of ☿, the party has some defect in his delivery or speech. ♃ in an airy sign, the body is more strong and corpulent; in a fiery sign more square made, and strong; in an earthy, a well-composed body; and in a watery, more fat and comely.

MARS IN THE TWELVE SIGNS

♂ in ♈

Represents a middle-statured person, well set, large boned; swarthy complexion, light hair, and curling, frequently red; austere countenance, and if ♂ be oriental, ruddy and smooth; bold and undaunted, confident, choleric, and proud; fond of war and dispute; one who often gains by those means.

♂ in ♉

Gives a middle stature, well set, rather short; dusky complexion, dark or black hair, which is rough and coarse; broad face, wide mouth; will generally have some scar or other mark in the face, which is often ruddy, but never fair; disposed to self-indulgence, speculative, headstrong, and inclined to selfish habits; generally unfortunate, but, if ♂ be near the Pleiades, remarkably so.

♂ in ♊

Gives a tall person, with black or dark brown hair (though if ♂ be in the first seven degrees of ♊, the terms of ☿, it will be light), sanguine complexion, and well-proportioned body. Restless and unsettled, but ingenious; unfortunate in most things, living in a mean way, generally shifting here and there, leaving debts unpaid, and exercising the wits for a livelihood; may be a *chevalier d'industrie*, or mere swindler. But good aspects of ☉, ♃, or ♀ will mitigate this evil tendency.

♂ in ♋

Describes a short figure and a bad complexion, without much hair, and it brown; the body is generally ill-made and crooked. The temper is uncertain; one who is given to unhealthy ways; a servile, unfortunate creature; mostly employed in some low business, being incapable of better.

♂ in ♌

Shows a well-proportioned body, rather tall; light brown hair, oval face, sanguine or sunburnt complexion, large eyes, stout limbs, and a brisk, cheerful aspect. Fond of robust sports, as hunting, riding, shooting, etc., and ready for warlike occupation at any time. A man dresses well, and is a favourite with women, but it is sometimes to his prejudice.

♂ in ♍

Produces a middle-sized body, and well made and proportioned; black hair or very dark brown; the first seven degrees give lighter hair than the rest of the sign, being the terms of ☿; the complexion is swarthy or darkish, and there is generally some scar, mark, or blemish in the face. A hasty, proud, passionate, and subtle mind; one who retains an injury, is hard to please, and generally very unfortunate in all undertakings.

♂ in ♎

Gives a neatly-made, rather tall person; the face oval, complexion sanguine, and hair light brown and soft, but, if in the last two degrees, his own term, it is more wiry and reddish. The disposition is brisk and cheerful, but fond of boasting and very haughty; one who is careful of dress. Much attached to the other sex, by whom he is also much beloved.

♂ in ♏

Produces a well-set form of middle stature, rather corpulent; swarthy complexion, black curling hair, broad and plain face. The temper is very unsociable and rash; they are generally revengeful, thoughtless, quarrelsome, and proud; yet of good genius and ready apprehension, excelling in medicine, surgery, naval, and martial occupations.

♂ in ♐

Denotes a tall person, with a well-proportioned body, compact and well-made; sanguine complexion, oval visage; a quick, penetrating eye; the mind is cheerful, merry, and jovial; but disposition hasty and passionate, high-minded and lofty, courageous, loquacious, and fond of applause; on the whole, a good character.

♂ in ♑

Represents a mean or small stature; thin, lean body, little head thin face; bad complexion, being sallow and obscure; black, lank hair. An ingenious mind, witty, shrewd, and penetrating; generally fortunate, and successful in undertakings.

♂ in ♒

Gives a well-composed body, rather corpulent, and inclined to be tall (though frequently not above the middle size), fair or clear complexion; sandy hair; a buoyant disposition, and addicted to controversy, etc.; not very fortunate in general.

♂ in ♓

Represents a middle stature, rather short and fleshy; a bad complexion, far from handsome; a debilitated look; light brown hair; of dull mind; self-indulgent, idle, and careless; not fortunate.

N.B.—If ♂ be in ☌, □, or ☍ of ♄, or with ☋, the disposition is capricious, especially if they be in angles, when the person he describes is very excitable. He is the giver of courage and resolution, which, if he be weak and afflicted, are very deficient. If ♂ be in fiery signs, he is hasty and choleric; and there is generally observed to be a falling in of the cheeks, and a lightness of feature, with an angry look; in earthy signs, a sullen, dogged temper; in airy signs, more free and obliging; in watery, more dull, and stupid, unless he be well aspected by ♃, ☉, or ☽.

THE SUN IN THE TWELVE SIGNS

☉ in ♈

Describes a good stature, strong and well made; a good complexion, though not very clear; light hair, flaxen or yellowish, and large eyes. Noble, valiant, and courageous; delighting in warlike actions and enterprise; gains victory, is famous, and a terror to enemies, etc.

☉ in ♉

Gives a short, well-set, rather ugly person; dusky complexion, brown hair, large broad face, wide mouth, and great nose. Confident, proud, and bold, fond of opposition, proud of physical strength, and one who generally is victorious.

☉ in ♊

Represents a well-proportioned body, above the middle stature, sanguine complexion, brown hair. Affable, courteous, and kind; not very fortunate, because so meek and mild-tempered as to be controlled and imposed on by others.

☉ in ♋

Gives a mean, ill-formed body, deformed in the face, with a very unhealthy aspect; the hair brown. A harmless, cheerful person, but indolent, and not fond of employment; one who spends time in sports and pastimes, dancing, etc., and is much addicted to roving.

☉ in ♌

Gives a strong, well-proportioned body, and a very portly person; sanguine complexion, light brown or yellowish hair, a full face, and large staring eyes, very prominent; there is generally a mark or scar on the face. Very just, upright, and honourable, scorning to do any meanness; punctual, faithful to friends, and magnanimous even to enemies; in short, a right royal disposition; very ambitious withal, fond of rule and authority, and given to war and dominion, conquest, etc.

☉ in ♍

Makes a person something tall of stature, and slender, but very well proportioned; good complexion, dark hair, and much of it, but not black; the mind ingenious, cheerful, and fond of honest recreations, especially agreeable convivial parties, etc.

☉ in ♎

Produces an upright, tall and slender body, full eyes, oval face, ruddy complexion, light hair, and frequently a rash or pimples in the face. The mind is honourable, and disposition good; but the party is unfortunate, especially in all matters of war or ambition, unless strong benefic influences concur.

☉ in ♏

Gives a remarkably square-built, full, fleshy person; broad face, cloudy complexion, dun or sunburnt; brown hair. The mind ingenious, but the temper rugged and overbearing; manners too brusque, disposition ambitious; one who will not admit of an equal. They are fortunate upon the seas, or as surgeons, physicians, etc.

☉ in ♐

Makes a tall, handsome, well-proportioned body, oval face, sanguine complexion, or rather olive-brown or sunburnt; light brown hair, but in the first eight degrees of the sign it is darker; one who is very lofty and proud-spirited, aiming at great things; austere and severe; and one who performs some honourable exploits, and often becomes ennobled, or receives titles, honorary distinctions, etc.

☉ in ♑

Represents a middle stature, ill-made, spare, thin body, oval face, sickly complexion; brown, soft hair, not curling, and, if in the first six degrees of the sign, it is light brown; the party is just and honourable in principles, has a tolerably fair temper, and gains love and friendship by agreeable manners; very hasty at times.

☉ in ♒

Describes a person of middle stature, well-made, corpulent body, round full face, clear complexion, and light brown hair (in the term of ♄ it is dark brown). The disposition tolerably good, free from malice or deceit, but yet vain, proud, desirous of bearing rule, and ostentatious.

☉ in ♓

Gives a stature rather short, body plump and fleshy, a round full face, and indifferent complexion; light brown hair; in the first eight degrees of the sign it is flaxen, and very soft; the party is extremely partial to society, very inoffensive, fond of pleasures, etc., and, though harmless to others, may ruin himself by extravagance.

Note.—The ☉ rising at birth generally produces a sunburnt or freckled appearance. It confers a degree of pride and a desire for fame.

VENUS IN THE TWELVE SIGNS

♀ in ♈

Describes a middle stature, rather tall and slender, light hair (if in the term of ♃, dark), good complexion, a pensive aspect, and usually a mark or scar in the face (often marked more or less with small-pox, according as ♀ may be afflicted or not). They are generally unfortunate both to themselves and others, unless ♀ have a ⚹ or △ of ♃.

♀ in ♉

Gives a handsome person, though the stature is not great; the body is extremely well made, plump, but not gross; and if ♀ be well aspected, they are very handsome; the complexion is ruddy, but not fair; generally females are handsome brunettes, and have much the face and figure of the *Venus de Medici.* The hair is generally brown, and, if ♀ be in her own term, it is very soft and luxuriant; if in the term of ♃, it is a shining black. The eyes are generally black, and very expressive. The temper is mild and winning, the disposition kind, humane, obliging, etc. They generally gain much respect from those with whom they come into contact or deal, and are fortunate.

♀ in ♊

Gives one above the middle height, slender, upright, and well-made body. The complexion clear and fair, with soft brown hair; frequently brown or hazel eyes. They are good-humoured, loving, liberal, just, and charitable; and rarely guilty of anything dishonourable.

♀ in ♋

Represents a short person, a fleshy body, round, pale, and sickly face, with light hair; and if the ☽ be with ♀, and they in the ascendant, the face will be quite white and wan, and the hair very light coloured; but if ♀ be in the term of ♂, the hair may be reddish, and a tinge of colour appear in the cheeks. They have generally small grey or greenish eyes. The disposition is idle and dull, and the sense of duty weak; they are fond of society and every form of pleasure; if it be a female, she is careless of her home and other duties. At the worst they are very fickle and timid, put the best side outwards, and seem to be in earnest when they are not; ever mutable and inconstant.

♀ in ♌

Gives a person reasonably tall of stature, well-composed body, clear complexion, round face, full eye, freckled and fair skin, hair reddish, or it may be flaxen. They are petulant and passionate, soon angry, and soon pleased again; free, generous, sociable, and good-humoured, but rather proud, and frequently indisposed, though not seriously.

♀ in ♍

Shows a tall, well-proportioned figure, oval face, dark hair, or, if in her own term, sad brown, and a dusky complexion. They are ingenious, eloquent, active, and clever; of an aspiring turn, but rarely successful in their pursuits; generally unfortunate.

♀ in ♎

Describes an upright, tall, elegant person, extremely well made, with a genteel carriage. The face is oval, and rather beautiful, having pleasing smiles and beautiful dimples; but they are frequently freckled; the hair is brown and soft, but rather grows long than plentiful. They are kind, affectionate, and very obliging; and generally well-beloved by all with whom they have any dealings. If ♀ be in the ascendant, and there be no afflicting aspects, but ♃ cast a △ from ♒, the party, if a female, will be a perfect beauty.

♀ in ♏

Denotes a short, stout, well-set, corpulent body, broad face and dusky complexion, and dark or black hair, one who has nothing very pleasant in the countenance. They are often envious, unhealthy, and foolish; given to contention, and, if ♀ be afflicted by ♄ or ♂, to very ungracious actions; and if both ♄ and ♂ afflict, and there be no assistance by ☉ or ♃, they are possessed of hurtful propensities.

♀ in ♐

Represents a person rather tall than otherwise, well made; clear or sanguine complexion, fair, oval face, and brown hair. They are generous, spirited, aiming at no mean things, rather proud, passionate, yet, in general, good-tempered, kind, and inoffensive. They delight in innocent recreations, and are, in short, very obliging, fortunate persons.

♀ in ♑

Describes a small-sized person, short stature, a pale face, thin and sickly; dark hair (but, if ♀ be in her own term, a sad-brown). They are generally persons of large appetite, fond of enjoyment, not fortunate, subject to sudden changes in life and strange catastrophes.

♀ in ♒

Gives a handsome, well-formed person, clear complexion, rather corpulent or large body, brown hair (if she be in her own term, flaxen). A good disposition, quiet, affable, courteous, not at all inclined to vicious actions, peaceable, obliging to all, fortunate in affairs, and respected by friends and acquaintance in general.

D

♀ in ♓

Personates a middle stature, a fleshy, plump body, a round full face, with a dimple in the chin, good complexion, between pale and ruddy. Good-humoured, just, kind, mild and peaceable, ingenious, but somewhat unstable, yet moderately fortunate in the world.

MERCURY IN THE TWELVE SIGNS

☿ in ♈

Gives a moderate stature, spare and thin body, oval face, light brown and curling hair, dull complexion. A mind rather ill-disposed, addicted to dispute, smart business tricks, and unworthy actions; in short, a cunning person.

☿ in ♉

Gives a middle-sized, corpulent, thick person, strong and well set, swarthy sunburnt complexion, dark short and thick hair. Idle, slothful, one who loves ease and luxury, and who hurts himself by his associations.

☿ in ♊

Shows a tall, upright, straight body, well formed, brown hair, good complexion, and a very intelligent look. An ingenious pregnant fancy, a good orator, a cunning lawyer, or clever bookseller; one who perfectly understands his own interests, and (if ☿ be not afflicted) one who is subtle, not easily deluded by the most cunning knave he may encounter.

☿ in ♋

Personates a low, short stature, or squat figure, an ill complexion, a thin sharp face, small eyes, sharp nose, dark hair; one who is fretful, inconstant, disposed to idleness, yet quick to take advantage, and not to be depended upon.

☿ in ♌

Gives a full large body and good stature, dull, swarthy, sunburnt complexion, light brown hair, round face, full eyes, a broad or high nose. A hasty, proud, conceited, ambitious, boasting, contentious, and troublesome character.

☿ in ♍

Denotes a tall, slender, well-proportioned person, dark brown hair or (if ☿ be in the terms of ♃ or ♄) black hair, not a clear complexion; a long visage, and austere countenance. A very witty, ingenious, talented mind; and, if ☿ be free from affliction, a profound scholar or linguist, and capable of any undertaking which requires great ability.

☿ in ♎

Personates a tall body, well made, but not thin; light brown, smooth hair, a ruddy or sanguine complexion. A just, virtuous, prudent person, a lover and promoter of learning, and having great natural abilities and many acquired accomplishments.

☿ in ♏

Gives a short, mean stature, full and well-set but ill-made body, broad shoulders, swarthy, dark complexion, brown curling hair. Not any way elegant or pleasing, yet ingenious and studious; very careful of their own interests, fond of the other sex, and partial to company and merry-making.

☿ in ♐

Denotes a person of tall stature, well formed, not corpulent, but rather large-boned and spare; an oval face, a large nose, and ruddy complexion. Hasty, but soon reconciled, rash in many things to their own injury, yet well disposed, striving after honourable things, but seldom attaining them; not very fortunate.

☿ in ♑

Gives a mean, small stature, often crooked made and bow-legged, a thin face and figure, dusky complexion, and brown hair. A very peevish, discontented, dejected, sickly, feeble person, yet active; one who is unfortunate to self and disagreeable to others, owing to a suspicious nature and ill temper.

☿ in ♒

Shows a person of middle height, rather fleshy and corpulent, a good complexion and clear skin, with brown hair and full face. An ingenious, obliging character, inclined to study, fond of arts and sciences, very inventive, and remarkable for talent, as well as being a humane, kind, charitable person.

☿ in ♓

Gives a short, squat, dumpy figure (though, if in his own term or that of ♄, rather thin), pale face, brown hair, sickly look, and very hairy body. A very fretful, repining, foppish person, disposed to irregular habits; if a man, very insignificant and contemptible.

THE MOON IN THE TWELVE SIGNS

☽ in ♈

Describes a person of indifferent stature, rather fleshy or plump, round face, tolerably good complexion, light brown or flaxen hair. The mind is rash, angry, ambitious, and aspiring, often changing; and such undergo various mutations in life; not often fortunate.

☽ in ♉

Gives a strong, corpulent, well-set body, rather short, pretty good complexion, dark brown or black hair. Gentle, obliging, kind, sober, just, and honest; one who gains esteem, is much respected, and attains preferment according to the situation in life.

☽ in ♊

Describes a tall, well-formed, upright, comely person, brown hair, good complexion, between pale and sanguine. The mind is ingenious, yet crafty and changeful; not of the best disposition, nor very fortunate, unless other good testimonies by aspects of ♃, ☉, or ♀ concur.

☽ in ♋

Represents a middle stature, well-proportioned, and fleshy person, a round, full face, pale, dusky complexion, sad-brown hair. The mind is flexible, given to change; a merry, easy, pleasant disposition, very harmless and peaceable, fond of good company; one who is generally well-beloved, and fortunate in most affairs; unsteady, but free from passion or rash actions; a great traveller.

☽ in ♌

Denotes a person above the middle size, well proportioned, strong and large-boned, sanguine complexion, light brown hair, large and prominent eyes, and full face. A lofty, proud, aspiring person, very ambitious, and desirous to bear rule; one who abhors servitude or dependence, and is generally an unfortunate person.

☽ in ♍

Describes a rather tall person, dark brown or black hair, oval face, rather ruddy, but tolerably clear complexion. An ingenious, reserved, covetous, melancholy, unfortunate person; not in general very well disposed, and one who seldom performs any very commendable actions.

☽ in ♎

Gives a tall, well-composed body, with smooth, light brown hair, handsome, and pleasant cheerful countenance, fine red and white complexion. They are merry, jocund, and pleasant, very fond of amusement, and much admired by the opposite sex; if a woman, she will be courted by numbers, but yet not be fortunate, unless ♀, the dispositor, be very strong and well aspected, etc.

☽ in ♏

Denotes a thick, short, and ill-shaped person, a fleshy obscure complexion, dark hair, often black. They are irregular, impulsive, contentious, and callous; and if it be a female, she is generally impulsive in her actions, and if the ☽ be afflicted by the □ or ☍ of ♄ or ♂, she will suffer thereby.

☽ in ♐

Represents a handsome, well-proportioned, and rather tall person; oval face, sanguine complexion, rather bronzed, and bright brown or shining chestnut hair. The disposition is good, open and generous, but hasty and passionate, yet forgiving; one who aims at great things, is fortunate, and much respected by those with whom he associates.

☽ in ♑

Gives a person of low stature, a thin, small, weak body, bad health, and feeble, especially about the knees; the complexion bad, black hair, and small features; one who is inactive, dull; not ingenious, generally very selfish in his conduct, and held in low esteem by his associates.

☽ in ♒

Represents a middle-sized person, well made, and rather corpulent, brown hair, clear skin, and sanguine complexion. They are ingenious, affable, courteous, and inoffensive; a lover of curious and scientific studies, having much invention, and a person rarely guilty of unworthy actions.

☽ in ♓

Describes a person of a mean or low stature, but plump or fat, pale and bloated face, light brown hair, and sleepy eyes; one not inclined to action except for pleasure; unfortunate both to self and others; inconstant.

N.B.—if ☽ be well aspected, and in a good house, the disposition is much improved.

———

[The student is warned to apply these descriptions with caution, more particularly in regard to the character ascribed to each.—S.]

TERMS OF THE PLANETS

According to the Egyptians

Sign.	Planetary Terminations.				
♈	♃ 6°	♀ 12°	☿ 20°	♂ 25°	♄ 30°
♉	♀ 8	☿ 14	♃ 22	♄ 27	♂ 30
♊	☿ 6	♃ 12	♀ 17	♂ 24	♄ 30
♋	♂ 7	♀ 13	☿ 19	♃ 26	♄ 30
♌	♃ 6	♀ 11	♄ 18	☿ 24	♂ 30
♍	☿ 7	♀ 17	♃ 21	♂ 28	♄ 30
♎	♄ 6	☿ 14	♃ 21	♀ 28	♂ 30
♏	♂ 7	♀ 11	☿ 19	♃ 24	♄ 30
♐	♃ 12	♀ 17	☿ 21	♄ 26	♂ 30
♑	☿ 7	♃ 14	♀ 22	♄ 26	♂ 30
♒	☿ 7	♀ 13	♃ 20	♂ 25	♄ 30
♓	♀ 12	♃ 16	☿ 19	♂ 28	♄ 30

Note.—This table of the " terms " or terminations of the planets will serve to indicate which degrees of the Zodiac are ruled by them.   Thus, Jupiter rules the first to sixth degrees of Aries, Venus the seventh to twelfth inclusive, of the same sign, and so of the rest in their order, as shown above.

NOTES TO BOOK I

.

ON THE DIVISIONS OF THE ZODIAC

WHETHER the influences and qualities of the several signs were revealed to man, or were read into them by empirical art in the course of ages, we can safely say that the influences are there, and that, as Paracelsus says, " Man is related to the stars by reason of his sidereal body," which, by modern astro-psychologists, is called " the astral." Personally we would incline to the belief that the celestial scroll, with all its images and symbols, came as a complete revelation to the God-man Adam, or such first of human kind as may be understood by that name, into whose nostrils was breathed the *nephesh cheyim*, the " breath of lives "—an inspiration as much spiritual, mental, and psychic, as purely physical; that God covered Himself with the spangled vestment of heaven, ordered the laws of human thought, and drew, by the celestial fires, man's mind to things that were not of earth. Then came the revelation, and the reading of the scroll.

Such is the immortality of tradition, that the same signs and symbols stand for the same things, and carry the same meanings, as in the days when, according to Josephus, Seth " engraved them upon pillars of stone." Some have imagined these pillars of stone to be the Pyramids of Egypt; but however that may be, the Jewish historian says they were to be seen in his day. Herein Josephus voices a tradition which clearly shows that, as we have said on our first page, the busy hand of man could not mar the sacred record. At first an inspiration, a revelation, the celestial language became a traditional knowledge, which spread over the whole earth, permeated the daily life of the nations, engaged the minds of princes and rulers, and finally became established as a sacred science in the temples of India, Babylonia, Assyria, Egypt, Greece, and Rome. As a tradition it was imperishable; for mankind can never be free from tradition. We are born in it; we breathe in it, and speak it from our infancy. We fashion our thought upon it; it moulds our life. We speak of *lunatics* and *jovial* men, of *martial* men and *venerables*, waking thereby the echoes of that old tradition which referred these qualities to the dominion of the Moon, of Jupiter, Mars, and Venus. So, while *mar* means a hurt, the red planet will be called Mars and nothing else; because, primarily, the names of things express their qualities.

It is the same in regard to the signs of the Zodiac. Our knowledge of them is purely traditional. If by daily experiment we find that knowledge to be true, it is the greater argument for primary inspiration, as well as for the immortality of tradition.

The signs of the Zodiac must not be confounded with the constellations bearing the same names. The fixed or intellectual Zodiac is counted from the Vernal Equinox, while the shifting or natural Zodiac is counted from the beginning of the constellation Aries. The two Zodiacs coincided in the year A.D. 498, as noticed by Varaha Mihira in his *Brihat Samhitâ*, already referred to, and confirmed by references to former authors. The precession of the equinoxes causes the constellations to retrograde through the signs of the Zodiac at the rate of about 50¼″ a year, so that at the present time the divergence amounts to about 19° 34′ 26″; *i.e.*, the first point of the constellation Aries is now located in 10° 25′ 34″ of the sign Pisces, and is moving towards Aquarius.

ON LILLY'S DESCRIPTIONS

WE have ventured to introduce Lilly's description of persons in the Appendix to this Book, because Lilly is a reputable author, whose " Christian Astrology " is a standard work on the horoscopical science, and much esteemed by modern votaries of Astrology.

For quite other reasons, which the polite reader will appreciate on reference to the original in the Ashmolean MSS., we have thought fit to paraphrase, refine, and otherwise temper the language of Lilly's delineations. The conditions of seventeenth century life, wherein the controlling influence of social and mental culture did not obtain so widely as in these days, no doubt would serve to bring into prominence many of the corrupt tendencies specified by our author in the forcible manner of one who illustrates by reference to extreme types. At the same time, it is proper to reflect that, although many of these illustrations are not likely to find their exact reflection in most modern instances, yet the possibility of corruption is inherent in human nature, and where the refining influences of good parental care, of mental and moral education, are lacking, otherwise venial faults and common failings may easily descend to the worse evils depicted by our author in the appropriate language of his day. Quite apart from the indications of character derived from Astrology, however, the influences of heredity, environment, education, hygiene, food, and climate, all play their part as factors in the development or suppression of inherent faculty, and must, therefore, be taken into consideration. Yet those who have marked and thought upon the wide differences of character existing in children born of the same parents, fed at the same table, taught in the same school, and otherwise brought up under like conditions, will be disposed to believe that, behind all these influences there is an Ego, in no sense to be regarded as the product of those influences, but which, on the contrary, is using them for the purposes of its own evolution—pushing through them, so to speak, into a fuller and more perfect expression. Those of our readers who hold the doctrine of reincarnation, or metempsychosis, will follow us more intelligently than others.

BOOK II

THE READING OF A HOROSCOPE

CHAPTER I

THE BODILY FORM, DEFECTS AND ACCIDENTS

THE rising sign, the ruler of the ascendant and that of the sign intercepted in the first house (if any), and the planets closely aspecting the ascendant, considered with the signs they are in, will determine much concerning the bodily form to which the native will arrive at maturity. (See Book i, chap. ii, and Appendix.)

Primarily, the ruling sign, or that which holds the eastern horizon, is the basis of the physical temperament, as set forth in the chapter on the " Signatures of the Zodiac." The modifying factors are the lord or ruler of the rising sign, and the planets in close aspect to the ascending degree, considered according to the signs they severally occupy. The peculiarities conferred by these signs will be found more or less reproduced in the body of the native.

Pluto in the ascendant, as indicated in the Appendix to Book i, affects the size of the body according to the sign which is rising. Thus Cancer, Virgo and Capricorn will shorten the height but Gemini, Sagittarius and Pisces, will increase the height. Taurus, Leo, Scorpio and Aquarius increase the width giving thickset bodies.

Uranus in the ascendant, or in close aspect thereto, gives length of limb and a slender body.

Mars gives a larger form than that indicated by the rising sign, if it be close to the horizon; and generally it contributes a ruddiness to the complexion, due to the presence of much iron in the system. If in exact conjunction or any aspect to the ascending degree, it operates to produce red hair and grey eyes, the ruddy colour and steel-grey being peculiar to the god of war. When rising it frequently gives a mole, a mark, or scar in the face.

Any of the earthy signs ascending, and two or three planets in the ascendant, makes a dwarf, or one much under the usual stature, more especially if Saturn be one of such planets.

Jupiter increases the vitality and gives bulk to the figure.

Saturn makes the complexion paler or darker. It was rising in Sagittarius in the horoscope of President Abraham Lincoln. His thin, pale, and somewhat melancholic face will no doubt be familiar to many of our readers from photographs and pictures of him. (See Book ii, chap. xv, " Rank ".)

Venus rising confers greater elegance on face and figure. When closely aspecting the ascendant or its ruler, it gives some claim to good looks.

Neptune causes the face to become prematurely wrinkled, owing to a sapping or wasting away of the vital fluids.

Venus and Jupiter in conjunction or opposition from any part of the figure gives blue eyes. It has been frequently noticed that when this position or aspect occurs, the native has very deep blue and almost violet eyes.

Leo, Sagittarius, Gemini, and Aquarius produce tall persons.

Aries, Libra, Virgo, and Scorpio give a medium stature.

Taurus, Capricorn, Cancer, and Pisces produce small persons.

But these observations are, of course, only general; they are subject to modifying influences.

The planets have each two complexions, the Sun and Moon only one each. They are as follows:—

Fair	☉	♌	—	♋	☽	Dark
,,		♒	♄	♑		,,
,,		♐	♃	♓		,,
,,		♈	♂	♏		,,
,,		♎	♀	♉		,,
,,		♍	☿	♊		,,

The Sun rules the first half of the male signs, and the second half of female signs; while the Moon takes the remaining halves of these signs. The Sun renders the complexion fairer, the Moon makes it darker, when ruling the half sign rising at birth.

PHYSICAL PECULIARITIES

The Eyes.—The Moon being with the Pleiades, in ♉ 29°, or in the Asselli, ♌ 6°, or with Antares in ♐ 8°, or the Sun in these places, afflicted by Mars from an angle, the person born may become blind.

The same result follows from the Moon in opposition to the Sun, or the Moon in conjunction with the Sun, in any of these nebulous parts of the Zodiac.

When either the Sun or Moon is in or near ♉ 29°, ♌ 6°, or ♐ 8°, and afflicted by any planet, defective eyesight is the result, the cause differing according to the afflicting planet.

The Sun in Aquarius, afflicted by Saturn, especially by the opposition or conjunction, stone-blindness frequently results. The sign Aquarius corresponds to the etheric vibrations, and therefore has affinity with the sense of sight.

The Sun and Moon being in opposition from Aries and Libra gives weak sight, and sometimes sore eyes. The same if the Sun or Moon be in Aries and afflicted by Mars or Saturn.

Pluto rising, squared by the Sun and Moon will also cause weak sight and accentuate the liability to blindness more especially if the signs Taurus, Leo or Aquarius are involved.

If a malefic planet occupy any of the nebulous parts of the Zodiac already referred to, and afflict the Sun or Moon by aspect, then danger of blindness will arise from an accident, more particularly if the malefic be elevated above the luminary.

In this matter it is better to have the Moon afflicted than the Sun, for it gives greater hope of relief.

The Ears.—Mercury ruling the twelfth house, and afflicted by the malefics, Uranus, Saturn, or Mars, or being in conjunction with the Sun, deafness ensues. The same happens when Mercury is *in* the twelfth house, and so afflicted by the malefics or in conjunction with the Sun. Mercury, ruling the intellect, is thus held in bondage, as denoted by the signification of the twelfth house.

The third sign of the Zodiac (♊), which is ruled by Mercury, corresponds to the atmospheric vibrations, and therefore has affinity with the sense of hearing.

The Tongue and Organs of Speech.—If Mercury, being ruler of the sixth house, is afflicted by Mars or Saturn, and posited in either of the watery signs—Cancer, Scorpio, or Pisces—the native will have a perceptible stammer, lisp, or other impediment.

Mercury anywhere in the figure in the watery signs, afflicted by Saturn, causes a stammer. If Mars add his influence by aspect, then the native will talk very fast, lisp, or pronounce his words badly.

When Mercury holds any of the first six degrees of Scorpio, and is in opposition to the Moon, the native will have a defect in his speech.

Saturn ascending in any of the bestial signs—Aries, Taurus, Leo, or Capricorn—or in any of the " mute " signs—Cancer, Scorpio, or Pisces—causes an impediment of speech.

Mercury in the sixth house, in conjunction with the Sun or afflicted by Saturn or Mars, causes a defect in the speech.

The second house (and the corresponding sign, Taurus) governs the vocal organs; and if a " sign of voice," *i.e.*, either Gemini, Libra, or Aquarius (the airy sign), be found in the second house of the horoscope of birth, more especially if Venus or Mercury be therein and free from affliction, then eloquence or some vocal gift may be predicted.

The Hair.—Mars exactly rising produces red hair. The greater the amount of iron, the more ruddy is the hair. Sulphur darkens the hair, and therefore Saturn rising produces black hair. The relative strength of Saturn and Mars in the horoscope, and their intimacy with the ascending degree, will determine whether the hair is naturally light or dark at maturity, consideration being always made of the characteristic of the rising sign.

Mars afflicting Venus, and elevated above Venus in the figure, causes the hair to fall off soon. Mars in Aquarius, Gemini, or Sagittarius, afflicting Venus, the same effect is produced.

Jupiter, being ruler of the ascendant, and occidental, *i.e.*, between the first and fourth, or the seventh and tenth cusps, produces premature baldness. The same if Saturn be ruler of the ascendant, and occidental.

The Limbs.—The Sun or Moon afflicted in the signs Capricorn, Aquarius, or Pisces often produces lameness, or, if any of these signs occupy the eastern horizon, and the rising degree be afflicted by the presence or evil aspect of the malefics, a similar defect is produced; and always that part of the body is afflicted wherein the Sun or Moon is found to be situated at birth, if in evil aspect or conjunction with the malefic planets.

Pluto rising in Gemini or Sagittarius afflicted by the Sun or Moon, together with Saturn brings a liability to partial or complete paralysis of either or both upper and lower limbs according to the severity of the affliction.

Thus far we see how certain defects in the body are brought about. Besides this, it is necessary to observe whether the afflicting planets are angular or out of their dignities, for then they increase the evils denoted. If however, Jupiter or Venus assist the afflicted planet by their benefic aspects, conjunction, or parallel, then the evils will be ameliorated, and assistance will proceed from the quarter indicated by the position of the benefic planet.

ACCIDENTS

When a planet, even a benefic, is in the ascendant, and afflicted by the evil aspect or conjunction of Uranus, Saturn, or Mars, it denotes injuries to that part of the body indicated by the sign ascending, or that occupied by the afflicting planet, more particularly if cardinal signs are involved.

Pluto rising in the common signs, Gemini, Virgo, Sagittarius, or Pisces and in affliction with the Moon, Mars or Uranus increases the liability to accidents through travel which break the limbs and can cause amputations.

The Sun or Moon rising, and thus afflicted, indicates similar dangers. Again, the Sun or Moon, being in the oriental quadrants, viz.: between the ascendant and mid-heaven or the descendant and nadir, and afflicted by the square or opposition of Mars or Saturn, will produce accidents.

The luminaries being afflicted by the malefics from Gemini, Aquarius, or Sagittarius denotes danger of gunshot or wounds if Mars be the afflicting planet; but Saturn disposes to produce falls and bruises, and hurts by falling things.

Mars or Saturn rising, and not in aspect to the luminaries, still denotes accidents at such time as they may form their exact conjunction with the ascending degree by oblique ascension. This calculation is explained in Book iii of this work.

If the malefics, Uranus and Mars, or Saturn and Mars, are in conjunction or opposition, especially when in cardinal signs and angles, they denote serious physical hurt to the native.

The first decanate of Leo and Aquarius, and the last of Taurus and Scorpio, dispose to drowning, as also the second decanate of Virgo, when the lights are afflicted therein, or the malefics afflict the lights from those parts of the Zodiac.

In regard to the nature of the accidents thus foreshown, Mars denotes cuts, burns, scalds, bites, etc., according to the sign it occupies, whether a fiery, airy, watery, or earthy sign, a human or animal sign, etc., taken together with the house it is in.

Saturn in this respect denotes blows, contusions, falls and dislocations.

Uranus denotes strange and unexpected hurts, accidents by machinery, electricity, etc. The part of the body liable to accident may be known by the sign and house the malefic is in.

Observe that the *odd* houses—first, third, fifth, etc.—denote the *left* side in a *male* horoscope, the *right* side in a *female* horoscope. The even houses—second, fourth, etc.—denote the right side in a male and the left in a female.

The first ten degrees of a sign show the upper part of that portion of the body ruled by it; the second decanate shows the middle part; and the last ten degrees show the lower part.

Thus Mars in ♉ 24° afflicting the Moon shows hurt to the *neck;* the twenty-fourth degree of Taurus shows the *lower* part of neck; and, if Mars be in the third house, the *left* side in a male, the *right* in a female. Thus all affections of the body may be localised.

CHAPTER II

THE PHYSICAL CONSTITUTION

A PRIMARY consideration in the horoscope of a newly-born child is that of its constitution and the likelihood of its reaching mature years; for, if life is denied at the outset, it will be manifestly absurd to predict anything concerning the fortunes, marriage, profession, and other incidents of adult age.

Consider, then, the nature of the rising sign, its lord or ruler, the nature of the planets rising (if any), the condition of the Moon, and the lord of the eighth house.

Pluto rising, afflicted by the luminaries or by the lord of the sixth or eighth shows difficulty in rearing an infant. There will be particular need for augmentation of natural feeding and for care during the teething period.

Should Saturn, Uranus, or Mars be found near the rising degree, afflicted by the ruler of the eighth house, and the Moon at the same time afflicted by the Sun, the premature death of the infant may be expected.

If the ruler of the ascendant be in the sixth house, afflicted by the ruler of the eighth, without assistance from Jupiter or Venus, then the child will be very sickly, and will die before reaching maturity.

In these and similar cases, the greater the affliction of the *significators of life, viz.:* the Sun, Moon, the ascendant, and its ruler, the shorter will be the life. When *all* of these significators are afflicted, without assistance from the benefics, the child is either still-born or dies immediately after birth.

A male child born at an eclipse of the Sun, or a female at an eclipse of the Moon, seldom draws breath, or is born only to see the light and die. This happened in the case of the Duchess of Fife's first child, which was born during an eclipse of the Sun on Tuesday, 17th June, 1890, the eclipse falling on the cusp of the fifth house in the horoscope of the Princess.

When, however, the ruler of the ascendant is found in the sixth house, assisted by the good aspects or conjunction of either Jupiter or Venus, or by planets in their dignities, even though afflicted by the ruler of the eighth house, the child, although sickly, will be reared.

The strength of the constitution mainly depends on the nature of the sign rising, and the condition of the Sun.

The signs are classified as follows:—

Aries, Leo, Libra, and Sagittarius are strongly vital signs, capable of withstanding considerable strain in the form of sickness during early years. They give much promise of continued life even in severely afflicted genitures.

Taurus, Gemini, Virgo, Scorpio, and Aquarius are moderately vital, and, with agreeable aspects, will bring the native safely to mature life.

Cancer, Capricorn, and Pisces are the weakest signs under which persons can be born. When they are rising, and the usual indications of weakness are shown, as explained above, then the child will be reared only with great difficulty, and may even die soon after birth.

The worst signs of short life are present when the Sun and Moon are both afflicted; when the ruler of the ascendant is in the sixth or eighth house, and the ascendant is vitiated by the presence of the malefics, Neptune, Uranus, Saturn, or Mars, the rising sign being either Cancer, Capricorn, or Pisces.

When Taurus rises with Mars or Saturn therein, the child will be subject to fits during dentition, and if the Sun or Moon be afflicted in a fixed sign, the child will die in a paroxysm.

It is important also to notice what aspect was last formed between the Sun and Moon, and what planets the Moon separates from and applies to. For if, in a weak nativity, the Moon be separating from a benefic, and applying by evil aspect or conjunction to a malefic, the child will hardly attain more than four years. On the contrary, if the Moon be separating from a malefic, and applying to the good aspect or conjunction of a benefic, then the child will be reared, though the nativity be otherwise a weak one.

In the horoscope of an adult, the duration of life may be judged by the sign rising, and the condition of the Sun, Moon, and ascendant. The Sun in a fiery sign and the Moon in a watery sign are indicative of a well-balanced temperament; and when the Sun or Moon is found in the first, tenth, eleventh, or second house, well aspected by Jupiter and Venus, a long life may be predicted.

Mars, in any aspect to the Sun or Moon, gives vital heat and a good circulation, with the power to throw off diseases. But if in evil aspect, it disposes to accidents.

When Saturn is rising, and the Sun and Moon are in evil aspect to one another, or when Saturn is in the sixth house, or the Sun or Moon therein badly afflicted, the native suffers much ill health, and easily succumbs to evil directions. If the rising sign be also a weak one, the life will be short.

When a malefic planet, afflicting the Sun or Moon, is elevated above the luminary, it is more evil than when the luminary is elevated above the malefic. And this holds good in regard to all horoscopical considerations. The more elevated the planet may be which favours or afflicts the significator of life or fortune, the more powerful is its action.

CHAPTER III

PHYSICAL INFIRMITIES

IN order to learn the various ailments to which the native will be liable, attention must be paid to those planets which afflict the Sun and Moon. The affliction from a benefic planet can only be by evil aspect, whereas in the case of a malefic the affliction may be by conjunction, parallel, or evil aspect.

In this matter, observe that the Sun becomes the significator of the radical constitution, of inherent tendency and hereditary transmission; while the Moon indicates acquired tendencies, and such affections as proceed from external causes, such as food, clothing, climate, habit, etc. Again, the Sun indicates chronic and lasting affections of the body; the Moon denotes acute ailments, and such as arise from the accidents of life. The Sun is organic; the Moon is functional.

Therefore, observe, first of all, the nature of the planets afflicting the Sun, taking note of the signs they occupy. These will declare certain hereditary and organic tendencies. Next, the Moon, in a similar manner, will indicate by its evil aspects those ailments which will arise after birth to the detriment of the native's health.

Thus, if Saturn were in Leo, the heart and dorsal region would be affected; if Saturn afflicted the Moon, the heart would *become* affected by weakness, debility, or grief; but if Saturn afflicted the Sun, the heart would *already* be affected from birth by hereditary transmission, and organic disorder would soon manifest itself.

The places occupied by the malefics are always points of affection. The planet's nature, considered with that of the sign it is in, will determine the character of the evil tendency and the part of the body likely to be affected.

When the malefics are in oriental quarters of the figure, the illness will be short, acute, and painful; but when occidental, tedious and prolonged illnesses are shown.

The Sun or Moon afflicted in the seventh house or in the sixth, much illness is shown. Again, the luminaries afflicted in the oriental quarters show acute pains and accidents. In the occidental quarters the luminaries afflicted show diseases.

The Sun and Mercury, afflicted in the sign Pisces, in the sixth house, when Virgo is rising (as sometimes happens with those born soon after sunset between 19th February and 20th March), shows a strong tendency to consumption.

When the Sun is afflicted by Saturn in square or opposition, and Saturn occupies the meridian of the horoscope, a wasting disease or consumption is shown. This is particularly true if Saturn be in any of the common signs, Gemini, Virgo, Sagittarius, or Pisces.

The student is referred to Book i, chap. ii, for the parts of the body ruled by the signs of the Zodiac. As regards the planets:

Saturn denotes colds, contraction, ossification, obstructions, compression, constipation, weakness, and festering diseases; dull, heavy pains and aches.

Jupiter denotes apoplexy, pleurisy, and corrupted blood, diseases arising from too full a habit, excess, and surfeit.

Mars denotes heat, inflammation, swellings, ruptures, sores, effusion of blood, fevers, and sharp pains.

Venus denotes such as are incident to the generative system, as also small-pox, measles, sloughings, etc., arising from weakness and poison.

Mercury denotes nervous complaints, restlessness, mental worry, sleeplessness, irregularities in food, overworked brain, etc.

The Moon, when afflicting the ascendant or Sun, denotes colds, humidity, dropsical swellings, weakness, and irregularities.

The Sun, when afflicting the ascendant or Moon, denotes fevers, sunstroke, and ills arising from excess of heat.

Pluto afflicting the ascendant or the luminaries brings disorders caused through the work carried out particularly in those industries where fumes, rays, radiation, etc., occur.   Those working in nuclear activities will be particularly susceptible.

Neptune in the ascendant, square to it or to the Moon will cause wasting diseases and ailments which have their origin in drugs, bites of animals, stings of insects, and through drunkenness.

Uranus near the ascendant or in square to the Sun intensifies the liability to heart trouble and to strokes.

In female horoscopes, the positions and affections of the Moon and Venus are of vital importance. The supreme function of maternity, the regularity of the system, and the health after puberty depend almost wholly on the condition of these two bodies in the horoscope of birth.

If, therefore, the Moon should be in square or opposition to Venus in a female horoscope, the catamenia may be profuse and weakening; and if, at the same time, Saturn afflict Venus, they are likely to be painful and irregular, and may even be entirely suppressed.

When Mars afflicts Venus, and the latter is in evil aspect to the Moon, there is a probability that the periods will be very painful, irritable, and profuse, and there is danger of a flooding haemorrhage.

When Venus is afflicted by both the Moon and Saturn, Venus being in the sign of Saturn, and the Moon in that of Venus, it denotes danger of the periods never occurring, and in some cases indicates barrenness.

Even when Venus does not afflict the Moon, but Saturn afflicts either Venus or the Moon, the periods may be irregular and liable to be suppressed.

Good health happens, in either sex, when the Moon is free from affliction and supported by the good aspects of Jupiter and Venus, and when the ascendant is free from the presence of evil planets. The health, under these conditions, will be such that even a feeble constitution will outlast the wear and tear of life, and bring the native to a mature old age.

The sixth house, the sign thereon, and its ruler, being free from the presence and evil aspects of the malefics, does much to confirm good health and to establish the constitution of the native. The conjunction of the rulers of the first and sixth, or the first and eighth houses, unless free from affliction, forewarns of continued sickness and early death.

THE POLARITY OF THE SIGNS

It has been found, by repeated and universal observation, that the signs of the Zodiac have a direct influence upon the human organism from head to foot. But apart from the *direct* influence exerted by a particular sign on a certain part of the human organism, there is also a *sympathetic* influence, extending from any given region or zone in the body to certain other zones. This is due to the polarity existing between opposite points of the zodiacal circle, and the diamagnetic currents instituted thereby between points at right angles thereto. Thus the polarity of Aries 1° is opposite to that of Libra 1°; the line between these two points forming the magnetic axis of a sphere whose equator lies between Cancer 1° and Capricorn 1°. Similarly each degree of the Zodiac has its polarity.

There is thus a magnetic relationship existing between all signs that are at right angles to one another, or in opposition; and as each of these signs has a direct influence upon a certain zone of the human body, it will be seen that each one of these zones exerts in its turn a sympathetic influence upon three others, *viz.*, those that are governed by the signs in square and opposition to its own.

The following familiar arrangement of the signs will show which are in sympathetic *rapport* with one another, and, therefore, what parts of the body exert a mutual and reciprocal influence:—

Thus Taurus governs the region of the neck, including the cerebellum, or *arbor vitæ*, and the ears, together with the gustatory process and the salivary glands, etc. These are in *rapport* with the heart and the dorsal region ruled by Leo; the generative and excretory system ruled by Scorpio; and the legs, or rather that part of them which is ruled by Aquarius; as also the blood, which is the life-fluid sent forth from Leo, and ruled by Aquarius. In general practice, however, it is sufficient to know what parts are ruled by each sign, and then it will be apparent to those versed in the theory of directions that, if a malefic planet be in Taurus at birth, the Moon will form a square or opposition to that radical position whenever it is directed to Scorpio, Leo, or Aquarius, and the effect will then fall on the part signified by Taurus, and will be of the nature indicated by the planet in that sign.

DISEASES OF THE PLANETS AND SIGNS

The following tabulation of the various ailments produced by the planets in the several signs when afflicting the Sun or Moon in the horoscope, or by direction, is taken from " Lilly's Astrology," where it is quoted as from the ancient Arabian writers. Consequently, many of the terms used are not those now employed in medical practice. But as " Zadkiel " remarks:—" As the human frame is still the same, so are its diseases, though called by other names."

The Diseases each Planet naturally signifies when it becomes the afflictor, and is posited in any of the Twelve Signs.

Diseases of Pluto

♇ in ♈ signifies a liability to brain tumours, blood-clotting in the head, fevers due to undue exposure to the Sun or intense heat and to tropical disorders such as sleeping sickness.

♇ in ♉ denotes pyorrhea, goitre, disorders of the thyroid gland, mastoidal ear, disturbance of the point of balance in the middle ear, shingles and painful skin complaints.

♇ in ♊ indicates lung troubles, catarrhal complaints, wasting or paralysis of the arms, softening of the bone formation of the arm.

♇ in ♋ shows abnormal conditions of the womb after childbirth, disorders of the mammary glands, ulcerated stomach and varied abdominal complaints.

♇ in ♌ causes holes in the heart, blue blood in babies, sportsman's heart, leukemia, difficulty in getting the blood to clot, spinal disorders, curvature of the spine and damage to the spine by accident.

♇ in ♍ signifies looseness of the bowels, diarrhoea, dysentery; blackwater fever, poisoning by eating of strange berries, roots or fungus, cramp in the wrists and fingers.

♇ in ♎ denotes floating kidney, uraemia, black jaundice, loss of function of excretion in old age, or of passing of urine. Affects the suprarenal glands.

♇ in ♏ indicates disorders of the spleen and pancreas. Illness through drunkenness or abuse of the sex function; blockage of the anus, piles and strangulated hernia.

♇ in ♐ shows loss of use in the lower limbs, accident through or injuries caused by animals, particularly horses, diseases of the arteries and of the liver; travel sickness, especially by sea.

♇ in ♑ signifies floating gout or rheumatism of a very painful nature; rickets, illness through exposure to extreme cold, wasting of the bone marrow and failure of the bones to knit should they be broken.

♇ in ♒ denotes synovitis of the ankles, diseases of the eyes, poisoning of the blood stream, varicose veins, elephantiasis, thrombosis.

♇ in ♓ shows odourous feet, webbed toes, a danger of venereal diseases, tumours, warts on the feet, king's evil, hallucinations and obsessions.

Diseases of Neptune

♆ in ♈ shows migraine, epilepsy, alopecia, encephalitis, atrophy of the mental processes, senile decay, conjunctivitis, cataract, myopia.

♆ in ♉ indicates glandular swellings in the neck, quinsy, laryngitis, angina gangrena, scrofula, polypus in the nose, asthma, dermatitis, softening of the brain.

♆ in ♊ denotes pneumonia, pleurisy, phthisis, St. Vitus's Dance, sickness through air travel, poisoning of the blood through radiation, nervous disorders, hallucinations.

♆ in ♋ signifies gastric catarrh, dropsy, pernicious anaemia, cardiac disorders, dipsomania, food poisoning, chlorosis, troubles in pregnancy, disorders through attempted abortion.

♆ in ♌ represents palpitation, syncope, varied forms of heart disease, spinal meningitis, locomotor ataxy, angina pectoris, aneurism, thrombosis.

♆ in ♍ indicates colic, enteric fever, neuralgia of the intestine, affections of the intestinal digestion, peritonitis, erysipelas, abscess on the appendix.

♆ in ♎ shows nephritis, Bright's disease, neuralgia of the kidney, yellow jaundice.

♆ in ♏ denotes affections of the generative organs, the prostate gland, the iliac regions or groins, the gall, rectum, the hydrocele vein, the vessels of the testicle, and the uterus.

♆ in ♐ signifies sciatica, hip-joint disease, dislocated disc, cramp or paralysis of the lower limbs, arterial disease.

♆ in ♑ denotes deformed knees, skin diseases such as impetigo, eczema, leprosy, coal gas poisoning or poisoning through inhalation of fumes from motor cars, diesel engines, etc.

♆ in ♒ shows dropsy, swollen ankles, excess of carbonic acid gas in the blood stream, loss of sight.

♆ in ♓ signifies mucous discharges, bunions, deformities of toes and feet, softening of glandular tissues, danger of drowning, or of poisoning through drinking impure water.

Diseases of Uranus

♅ in ♈ signifies injuries to the head through blows, cuts, fractures; nodding head spasms, rumbling noises in the head, apoplexy, migraine and nervous headaches, loss of sleep.

♅ in ♉ shows exanthematous sore throat, membranous exudation in the throat, glandular swellings, mumps, stenosis or stricture in the throat, paralytic strokes, sudden loss of voice.

♅ in ♊ denotes croupous pneumonia, disturbance of capillary oxygenation, bronchial colds on the chest, spasmodic lung cough, pneumoconiosis, paroxysmal dyspnoea.

♅ in ♋ indicates antiperistalsis, colic in stomach, stomach cramps, dyspepsia, hiccoughs, catamenial disorders, carcinomas, fractured or broken ribs, accidents to the breasts.

♅ in ♌ represents diseases, affections and injuries to the back and spine, trembling of the heart, sunstroke, yellow fever, disorders of the pituitary body, vavular lesions, convulsions.

♅ in ♍ shows digestive disorders due to nerve strain, barrenness, duodenal ulcers, neurasthenia, electric shock, homosexuality, appendidicular colic.

♅ in ♎ signifies inflammation of the kidneys and ureter, diseases of the reins, retention of urine, sugar diabetes, shooting pains in the lumbar region, accidents to the lumbar vertebrae of the spine.

♅ in ♏ denotes puerperal fever, inguinal hernia, haemorrhoids, renal stone, hydrocele infections, stricture of urethra, diseases of the ovaries, scurvy, spasm of bladder.

♅ in ♐ indicates baldness, over-heated blood, endemic diseases, bites from animals, hurt through falls from horses, diseases in the buttocks, fractures of the hips, thighs and femurs.

♅ in ♑ shows dryness of the skin, articular rheumatism, cutaneous complaints, dislocations, hypochondria, injuries to the knees and kneecap, nettle rash, urticaria, parasitic diseases.

♅ in ♒ signifies diseases through working under increased air pressure, disorders and hurts to the calves and the ankles, impure blood, astigmatism, colour blindness, glaucoma.

♅ in ♓ denotes club feet, corns and bunions, delirium tremens, lameness, relaxation of tissues, scabies, phlegmatic diseases, suppurative inflammation of areolar tissue, phobias.

Diseases of Saturn

♄ in ♈ signifies rheum, melancholy, vapours, cold in the head, obstructions, stoppage in the stomach, pains in the teeth, deafness, etc.

♄ in ♉ signifies swelling in the neck and throat, king's evil, scurvy, hoarseness, melancholy, and chronic distempers about the neck and throat.

♄ in ♊ signifies infirmities incident to the arms and shoulders, consumption, black jaundice, and diseases proceeding from bad blood.

♄ in ♋ denotes phthisis, ulcerations in the lungs, obstructions and bruises in the breast, ague, scurvy, cancer, etc.

♄ in ♌ signifies the heart afflicted by grief or poison, consumption of the reins or inward parts, vapours, weakness, and pains in the back, etc.

♄ in ♍ shows the blood corrupted, obstructions in the bowels, costiveness, weakness in the thighs, melancholy, gripings, stone, etc.

♄ in ♎ shows the blood corrupted, back and kidneys distempered, strangury, consumptive pains in the knees and thighs, sciatica, gout, and liver complaint.

♄ in ♏ denotes swellings or distempers of the secret parts, melancholy, piles, palsy, gout in the hands and feet.

♄ in ♐ signifies weakness in the hips and thighs, old aches and bruises in those parts, and sciatica or gout.

♄ in ♑ denotes the gout in the lower parts, pains and obstructions in the head, ague, etc.

♄ in ♒ signifies disorders in the head and teeth, defects in the ears, pains in the joints, bruises, swellings in the legs, and sometimes a sore throat.

♄ in ♓ gives defluxions of rheum, king's evil, consumption, all distempers of the feet and toes, such as the gout, and illness by colds.

Diseases of Jupiter

♃ in ♈ produces distempers in the head, a quinsy or swelling in the throat, chiefly from ill blood in the veins of the head; and causes strange dreams and imaginations.

♃ in ♉ brings distempers in the throat, wind in the blood, gripings in the bowels, and goutish humours in the hands and arms.

♃ in ♊.—A pleurisy, or some disorder of the reins.

♃ in ♋ gives the dropsy, the stomach offended, bad appetite, corrupt blood, scurvy, surfeits, etc.

♃ in ♌ indicates a fever, pleurisy, the heart ill affected.

♃ in ♍ indicates a consumption, obstructions of the lungs, melancholy, cold and dry liver.

♃ in ♎ shows the patient hath too much blood, whence arise obstructions, corrupt blood, fever, piles, tumours, inflammations, etc.

♃ in ♏ signifies the strangury, piles, the blood surcharged with watery humours, whence arises dropsy, etc.

♃ in ♐ denotes some choleric distemper, arising from putrefaction of the blood; a fever, pains and swellings about the knees, etc.

♃ in ♑.—The patient is afflicted with melancholy, obstructions in the throat, etc.

♃ in ♒.—The blood abounds too much, whence it is corrupted, and many diseases and flying pains afflict the body. It gives lumbago.

♃ in ♓.—The blood is too thin and waterish, which breeds dropsy.

Diseases of Mars

♂ in ♈ signifies the patient is almost distracted with a violent pain in his head, rheum in the eyes, want of rest, etc.

♂ in ♉ denotes extreme pain in the throat and neck, king's evil, weakness in the loins, and the gravel or stone.

♂ in ♊ shows the blood is corrupted; itch, breakings out, surfeit, fever, pains in the arms and shoulders, disorders in the secret parts, strangury, etc.

♂ in ♋ indicates pains in the breast and stomach, a dry cough, or a tumour in the thighs; accidents to the feet.

♂ in ♌ denotes affliction at the heart, choleric humours, gravel in the kidneys, pain in the knees, etc.

♂ in ♍ signifies choleric humours, obstructions in the bowels, bloody flux, worms in children, humours in the legs.

♂ in ♎ produces diseases in the reins and kidneys, stone or gravel, urine hot, lues, etc., as may be suspected.

♂ in ♏ shows a suspicion of some venereal distemper, or ulcer in the secret parts, pains in the bladder, pains in the head, overflowing of courses, etc.

♂ in ♐ produces pain or ulcers in the hips and thighs by humours settled in those parts, and an extreme heat in the mouth and throat.

♂ in ♑ denotes lameness in the knees, hands, or arms, or a flying gout.

♂ in ♒ signifies blood overheated, pains in the legs, surfeit, or fever.

♂ in ♓ gives lameness in the feet by corrupt humours settled there; sometimes the heart is afflicted, etc.

Diseases of the Sun

☉ in ♈ produces sore eyes, megrims, head disturbed, fevers, etc.

☉ in ♉ denotes tumours in the knees, quinsy or sore throat, breakings out and swellings in those parts.

☉ in ♊.—Blood inflamed, pestilential fevers, breakings out in several parts of the body, scurvy, pains and weakness in the legs.

☉ in ♋ shows the measles or small-pox, a disordered stomach, hoarseness, dropsy, or swelling in the feet.

☉ in ♌ indicates violent pains in the head, madness, stone, pains in the back, plague, spotted fever.

☉ in ♍ produces humours in the bowels, obstructions in the stomach, bloody flux, sore throat, or swellings in the neck.

☉ in ♎.—Inflammation of the blood, pains in the arms and shoulders, stone and gravel, the venereal distemper, etc.

☉ in ♏ indicates distempers in the secret parts, sharpness of urine, obstructions in the stomach and female courses, also *phlegmatiæ dolens*.

☉ in ♐.—The thighs are afflicted by hot humours; a fistula, fevers, swoonings, etc.

☉ in ♑ signifies lameness about the knees, bowels disordered, and a fever.

☉ in ♒.—The blood inflamed, breakings out, reins disordered, gravel, stone, strangury, etc.

☉ in ♓.—The secret parts afflicted, strangury, and violent pains in those parts.

Diseases of Venus

♀ in ♈ indicates the disease is in the head from abundance of moist humours; lethargy, reins afflicted, and head disordered by cold.

♀ in ♉ signifies pain in the head or secret parts, swellings in the neck from moist humours in the head.

♀ in ♊ denotes a corrupted blood, king's evil, dropsy, and a flux of rheum.

♀ in ♋ shows the stomach is much offended with cold, raw, undigested humours; many times with a surfeit, etc.

♀ in ♌.—some ill affection of the heart, love passion, etc., pains in the legs, of bad consequence.

♀ in ♍ shows some distemper in the bowels, a flux, or the worms, mucus in the bowels.

♀ in ♎ denotes a gonorrhœa or distemper in the reins, or surfeit by too plentiful eating or drinking, and windy disorders.

♀ in ♏ produces some venereal distemper, and pain in the private parts, etc.

♀ in ♐.—Hip gout, surfeits, cold and moist humours.

♀ in ♑ produces gout in the knees and thighs, and swellings in those parts.

♀ in ♒.—Pains and swellings in the legs or knees from a cold cause, and the heart afflicted.

♀ in ♓ indicates lameness in the feet, swellings in the legs, a flux, windy complaints, etc.

Diseases of Mercury

☿ in ♈ shows the disease lies in the head and brain, vertigo and spasms in the head, and sometimes disorders of the womb.

☿ in ♉ produces defects in the throat, swellings in the neck, hoarseness, and also pain in the feet.

☿ in ♊ signifies windiness in the blood, gouty pains in the head, arms, etc.

☿ in ♋ produces a cold stomach, gripings, windiness, distillation of rheum, lameness in the legs and knees from colds, etc.

☿ in ♌ indicates tremblings, melancholy, pains in the back, occasioned by colds caught in the feet.

☿ in ♍ imports much wind in the bowels, obstructions, pains in the head, short breath, and wind cholic.

☿ in ♎ shows stoppage of urine, obstructions, blood disordered; breast, lungs, and reins afflicted.

☿ in ♏ denotes distempers in the secret parts, afflictions of the bowels, running pains in the arms and shoulders.

☿ in ♐ shows distempers in the reins, weakness in the back, stoppage at the stomach, coughs, swellings in the hips and thighs.

☿ in ♑ denotes stoppage of urine, goutish humours above the knees, pains in the back, melancholy, etc.

☿ in ♒ imports wind in the blood, running pains in different parts of the body, fluxes and disorders in the bowels.

☿ in ♓ signifies pains in the head, weakness in the legs and feet, a gonorrhœa or a distemper in the reins, etc.

Diseases of the Moon

☽ in ♈ signifies convulsions, defluxions of rheum from the head, lethargy, weakness in the eyes, and pains in the knees.

☽ in ♉ produces pains in the legs and feet, swellings, stoppage in and sore throat, etc.

☽ in ♊ denotes a wandering gout in the legs, arms, hands, and feet, surfeits, and great obstructions.

☽ in ♋ shows the stomach much afflicted, a surfeit, small-pox, convulsions, falling sickness, tympany, or dropsy.

☽ in ♌.—The heart afflicted, sore throat, quinsy, king's evil, etc.

☽ in ♍ signifies great pain and disorders in the bowels, melancholy blood, obstructions, weakness in the arms and shoulders.

☽ in ♎ denotes the reins are distempered, obstructions in the stomach, weakness in the back, whites in women, surfeits, pleurisy, etc.

☽ in ♏ shows the distemper is in the secrets; small-pox, dropsy, poison, the heart afflicted, swoonings, etc.

☽ in ♐ imports lameness or weakness in the thighs, distempers in the bowels, etc.

☽ in ♑ signifies the stone, weak back, gout in the knees, whites in women, etc.

☽ in ♒.—Hysterics, swellings, and pains in legs and secret parts.

☽ in ♓ shows cold taken in the feet, and body disordered thereby; swellings in the legs, dropsies, and the body overcharged with moist humours.

CHAPTER IV

MENTAL QUALITIES AND INFIRMITIES

THE sign ascending, and those wherein the Moon and Mercury are posited, have chief influence on the mental qualities. The nature of these signs, also, which contain *the majority of the planets*, will determine the direction or bent of the nature. Thus:

Cardinal signs indicate active, useful, energetic, ambitious, and persevering persons;—busy people, the workers of the world, the best business men and women, pioneers and organisers, such as are capable of cutting out a line in life for themselves, and of making headway against obstacles. They are very independent, capricious, and averse to humble service.

Fixed signs denote plain, rigid, unbending natures. Disciplinarians; obstinate and dogmatic people; very patient, steadfast, and thrifty, but self-absorbed and difficult to know. They are thoughtful, philosophical, plodding, inventive, austere, and reserved. They achieve results slowly, but surely; and effect by patient work what others do by a stroke of luck, or by well-timed action. They are reliable friends and unrelenting enemies. They originate, while others of the *cardinal* type execute. They have a tendency to contract habits of life and to get into a groove; always independent, self-reliant, and never servile.

Common signs denote subtle, versatile, and changeful natures; oftentimes repining and regretful, inconstant and imitative; of no set purpose; much affected by their surroundings and those with whom they come in contact; capable of simulating qualities not inherent in them; dabbling, volatile, and superficial generally. They have very acute feelings and sensitive natures; likely to go under when opposed. They are the natural servants of the world, waiting upon the intellect and industry of others. Unless born well-off, they seldom make their way in life. With the majority of the planets in common signs, a person is very sympathetic, but often of weak character.

These general tendencies, however, are modified by the aspects to the Moon and Mercury, and by the signs containing the planets thus in aspect.

If the planets aspecting the Moon and Mercury are in the first or tenth house, their influence is greatly increased. Planets in the third and ninth houses, even when not in aspect to the mental rulers,

Moon and Mercury, must nevertheless be taken into consideration, on account of the influence these houses have over the mind.

Pluto squaring the Moon or Mercury from the third or ninth houses will bring mental instability resulting from too great a concentration upon or speculating regarding the problems of space, time and infinity. Fear of the unknown and the future will result and if persisted in can cause insanity.

Pluto in favourable aspects to the Moon and Mercury especially from the third or ninth houses will strengthen the mind, giving great powers of visualisation, of literary, psychic and prophetic ability.

Thus, when so placed, or in aspect to the Moon or Mercury, Neptune confers a strong taste for æsthetic and mystical subjects, a strong imitative faculty, capable of absorbing the views of others, and emulating characteristics foreign to the native. It gives mediumistic powers; renders the nature unreliable and chaotic, full of strange tastes and fancies, and highly neurotic. The disposition is dreamy, indolent, and self-indulgent, allowing the responsibilities and duties of life to fall into neglect.

Uranus confers original and inventive faculty, a wayward, obstinate nature, love of romance, strange sights, eccentricities, curious studies. Indulging in reveries, the native is argumentative when aroused, very determined and headstrong; oftentimes affected with Utopian ideas and unpopular projects.

Saturn gives a thoughtful, melancholic mind, oftentimes a desire for seclusion, bodily fears, anxious disposition, cautious in action, doubtful of others, timorous, secretive, taciturn. The native is much attached to the home and relatives. It confers depth and steadfastness of character, makes the native a faithful friend or persistent enemy. It gives a profound and sincere nature, and produces a reliable disposition.

Jupiter produces an open, free, generous, and frank mind, truthful, despising all mean and underhand actions; gives a strong sense of justice, erring rather on the side of leniency and moderation; renders the native jovial, confident, humane, and conscientious. It gives nobility of character, and does much to enrich the nature.

Mars produces a military spirit, contentious, free and courageous; gives a desire for conquest, a proud spirit, warmth of feelings, ardent passions, an extravagant nature, impetuosity, want of foresight; a rash and ungovernable character, disposed to gain by force what cannot be obtained by other means.   The sense of freedom dominates the nature.

The Sun gives a proud nature with a love of display, ambitious of honours; a thirst for renown, love of approbation, self-confidence, a profuse nature, and in most cases upright and noble; opposed to all underhand actions and covert deeds.

Venus produces a love of refinement, ease, and luxury; gives some artistic faculty; inclines to poetry, music, and the drama, refined and elegant tastes; fondness for scents, jewellery, and personal adornments; amorous, quiet, amiable, inclined to society, fond of children and pets, disposed to kiss and fondle.   It confers beauty and tenderness, and makes men and women much beloved for their kindness.

Mercury when rising, or aspecting the Moon, gives a desire for knowledge, inclination for reading, writing, travelling and talking; quick intellect, adaptability to all kinds of mental work; cunning and alert, active, nimble, and excessively busy.

The Moon when rising, or aspecting Mercury, makes people fond of travelling, constant change, and roaming about; it confers a strong imaginative faculty, love of romance; gives grace and elegance to the manners; renders the native inconstant and uncertain in action and thought.

The *elemental* nature of the signs occupied by the majority of the planets must also be considered.   Thus, when the majority of the planets are found in either the Fiery, Airy, Earthy, or Watery signs, it modifies the expression of the mental qualities.   Thus:

Fiery signs are inspirational;   *Airy* signs, cogitative and intellectual; *Watery* signs, psychic and emotional;   *Earthy* signs, worldly and hard.

The majority of planets in any of these triplicities will generally indicate the trend of the nature, or the sphere in which the life will chiefly find expression.

It must always be remembered that the good aspects of the planets produce good effects, and the bad aspects evil effects.   Therefore, the more laudable traits are the result of the favourable aspects of the planets to the Moon and Mercury.   Everything depends upon the *aspect* of a planet to the significators, whether in health, fortune, or character.   We must note, too, whether a planet is essentially dignified by being in its own sign or a congenial one, or debilitated by being in an adverse sign—all of which should enter into the consideration of the student.

The larger planet always controls the action of a minor one. So Saturn can overrule Mars, being of a more ponderous nature, and of slower motion.

The mutual aspects existing between the planets Neptune, Uranus, Saturn, Jupiter, Mars, and Venus, also confer their influences on the native's character. Thus:

Mars afflicting Jupiter causes boasting and extravagance. Afflicting Venus, he causes an ardent, passional nature, prone to waste its energies and substance on the opposite sex. Afflicting Saturn or Uranus, he gives an ungovernable temper, subject to sudden storms of passion, often accompanied by violence. Afflicting Neptune, he causes some mania, generally of a neurotic character.

Saturn afflicting Jupiter gives a doubtful and hesitating nature, often penurious and grasping, harsh, and lacking in sympathy. Afflicting Venus, he causes secret vices, a sorrowful spirit, apt to shed tears, very sensitive, and liable to severe disappointments.

Uranus in aspect to Venus gives a strong attraction to the other sex, romantic attachments, liability to seductive influences.

When Venus or Mercury, badly afflicted by Mars, Uranus, Neptune, or Jupiter, is found in watery signs, there will be a tendency to debauchery or drunkenness.

In female horoscopes, Saturn in conjunction with the Moon, or in evil aspect thereto, with Mars also in bad aspect, the native is liable to be led astray. The conjunction and bad aspects of Mars to the Moon always tend to produce unwomanly freedom.

If Saturn afflicts the Moon, and Mars at the same time afflicts Mercury, the same evil is to be feared. In either case the evil is greater when the malefics are elevated above the Moon and Venus. Mars in any aspect to Venus disposes to flirtation, and gives intensity to the affections, without conferring stability.

Venus afflicting the Moon makes the native untidy and slovenly, though outwardly inclined to preserve appearances. It also makes the native squander money on fineries and frivolities of various kinds.

With Neptune afflicting the Moon or Venus, chaotic sex relations are liable to ensue.

Mental Infirmities

are produced by the affliction of Mercury or the Moon, or both, in certain signs of the Zodiac.

When Mercury, the Moon, and ascendant are in no aspect or familiarity (mutual disposition, conjunction or parallel) with one another, it is a sign of danger to the mental faculties. If, at the same time, Mercury be afflicted by the presence or bad aspects of the malefic planets, Neptune, Uranus, Saturn, or Mars, insanity may result. The effects are more striking when the affliction is from the angles of the horoscope.

In a *day* nativity, *i.e.*, when the Sun is above the horizon, Saturn afflicting Mercury indicates epilepsy, but Mars denotes insanity.

In a *night* nativity, Saturn shows insanity when afflicting Mercury, and Mars shows epilepsy.

Mercury in Pisces, and angular (in the first, fourth, tenth, or seventh house), afflicted by Mars or the Sun, makes a fanatic. The same if the Sun be angular in Capricorn and thus afflicted. Mars afflicting Jupiter gives religious enthusiasm, and with other testimonies it makes a rabid sectarian.

Mercury afflicting the Moon, and itself afflicted by the presence or aspect of the malefics, indicates a tendency to mental disorder.

When either the Sun or Mercury is in one of the common signs, Sagittarius, Pisces, Gemini, or Virgo, and afflicted by Saturn, Uranus, Mars, or Neptune, there is strong disposition to insanity or mental disorder of some sort.

In all cases, the good aspects of Jupiter or Venus will assist for a while, and in some circumstances may prevent the calamity foreshadowed. Affliction from angles or from planets out of their dignities makes the evil more certain.

CHAPTER V

FINANCIAL FORTUNES

The condition of the Moon in a male horoscope, and of the Sun in a female horoscope, determines the fortunes to a very great degree. The planets occupying the second house, and the tenth, must also be considered in this connection, together with the condition of the ruler of the second house.

Remember always that good aspects, whether proceeding from Saturn or Jupiter, from Mars or Venus, or any other planet, denote good effects.

For general good fortune, nothing is better than the good aspect of the Sun to the Moon, and the benefic configuration of Jupiter and Venus, more especially when the latter are in elevation, or else in the ascendant.

In a male nativity, look to the Moon and those planets which aspect it. If the aspect be good, say good will result from such sources as are ruled by those signs and houses in which the planet is posited; also from things and persons ruled by those houses over which it has dominion in the figure, as well as those indicated by the nature of the planet itself. Thus, if Jupiter were in trine aspect to the Moon from the sign Leo in the tenth house, and ruling the fifth and second house, it would show benefits to arise from high offices and business affairs generally (tenth house position), from theatres, speculations, etc. (Leo, fifth sign of the Zodiac); again confirmed by its rulership of Pisces, the sign occupying the cusp of fifth house, and by financial transactions (ruled by second house, occupied by the sign Sagittarius), and generally by clerical and legal affairs (denoted by Jupiter itself). In a similar manner, judgment is made of the good aspects of other planets. Of bad aspects, evil results may be predicted from corresponding sources. A planet that has no aspect to the Moon must, in this respect, be judged from its position and rulership in the horoscope, as given in Book i, chap. vi.

Jupiter, though benefic, cannot do much good if badly placed and aspected, but its good aspect to the Moon, or ruler of the second house, gives a fortunate life, and many chances of success. Saturn, on the contrary, though a malefic, may effect many benefits if well placed and aspected, and especially when in good aspect to the Moon.

Saturn or Uranus in trine or sextile to Jupiter produces legacies, gifts, etc., especially if either be ruler of the eighth house, or placed therein. If ruling the fourth, or placed therein, and thus in aspect to one another, they give gain by inheritance. If either be ruler of the seventh, or Jupiter be therein, it shows gain by marriage, or by any partnership whatsoever.

The second house must have attention, because it rules over money matters, and the tenth, because of its influence over business matters.

Saturn or Mars therein is bad, and success cannot be expected unless Jupiter or Venus throws a trine or sextile to them, or the lights receive their good aspect.

If Mars, or Saturn, or Uranus in the second house afflicts the Moon, and no assistance is given, the life will be a continual struggle against adversity.

Jupiter afflicting the Moon in any position makes the native improvident, and conduces to losses through indiscreet actions and generous impulses.

Mars in the second house, the native is too liberal. When so placed, and afflicting the Moon, it shows loss by fire, theft, and strifes.

Neptune in the second house afflicting the Moon, makes the native the victim of a bubble company, or some big fraud.

Jupiter in the eighth, money by marriage; the eighth house being that of partners, whether in marriage or business. The condition of the native after marriage can generally be seen from the condition of the seventh and eighth houses, their rulers, and the planets therein.

Pluto in the second house in good aspect to the Moon, Venus or Jupiter will bring financial gain through personal skill and ingenuity. If this combination occurs with Pluto in the fifth house, extraordinary gains by speculation, lotteries, sweepstakes and football pools are denoted, and if Pluto is in the eighth house this combination would bring unexpected gain through legacy. Adversely aspected in these houses the Pluto influence would cause crippling losses, bankruptcy, profligacy.

With the majority of the planets in cadent houses, especially in the sixth, the native makes little headway in the world. When Uranus is the afflicting planet, it shows great financial danger. In the second house, it shows many sudden changes, success and failure coming in rapid succession. If in good aspect to the Sun and Moon it denotes gain through things and persons governed by it. (Book i, chap. iii).

Saturn or Uranus in evil aspect to Jupiter shows loss by law, and deception of trustees and others having charge over the financial affairs of the native. The house wherein Saturn or Uranus is placed will indicate more exactly the source whence the trouble will proceed. If Mars adds his evil influence to these planets, then loss by speculation, betting, etc., is shown.

Saturn in the seventh house is bad for trade; and in evil aspect to the Moon it shows financial failure.

When Uranus is in the seventh, and badly aspected, the native is harassed by his creditors. He gets into difficulties after marriage. But if in good aspect to the Moon, the native will rise above his difficulties.

Uranus or Saturn in the seventh, afflicting the Moon, the native should be warned to keep out of partnership, and to avoid public affairs. When the malefics are afflicting the Moon, and elevated above it, financial failure is shown.   If Saturn be in the tenth house, the native never recovers his fortune.

Again, Jupiter or Venus lending their assistance, the native will overcome his difficulties; the source of help being shown by the position of Jupiter and Venus.

Property is largely controlled by the position and aspects of the Part of Fortune. Its place in the horoscope is found by adding together the longitudes of the Moon and ascendant, and subtracting therefrom the longitude of the Sun.   Thus:

☽ in ♉ 14° 20′	..	..	..	..	..	S. 1	14°	20′
Asc. in ♐ 25° 2′	..	..	..	..	..	8	25	2
	Sum.		..	..	..	S.10	9°	22′
☉ in ♈ 20° 1′	..	..	..	..	..	0	20	1
⊕ in ♑	..	..	..	..	..	S. 9	19°	21′

Some authors omit this symbol, but without sufficient reason for so doing. When in conjunction with Jupiter, Venus, or the Sun or Moon well aspected, or itself well aspected by the planets, it gives success in the accumulation of property.

We confidently affirm that the " imaginary nothing," the " airy myth," called the Part of Fortune (⊕), is of immense consequence in practice; and its actual significance will be apparent to any who will take the trouble to notice the transits of Saturn, Uranus, Jupiter, and Mars over its place and aspects in the horoscope.

When misfortune is strongly indicated in a horoscope, it is better for the native not to go into business for himself, but to link his fortunes with those of a person born under more favourable influences, in a subsidiary function. A well-paid servant is better than a bankrupt master. But if the Sun and Moon are in evil aspect to each other, it will be difficult even to get into service.

In female horoscopes, more attention is paid to the position of the Sun, as chief significator of the fortunes; but both luminaries should always be considered in every horoscope.

CHAPTER VI

THE RANK OR POSITION

IN order to know to what rank or position the native will attain in his sphere of life, look to the position of the planets and see where the majority are situated.

E

If the majority of the planets, including the Sun and Moon, the ruler of the ascending sign and mid-heaven, are rising between the meridian and the fourth house, the native will rise in life and become his own master. If the majority of the planets are in cardinal signs, and in the quadrant between the ascendant and meridian, the native will rise to a very good position in his sphere of life, and will outrun his compeers.

The majority of planets in angles and cardinal signs, make the native a prominent figure in his own walk in life. Most of the planets being in the cardinal signs bring the native into prominence early in life. In fixed signs success is slower, but more enduring; in common signs it only comes by the assistance of others, or in the service of others, and the native generally has " too many irons in the fire," and goes from one pursuit to another, a " rolling stone, gathering no moss."

The planets essentially and accidentally dignified, *i.e.*, in their own signs and in angles, give much hope of success.

Jupiter or Venus in the meridian always raises the native to high positions in his own sphere, and often far above that of birth.

When several planets are in square or opposition from cardinal signs, the native strikes out some original and remarkable line in life, gaining thereby a certain renown, but liable to much opposition and criticism.

Many planets well placed between the fourth and seventh cusps, is a good augury of success after marriage; or in a horoscope where marriage is denied, success in the latter part of life.

Planets well aspected in the fourth house indicate a successful termination to the career.

Saturn in the tenth house, the native rises to a good position, but suffers a downfall. This position is exemplified in the horoscope of Napoleon Buonaparte.

Mars in the tenth, in a male horoscope, affects the native's credit. He will be a constant victim of criticism, chiefly owing to his own impatience and pugnacious character. He has many jealous and envious rivals, who throw aspersions upon his character and honour. In a female horoscope, this position of Mars makes the native a constant victim of slander and ill repute, whether it be warranted or not. When the Moon is there with Mars, there are probably good grounds for suspicion and talk, however despicable such scandal may be. It frequently affects the credit and honour of the parent involved.

The Sun in square or opposition to the Moon in a male horoscope, shows troubles with superiors, difficulty in retaining office, and, at least once in every seven years, the native loses his appointment and gets into difficulties with his employers or those in office above him. In general, it shows fleeting honours, unstable reputation, and many difficulties. The same or similar events happen in a female horoscope under the configuration of the luminaries. It ruins the energies of the native, and, if Saturn afflicts at the same time, the native may become an ambitionless and impotent loafer.

The Sun or Moon afflicted by the malefics from cardinal signs, the native attains a questionable fame, and sustains it only by *outré* and unpopular actions. The Sun in sextile or trine to Uranus, gives success in governmental circles, public offices, and honours thereby. It also gives a wide popularity.

If the majority of the planets are setting, between the tenth and seventh houses, or out of their dignities, and in adverse signs, or retrograde and afflicted, the native will not improve his position in life, the family fortunes will fall off, and his progeny will not enjoy the benefits of a good patrimony. Indeed, the position of the native will decline with advancing years.

Any planet in the tenth or first houses, in its own sign or exaltation, and well aspected, denotes success and honours, especially if the planet be either Jupiter, Venus, Sun, Moon, or Mercury.

Chiefly, however, look to the fourth house for the condition of the native at the close of life. If planets, dignified and well aspected, are found therein, particularly if these be the lights or benefics, the end will be successful, happy, and contented. Saturn there shows retirement or seclusion. Uranus indicates an eccentric existence, and disposes to miserliness. Neptune shows some enforced retirement, and the native usually ends his life in some asylum or other institution.

Pluto in the fourth house if badly aspected shows a breaking up or disintegrating of domestic and family life during the closing years of life and sometimes shows the complete disappearance of the native with the nature of the death never being ascertained. From another standing it can show that the end of the life will be passed either in exile or in uncongenial conditions in a place far removed from the place of birth. If, however, Pluto is well aspected, particularly by Venus or Jupiter then the end of life will bring contentment and the material position will be good.

The malefics in the fourth house, in uncongenial signs, show the end of life to be fraught with troubles and dangers. But if well aspected by Jupiter or Venus, and in their own signs or exaltations, then success is shown.

CHAPTER VII
THE PROFESSION OR OCCUPATION

JUDGMENT is made from the nature and condition of the planets occupying the angles of the horoscope, and from those also which aspect the Sun and Moon.

The planet which is in nearest conjunction with the Sun, rising either just before or after it, has much influence in this question; and the condition thereof, by aspect and position, will indicate the success attending the occupation. The planet in nearest aspect to the Sun has also great influence, and those also which aspect the meridian.

The signs occupied by the significators of the profession generally determine its nature.

The signification of each planet will be found under the head of " Planetary Occupations " in Book i, chap. iii. These must be considered in relation to the signs they occupy—as for instance, Jupiter in Virgo would denote gardeners, dealers in garden stuffs, timber merchants, farmers, clothiers, bootmakers, etc., owing to the influence of Virgo upon food and clothing. Similarly, Venus in Virgo would denote makers of sweets, cakes, and other delicacies and artistic foods, art fabric makers, vendors of dress and food luxuries, silk merchants, etc. Mars, on account of its more practical nature, and its association with fire, steel implements, etc., would in the same sign denote builders, carpenters, house-repairers, and workers in sanitary structures. Gemini, Pisces, Sagittarius, show double occupations and a multitude of interests; the native generally runs two lines of business at the same time.

Therefore, in judging this question, which is perhaps the most difficult to define, consideration must be made of the planet or planets in the tenth house, those nearest the Sun, their natures, and the character of the signs they occupy. The signs in this connection must always be referred to the nature of the houses to which they correspond—as Gemini to the third house, Virgo to the sixth, Sagittarius to the ninth, and so on. The things over which those houses naturally have dominion, will determine the sphere in which the significator will be employed.

Thus, if the planet in the tenth house be Mercury, or that planet be nearest to the Sun, or rising next before it, it denotes the use of the pen. If Mercury be in Pisces, then it is employed in twelfth house affairs, occult things, secrets, private correspondence, etc.

Pluto in the tenth house, particularly in the earthy signs, Taurus, Virgo or Capricorn gives capacity for trading and commercial activities but if in the fiery signs, Aries, Leo or Sagittarius would give more capacity for architecture, building and demolition.

Neptune in the tenth house shows ability for interests to do with oil, motoring, aviation, especially if in the watery signs Cancer, Scorpio, Pisces, but denotes that there will be fluctuations and periods of uncertainty with a need for guarding against fraud.

The nature of the signs wherein the majority of the planets are posited will show the line of greatest success and natural aptitude.

The airy signs show intellectual pursuits, head work, literary and artistic occupations.

The watery signs show occupations in which water is the motive power or chief element—dealers in soft goods, textiles, and fabrics; painters, sailors, brewers, chemists, etc.

The fiery signs show those in which fire, iron, and the metals generally are employed; soldiers, surgeons, etc.

The earthy signs show manual labour, all agricultural pursuits, corn-dealers, dealers in the produce of the soil in whatever capacity or kind. The places and signs occupied by planets in good aspect to the Sun or Moon, especially if such planets are Jupiter or Venus, should be observed as potent sources of benefit.

Uranus in aspect to the Moon produces changes, and the Sun afflicting the Moon is evil, and depletes the native powers, giving also disfavour of superiors.

Pluto or Neptune in the seventh house signify especial need for discrimination in matters to do with business partnership or any form of business co-operation owing to the liability of the partner either concealing certain of his activities or exercising a degree of deception or intrigue.

Uranus or Saturn in the seventh house, unless well aspected, shows opposition and loss in all public affairs, and the native will do well to live quietly, and not come prominently before the public, and all business should be done through a third party or agent, or by correspondence.

For the degree of success the native will achieve in his work, judge by the rules given for the rank or position in the previous chapter. Unless the majority of the planets be rising, or above the earth, or the Sun well aspected in such position, the native will not be successful in business for himself, but may be so in the service of others.

CHAPTER VIII

MARRIAGE

THE promise or denial of marriage depends largely upon the condition and aspects of the Moon and Venus in a male horoscope, of the Sun and Mars in a female horoscope. With men the signs of marriage are: Mars in aspect to Venus, and the latter strong in the figure; the Moon strong in a fruitful sign; Venus similarly placed; Jupiter or Venus in the seventh house; the fruitful signs, Cancer, Pisces, Scorpio, on the seventh, or intercepted therein; the Moon in a fruitful sign in the first, fifth, tenth, or eleventh; Venus similarly placed; the Moon and Venus unaspected by Saturn, and stronger than Saturn in the horoscope; the lords of the first and seventh house in conjunction or good aspect.

Pluto or Neptune being in the seventh house although emphasising the idealistic conception of marriage again brings a liability towards unfaithfulness on the side of the marriage partner with a possibility of experiencing personal temptations towards adultery which, if given way to, will break the marriage.

All these are indications of an inclination to marriage, and of opportunities thereto.

The indications of marriage being denied are—

When Pluto or Neptune square the Moon in a male horoscope or the Sun in a female horoscope there is a danger of the engagement being broken and of marriage not being consummated. Pluto can cause the prospective partner to disappear before the wedding day whilst Neptune gives an indication of the possibility of bigamy.

Saturn in evil aspect to the Moon and Venus, or the Moon alone aspected by Saturn, if Saturn be strong and they weak in the figure.

The Moon or Venus in either Capricorn, Gemini, Leo, Virgo, or Aries, and cadent, and afflicted by Saturn, the marriage is difficult to achieve.

The Moon in Scorpio in evil aspect to Saturn, or in the signs of Saturn, conjoined to the Sun, and afflicted by Saturn.

The Moon in the occidental quarters of the figure in conjunction, square, or opposition to the Sun, and also afflicted by Saturn.

All these are indications of the marriage being wholly denied, or accomplished with great difficulty.

In general, consult the condition of the seventh house, its ruler, the Moon and Venus. If you find them cadent or in barren signs, and afflicted by Uranus or Saturn, then judge that marriage will not take place. Otherwise, it goes without saying that the native will marry at some time in life.

Delay is shown when the Moon or Venus is afflicted by Uranus or Jupiter, the Moon being in an occidental quarter of the figure; or when the Moon and Venus are in evil aspect to one another. For these aspects show disappointment in early love affairs, crosses, and delays.

THE TIME OF MARRIAGE

The Moon in a male horoscope, being in any of the fruitful signs in aspect to Saturn, disposes to a late marriage.

The Moon oriental and unafflicted, Mars in aspect to Venus, Venus or Jupiter in the seventh, or the lord of the first going to an aspect with the ruler of the seventh—these dispose to an early marriage.

The position of the Moon must chiefly be considered in this respect. The Moon and Venus well placed in congenial or fruitful signs, and not in aspect to Saturn or Uranus, the native is left free to marry. If the Moon is found oriental of the Sun, *i.e.*, increasing in light, and in an oriental quarter of the figure, *i.e.*, between the fourth and seventh, or the first and tenth cusps, the native will marry early. But if the Moon be in an occidental quarter, and decreasing in light, marriage takes place later in life.

When the Moon and Venus are in good positions, and not in aspect to Saturn or Uranus, but the Moon occidental and decreasing in light, marriage takes place at a moderate age, neither early nor late.

The testimonies must be weighed carefully, and judgment made accordingly.

HAPPINESS OR SORROW

Jupiter or Venus in the seventh house, well placed and aspected, is the best sign of felicity in marriage. Even if well placed in the seventh, and afflicted, Jupiter or Venus will give happiness, but will denote some affliction to the partner. Again, Mercury, Moon, or

Sun in the seventh, well aspected, shows happiness in wedlock.

The Sun and Moon in good aspect to one another is a sign of happiness. The reverse of this, if the aspect be evil.

The malefics in the seventh denote unhappiness, unless very well aspected, or in good aspect to the Moon, in which case the wife dies early.

Uranus in the seventh, badly aspected, estrangement or divorce follows. If Mars adds the weight of his influence by evil aspect, then violence occurs.

Venus or Jupiter in good aspect to the Moon, happiness is almost certain.

The Moon afflicted by Saturn, Mars, or Uranus, a man is not fortunate in the choice of a wife, more especially if the afflicting planet be in the seventh house.

Good planets in the eighth house, or the Moon there, well aspected, denotes gain by marriage.

Venus afflicted by Uranus or Saturn, domestic troubles ensue. But if in good aspect to these planets, sincere attachment and well-ordered affections are shown.

The Moon in opposition to Jupiter or Venus shows troubles after marriage, or grief through bereavement.

If Mars be in the seventh or eighth, in bad aspect to Jupiter, the native is ruined by an extravagant wife.

The Moon afflicted by Mars shows a wife who is difficult to control, if not altogether loose in her conduct. If Mars be thus placed, and in Cancer, Pisces, or Scorpio, the wife may be addicted to drink.

Mercury in the seventh, afflicted by Mars or Uranus, shows a wife of unsound mind, or suffering from a severe nervous disorder.

Neptune there (in the seventh), badly placed or afflicted, or in evil aspect to the Moon, denotes a negligent and self-indulgent wife.

Uranus afflicting Venus in any part of the horoscope, shows intrigues with unmarried girls; but when afflicting the Moon, the attraction is to married women. If either Uranus or Moon or Venus be in the first, fifth, or seventh house, it will lead to complications. If Mars add his influence it will be much talked of, and may form the subject of a public scandal. This is certain to be the case when the planets thus in aspect are in the tenth house. But when Saturn gives his influence by aspect or conjunction, the matter is a secret one. Jupiter assisting brings the native safely through his troubles. Mercury is a great talker, and his influence is to be feared in this matter.

Neptune afflicting Moon or Venus disposes to illicit and unnatural appetites, chaotic relations, and lascivious habits. The conjunction and opposition are most to be feared, especially if no benefic aspects intervene to ward off the evil.

Pluto afflicting the Moon or Sun shows that the marriage can turn " sour " as it were, as a result of frustrating or disappointing conditions occurring, with the possibility that one or other of the partners (the marriage partner if Pluto is in the seventh) walking out and disappearing.

The good aspects of Jupiter or Saturn to the Moon and Venus, do much to steady and regulate the expression of the sex feeling. The evil aspect of Saturn, however, tends to produce morbid feeling and unnatural restraint. Mars being in evil aspect or conjunction with Venus, or Venus in the signs of Mars, stimulates the sex feeling, and disposes to freedom of expression. Uranus, on the other hand, makes the native erratic in this respect; while Neptune conduces to chaotic and highly sensuous appetites.

Pluto in good aspect to the Moon or the Sun will bring about happy conditions in the marriage, the native in many respects being able to " lift " the prospective partner from out of unhappy or deplorable conditions as a result of marriage.

The planet with which the Moon forms the first aspect after birth must be taken into account chiefly. If this be a benefic, or the aspect be a benefic one, then the evils signified by evil planets in the seventh house will be overruled, but the wife will die before the native. In such cases if Uranus be there, a sudden death is shown, and if Mars, a violent death. Saturn, under such conditions, produces death by disease.

If, with the malefics, or one of them, in the seventh house, the Moon, applying to Jupiter or Venus, is found to be in a fruitful sign—Cancer, Pisces, or Scorpio—or in aspect to many planets from Gemini, Sagittarius, or Pisces, or the Moon therein herself, then the native marries again, and, making a bad choice, fulfils the destiny noted by the malefic in the seventh house.

If the Moon be applying to Jupiter or Venus, the marriage will be happy; but if, at the same time, the malefics, or one of them, shall afflict the Moon or the wife's significator, then the wife dies before the native.

When, in the horoscopes of the native and his partner, Saturn, Uranus, or Mars in the one is found on the ascendant of the other, then hurt will fall to that person whose ascendant it is. If Saturn in one shall be on the place of the Sun or Moon in the other, the person whose Sun or Moon is thus afflicted will suffer by the marriage. The same if Uranus be the afflicting planet. Mars thus situated in regard to the Moon in the partner's horoscope, shows trouble to the latter, and continual disagreement. The Sun and Mars are in more affinity by nature, and their interchanges in the horoscopes of man and wife are rather fortunate than otherwise. But Mars in one in opposition to the Sun in the other horoscope is evil.

On the contrary, if Jupiter or Venus be thus situated in respect to ascendant, meridian, Sun, or Moon, in the partner's horoscope, good results will follow from the marriage.

The agreement or disagreement of the two contracting parties can be infallibly judged by the mutual interchange of positions and aspects in their horoscopes.

DESCRIPTION OF WIFE

Take the planet to which the Moon first forms an aspect after birth, either by conjunction, sextile, square, trine, or opposition, and this planet, together with the sign it is in, will describe the wife. If, however, that planet is *retrograde*, reject it; it denotes an attachment which will be broken off. But if it be the ruler of the seventh house, it must be taken as the significator of the wife, who will die before the native. The successive aspects formed by the Moon after birth will show the several attachments of the native, until the ruler of the seventh house is reached by the lunar aspect or conjunction. Then, the sign occupied by the ruler of the seventh, together with the sign on the seventh cusp, describes the first wife in legal bonds with the native. Any other planet in the seventh house will describe the second wife, if more than one marriage is shown.

Therefore, unless the Moon comes first to the aspect of the lord of the seventh, or a planet in the seventh, the various applications of the Moon must be regarded with caution, lest a lover be mistaken for a wife. The character of the wife must be judged from the condition and aspects of the significator.

The circumstances under which the native meets his wife are

judged from the house occupied by her significator; as, if in the
eleventh, among friends; in the fourth, at his own home, or in his
native town; in the third, among relatives, or on a short journey;
in the ninth, abroad, or on a voyage, or the partner may be a
foreigner; and so of the rest.

SECOND MARRIAGES

The Moon in Cancer, Scorpio, Pisces, Gemini, or Sagittarius,
and in aspect to many planets, shows a possibility of a second
marriage, especially if a planet, not in aspect to the Moon, be
found in the seventh.

The Moon in aspect to two or three planets in double signs—
Gemini, Pisces, Sagittarius—especially if she be in one of these
signs herself, shows plurality of wives.

If the Moon be in aspect to no planet at all, but two or more
planets are in the seventh house, and the ruler of the seventh is in
a double sign, or such a sign on the cusp of the seventh, these are
indications of more than one marriage.

The ruler of the ascendant in a double sign in the seventh,
associated with other planets similarly placed, denotes plurality.

The ruler of the ascendant in conjunction with ruler of seventh,
in a double sign, denotes plurality.

FEMALE HOROSCOPES

are judged in all particulars like those of the male sex in regard to
marriage, taking the Sun instead of the Moon, and Mars instead of
Venus. The following observations apply particularly to female
horoscopes:—

Mars, being weak in the figure, and in no aspect to the Sun, has
a tendency to prevent marriage. The same if Mars be in no aspect
to the Sun, and afflicted by Saturn or Uranus.

Mars in the fifth house delays marriages; and if, at the same
time, Saturn afflicts the Sun, the native does not marry, unless
Jupiter be in the seventh house, or two of the foregoing planets
(Mars, Sun, Saturn) be in fruitful signs.

Mars afflicting the Sun by parallel, conjunction, or otherwise,
renders the married life unhappy, or the husband dies suddenly.
If Mars be in Cancer, Scorpio, or Pisces, and afflicting the Sun, the
husband will drink, and be of a profligate nature.

Uranus afflicting the Sun delays a woman's marriage, and also tends to produce an elopement or seduction. This latter calamity is almost certain to follow if Uranus afflicts the Sun, and Mars afflicts the Moon or Venus at the same time. In all cases the evil aspect of Uranus to the Sun produces trouble in the married life.

Neptune afflicting the Sun increases the liability to deception before marriage and unfaithfulness after marriage. It shows that the husband can develop traits of drunkenness, drug taking and immorality. Pluto afflicting the Sun shows that the marriage partner's business or private activities can take him far away from the marital home causing absences of long duration that can disturb the marital life, or alternatively can compel the wife to go with him and thus have no settled home life. Sometimes circumstances or the deliberate design of the husband can cause him to disappear so that his whereabouts are unknown. In certain instances he can reappear without warning and expect to resume marital life as if nothing had happened.

When the Sun first applies to the evil aspect of Saturn, the native marries a poor or worthless husband, without enterprise or nobility of character; and if Saturn be in a watery sign he will be given to drink; in a sign of Venus, he is unfaithful; in a sign of Jupiter, unfortunate; in his own signs, miserly and selfish.

Note.—The Sun is said to " apply " to that planet to which it forms the first complete aspect by its motion after birth; and generally the sextile, square, trine, and opposition are the only aspects which need be considered in this connection. We are disposed, however, to think that the Sun's first aspect *in the ephemeris* after birth should be taken chief notice of, and not its aspect by *direction*, as former authors state.

When the Sun is found in a barren sign—Aries, Gemini, Leo, Virgo, Capricorn—and afflicted by Saturn, the native does not marry. If Saturn be in the seventh house, and the Sun in trine or sextile to it, the native marries a widower; and if, at the same time, Mars be in aspect to Saturn, she will marry a widower with a family. The same happens if Saturn be in the seventh in aspect to Mars, and the Sun applying to some other planet in the figure.

If the Sun applies to Saturn in the seventh, and Saturn be in its own dignities, Libra or Capricorn, or in good aspect to Jupiter, then the native marries a widower who is wealthy, and by whom she will gain.

The position of Mars in a female horoscope is of great importance. For if it be found afflicted by Uranus or Saturn, and in a barren sign, it delays marriage or wholly prevents it. Thus, in a lady's horoscope, I find the Sun oriental, and in a fruitful sign, Cancer, in trine to Jupiter in Scorpio, Jupiter being ruler of Pisces on the cusp of the seventh house—all excellent signs of marriage. But Mars is in the tenth house in Gemini, and in conjunction with the Moon, afflicted by Uranus from the seventh house, and in opposition to Saturn, Mars at the same time being in no aspect to the Sun. At fifty-seven years of age she remains unmarried.

LENGTH OF MARRIAGE

The years of married life are measured by the distance of the significator of the wife or husband from the evil aspect of the malefic to which it is directed. Thus, if Jupiter were the significator in Aries one degree, and the planet Saturn were in Cancer eleven degrees, then ten years of married life would be experienced, as the distance of Jupiter from square of Saturn is ten degrees. Again, if Venus be significator in Libra ten degrees, and Saturn in Libra eighteen degrees, then Venus to conjunction Saturn gives eight years of married life. Or, if Uranus were the significator, and the Sun were eight degrees distant from it, then Uranus to conjunction Sun would indicate the marriage years as extending over eight years. Thus the significator to the conjunction or evil aspect of the malefics will show the period of married life.

CHAPTER IX

CHILDREN

THE condition of the Moon is of importance in this enquiry, inasmuch as it shows the inclination in the male, and the power in the female.

If the Moon be found in Cancer, Scorpio, Pisces, Gemini, Sagittarius, it makes the nature fruitful. In Taurus, Virgo, Libra, Aquarius, the nature is moderately fruitful. In Aries, Leo, Capricorn, the nature is disposed to barrenness.

The Moon angular in the first, tenth, or seventh house, the number of children is increased.

The Moon in Aries, Leo, or Capricorn, afflicted by Saturn, Mars, Sun, or Uranus, there is small chance of children being born.

The Moon in Cancer, Scorpio, or Pisces, in good aspect to Jupiter or Venus, a full family may be expected.

The signs on the cusps of the fifth and eleventh houses and the planets in those houses must also be considered. Thus, Cancer, Scorpio, Pisces, Taurus, or Virgo on the cusp of the fifth house promises a large family, if the Moon be also well placed and aspected.

The malefics, or the Sun, in the fifth or eleventh are bad, and afflict the offspring.

The benefics, or the Moon, in these houses increase the strength and number of the progeny.

The malefics in fruitful signs in the fifth or eleventh, show that children will be born, but some of them will not live.

The benefics, or the Moon, in these houses, afflicted by the malefics, show the same result.

The malefics in the fifth or eleventh, and in good aspect to Jupiter or Venus, the children will be reared, but with difficulty.

The fifth house denoting the birth of children, and the eleventh house denying them, shows the death of some in infancy. The same if the eleventh promises and the fifth denies them.

The Sun in the fifth, or Leo on its cusp, and the Sun afflicted by any of the malefics, no progeny will live beyond childhood.

The Moon in the tenth or fourth, afflicted by the malefics, shows death among the progeny.

Pluto in the fifth house well aspected, particularly by the Moon, Venus or Jupiter will give children of outstanding merit and genius which can be of an artistic, scientific or administrative nature, but if Pluto be afflicted it will show progeny whose subsequent actions and way of life will cause distress and in extreme instances bring dishonour or disaster to the family.

Neptune in the fifth house favourably aspected shows children of musical, theatrical and diplomatic ability and, in certain instances stresses capacity of a religious and psychic nature. If badly aspected it gives a very marked warning to guard children against the possibility of drowning in early life through such agencies as ornamental ponds, etc., and shows a danger as well of being kidnapped or, with girls, of them being forced into the white slave traffic.

The ruler of the fifth house, in conjunction with the ruler of eighth, or afflicted by the malefics, kills the children. Saturn in an angle, afflicting both Venus and Moon, is a sign of sterility. The same if Saturn be with Venus in the seventh house.

The fifth house in a male horoscope denotes the first child; the seventh shows the second; the ninth the third, and so on, taking every alternate house. In a female horoscope the first child is denoted by the fourth house; the second by the sixth, and so on.

The planets ruling each alternate house, and those posited therein, will show the sex and condition of each child, by the sex of the signs they occupy and their own natures. Thus, if Saturn, Uranus, or Mars be in any of these houses, badly placed, or the luminaries afflicted therein, then judge that child to which the house corresponds to be weak and ailing, and likely to die. For example, in a male horoscope, the sign Cancer on the fifth and Saturn therein, with the Moon in Taurus, the first child would be a girl, and would be very sickly, and only reared with great difficulty.

The majority of the planets in male signs shows a predominance of male progeny, and *vice versa* if in female signs.

The fortunes of the progeny are, in a general way, judged from the condition and aspects of the significators or rulers of the alternate houses.

CHAPTER X

FRIENDS AND BENEFACTORS

THE eleventh house, the ruler of the eleventh, Mercury, and the luminaries, are the chief significators.

If the luminaries, the benefics, or Mercury, are found in the eleventh house, well placed and aspected, the native will have many friends by whom he will benefit. But if the benefics be retrograde in the eleventh, or afflicted therein, those who would befriend the native oftentimes cannot. The same if the luminaries or planets, otherwise well placed, be afflicted in the eleventh.

The malefics in the eleventh, the native will suffer through his friends, and great care will be needed in the selection of them. If a malefic planet be in the eleventh, in its own sign or exaltation, then the injury denoted will not be the result of unfaithfulness, but some of the friends will be the cause of unconscious wrong to the native. But if the malefics be found in the eleventh, afflicting the Sun, Moon, or Mercury, then the friends are false, designing, and in every way harmful to the native.

Saturn therein causes deceit; Uranus, estrangement and quarrels; Mars, all kinds of extravagance and strife. Neptune causes plots and deceptions, frauds and seductions.

Pluto brings the forming of strange friendships, on occasions through extraordinary happenings such as when disasters occur and if well aspected shows subsequent benefit. If adversely aspected the presence of Pluto in the eleventh house shows a loss of genuine friends through disasters, wars and such-like conditions, and an encountering of abnormal difficulties through the treachery of those with whom friendly associations have been made.

If the malefics in the eleventh house be elevated above the luminary it afflicts—*i.e.*, nearer to the meridian—then the friends will be the cause of the native's ruin.

The Moon anywhere in the horoscope, afflicted by Saturn, shows false friends.

If the luminaries and Mercury be found powerful, and free from the affliction of the malefics, or in good aspect to Jupiter or Venus, or indeed to any planets, a quiet and successful life will be experienced, with many sincere friendships and happy associations.

Several planets in the same sign show many acquaintances, but few real friends, unless these planets be in good aspect to the Sun or Moon.

Mercury in good aspect to Jupiter or Venus gives many true friends. The same if Mercury be in good aspect to the luminaries.

When a fixed sign occupies the cusp of the eleventh house, and the lord of the eleventh is found in a fixed sign, the friends of the native will be faithful and reliable; if in common signs, doubtful and inconstant; in cardinal signs, ambitious and time-serving.

The ruler of the ascendant being in the twelfth house conduces to a reclusive life.

The ruler of the ascendant in the eleventh house, or the ruler of the eleventh in the ascendant, or these rulers in conjunction and good aspect to one another, the native makes many friends, and is much benefited by them.

Chiefly, however, regard the Sun, Moon, and Mercury; for if these be well aspected or well placed and free from the affliction of the malefics, the associations of the native will be happy and fortunate.

The dates shown by the longitude of the benefic planets will indicate the birthdays of persons who will benefit the native, should they come into his or her life; while the longitude of the malefics will show the birthdays of persons who will work mischief therein.

Persons born on the dates corresponding to the mid-heaven and the ascendant, will be found to dominate the native's fortunes to a large extent. The opposite points will give the birthdays of persons who may prove disastrous to the native, or such whose interests will be opposed to his.

CHAPTER XI

ENEMIES

THE rulers of the twelfth, eighth, seventh, and fourth houses must be taken into consideration, together with the planets therein. These houses are opposed to the first, second, sixth, and tenth, which denote the material welfare of the native.

In addition to these natural significators, the planets which may afflict the Sun or Moon or ascendant must also be taken, with the houses they occupy, as being indicative of probable sources of loss or trouble.

Thus, if evil planets be in the seventh, they will oppose the ascendant, and will denote many strifes and open contests from persons whose avowed interests are contrary to those of the native.

Uranus in the seventh house shows public rivals; Saturn shows deceitful opponents who will use fraudulent means to overcome the native; Mars denotes such as may use violence and do him bodily harm; the Sun therein denotes open and powerful rivals; Mercury indicates petty traducers and commercial rivals.

Neptune in the seventh produces ambushes, plots, and nefarious schemes designed to bring the native into trouble.

Pluto in the seventh house if badly aspected shows an encountering of enmity in public life. Enemies will seek to harm through attacking the marriage or business partner or attempting to involve the partner in something of a scandalous moral, social, financial or business nature.

The evil planets in the fourth house denote such as are opposed to the dignity, honour, and credit of the native; those in the twelfth show enemies to his personal comfort, secret foes, and those that lie in ambush around him.

The benefics in these houses need not be considered as enemies, unless they afflict the Sun or Moon.

The malefics in these houses are very evil.

Any planet afflicting the Sun or Moon, from any part of the horoscope, may be taken as an enemy, and judgment is made according to its nature and the house it occupies.

The malefics in any of the houses cited, and in good aspect to the Sun or Moon, and having a good aspect from the benefics, denotes that there is little or no danger of serious enmity.

Similarly, if the malefic be in its own sign or exaltation, and in good aspect to the Sun and Moon, or in no aspect to them, but itself configurated with Jupiter or Venus, then the enmity will produce only good.

The lord of the tenth house, afflicted by the lord of the sixth, or a malefic in the sixth, the native will be in danger of hurt and reversal through his inferiors.

An enemy to be feared is denoted by a malefic in the seventh, twelfth, fourth, or eighth house, in the sign of its detriment or fall, and afflicting the Sun or Moon.   Such conditions produce persistent and malicious enemies, who will injure the native continually and effectually.   Mercury badly aspected in any part of the figure shows enemies to abound.   If afflicted by Mars it produces scandal and slander; by Uranus it produces quarrels, legal disputes, and much controversy; by Saturn it brings deceit and treachery; by Neptune, plots and frauds.

Pluto badly aspected by Mercury shows that enemies will try to lower the prestige and reputation by libellous and lying statements which so distort the true facts that litigation to prove the truth would be almost ruinous.

The lord of the ascendant elevated, well placed, and well aspected, denotes that the native will never fear his enemies; and if the lord of the horoscope be stronger than the ruler of the seventh house, and the ruler of the tenth stronger than the lord of the fourth, the native will rise above his enemies and vanquish them entirely. Otherwise, the reverse of this will happen.   If good aspects are the only source of strength to the lord of the horoscope, the native will rely on the assistance of others to overcome his enemies.   If, however, it be itself essentially dignified and elevated above the ruler of the seventh house, the native will of himself overcome his rivals and opponents.

When, therefore, Jupiter is found in the ascendant or tenth house, and the ruler of the ascendant strong and well aspected, the native overcomes all his enemies.

The horoscopical causes of friendship and enmity are explained in the succeeding chapter.

The longitude of the malefic planets in the horoscope should be noted, and the dates corresponding thereto will indicate the birthdays of the persons who will oppose the native's fortunes.

CHAPTER XII

SYMPATHY AND ANTIPATHY

EVERY observer of human life will have been struck by the strange instinctive likes and dislikes which some people manifest towards others of their own or the opposite sex.   Two friends will take opposite views regarding the same person at first sight.   There is a cause for it; and the science of horoscopy affords a useful and satisfactory explanation.

Suppose a person to be born under the sign Libra—*i.e.*, with Libra rising at birth; another is born with Sagittarius rising.   They are friends.   Their ascendants are in sextile aspect.   Another person is born under Aries.   He comes into the lives of these two people born under Libra and Sagittarius.   He proves agreeable to the one born under Sagittarius, and disagreeable to the one born under Libra.   The reason is obvious: Aries is in trine to Sagittarius, and in opposition to Libra.

Had the person born under Aries been a female, and the one under Libra a male, there would have been an attraction instead of a repulsion.   Persons of the *same sex* born under opposing signs rarely effect a lasting friendship, but, on the contrary, will be disposed to injure one another by diversity of interests.   The square aspect between ascendant signs is bad for both sexes.

In horoscopes of opposite sexes, Mars in the one on the place of Venus in the other, is a strong sex attraction.   The result of close association between the two persons would be dangerous, unless marriage were in question; or, otherwise, unless some modifying influence also existed in the two horoscopes.   The Sun in one horoscope in conjunction or parallel to the Moon in another, is a strong friendly tie, and occurring in the horoscopes of opposite sexes, it disposes to marriage.   Venus in one horoscope in the place of Sun or Moon in another, of the opposite sex, denotes strong attachment and affection.

The strongest sign of friendship between two persons is when the Sun in one is in trine to the Moon in the other, and the Moon in similar relations with the Sun also. Thus: if one person had the Sun in Pisces 20°, and Moon in Sagittarius 10°, the person who would best agree with him would be one whose Sun was in Aries 10°, or Leo 10°, and whose Moon was in Cancer 20°, or Scorpio 20°. The two luminaries would then be in mutual trine aspect. It is the most felicitous augury when happening between the horoscope of friends of opposite sex.

Benefics in one nativity on the ascendant, Sun, or Moon of another, denote that good will result to that person whose benefics are so placed. The person whose Sun, Moon, or ascendant it is, will be the cause of good to the other.

The opposite effect will be experienced when the malefics in one horoscope occupy the places, or afflict the places of the Sun, Moon, or ascendant in another. Satisfactory relations will not transpire between the persons whose planets are thus mutually placed.

When such or similar relations as the foregoing are found to exist between the horoscopes of individuals, there is radical sympathy or antipathy between them. Such radical dispositions of the planets are never overcome, though under certain circumstances they may be liable to interruption.

Temporary sympathy or antipathy is caused by the motion of planets in one nativity to the body or aspect of planets in another, after birth.

Thus, the planet Mars in one horoscope passing over the place of Venus in another, will produce a temporary magnetic attraction. The same may occur if Venus in one be passing over the place of Mars in the other.

The Sun in one progressing to the place of the Moon in another, will produce a strong friendship. But this will not last unless there are radical indications of friendship between the parties concerned.

The Moon progressing to the opposition or square of the Sun in another horoscope produces breaches and quarrels. These will pass away if the horoscope show radical points of sympathy. The Moon progressing to the body of a malefic in another horoscope will cause trouble between the parties concerned, and he whose malefic it is will suffer injury according to the nature of the planet and its signification in the horoscope.

The Sun progressing to the place of Jupiter in another horoscope is an exceedingly good sign of friendship, out of which benefits will arise.

If students will observe the progressive places of the Sun and Moon at the time of making the acquaintance of any person, and compare them with the places of the planets in the horoscope of that person, the truth of these observations will be at once apparent. The progressive position of Sun and Moon in that person's horoscope, compared with the radical positions in the horoscope of the subject, will further point to the results of the acquaintance. In all cases, that person whose planet, Sun, or Moon, progresses to the radical position of the other's, will be the one who *makes* the overture or advance, or who *causes* the evil or *commences* the quarrel, as the case may be.

Thus, if Mars in a man's horoscope progresses to the radical place of Venus in a woman's horoscope, the man will at that time make advances of an amorous nature. The result of this would depend wholly on the radical sympathy or antipathy of the two horoscopes. Reason similarly in regard to other relationships, whether good or evil.

The method of computing the progressive positions of the planets will be explained in Book iii.

CHAPTER XIII

TRAVELLING AND VOYAGES

THE third and ninth houses, their rulers, and the planets therein, have chief influence in this question. The Moon, Mercury, and Mars have also much influence in regard to journeys.

If the majority of these, *viz.*, Moon, Mercury, Mars, and the rulers of the third and ninth houses, be in movable or common signs, many journeys and changes will take place. If the majority are in watery signs, Cancer, Scorpio, Pisces, or these be on the cusps of the third or ninth houses, voyages are denoted.

The ninth house shows long journeys in foreign countries, and voyages. The third house denotes railway and inland journeys. The Moon signifies all kinds of changes, and Mercury the inclination thereto. So, if the majority of the planets are found in Aries, Cancer, Libra, Capricorn, Gemini, Virgo, Sagittarius, or Pisces, then judge that journeys and changes will take place.

Many planets in watery signs show many voyages, especially if these signs occupy the ninth or third house.

Saturn strong and in the ascendant, gives a love of a locality, and counteracts the influences which tend toward changes.

The Moon in any aspect to Uranus, either being in the first, third, fourth, seventh, ninth, or tenth, produces sudden changes and frequent removals.

The Moon, Sun, or Mars cadent in the third, ninth, sixth or twelfth, denotes many journeys; and if in watery signs or in Sagittarius, voyages and life in foreign countries.

Pluto in the third or ninth house shows travel of an unusual nature or brought about by an arising of unusual circumstances connected with relatives, family or marital affairs. If in the third house, these unusual circumstances will be connected with the native's relatives but if in the ninth house will be connected with or caused by the marriage partner or the marriage partner's relatives.

Neptune in either of these houses increases the indication of travel by sea and by air, the third house showing relatively short journeys but the ninth house indicating long distance travel unless the sign Gemini is involved when it denotes continental rather than long distance travel. If Neptune should be badly aspected there will be liability to sickness or danger through storms at sea, or through hazards affecting the airplane.

Planets in a watery sign in the twelfth, tenth, or first, denote a voyage early in life.

The more planets there are in cadent houses and common signs, the greater is the tendency to lead a roaming life.

The Moon in Gemini or Sagittarius, rising or in the mid-heaven, produces long voyages and a taste for travelling and foreign life.

When Jupiter, Mercury, Mars, are all in either movable or common signs, the same tendency is shown.

Mars in any aspect to Sun or Moon tends to produce changes and journeys.

If, however, *fixed* signs are found in the third or ninth house, and most of the planets in fixed signs, then the native will not travel much.

The Sun or Moon in aspect to Saturn, and the latter strong in the figure, makes the native adverse to travelling.

Similarly, Mars, Uranus, or Mercury strong, and aspecting the Moon or Sun, produces a restless life.

SUCCESS OR LOSS BY TRAVELLING

Success abroad is shown by the benefic planets, Jupiter, Venus, or the luminaries well aspected, in the ninth house.

But the malefics in the ninth house, or the luminaries therein, and badly aspected, show dangers and losses in foreign lands. By a " foreign land " is meant one that is distant from the place of birth, no matter of what nationality the native may be.

The malefics in the ninth house, afflicting either luminary, show dangers according to the signs they occupy.

If in *airy* signs, the voyages will be dangerous through lightning, tempests, and falls from high places; in *earthy* signs, by foundering or running aground, by famine, falls, avalanches, and privations generally; in *fiery* signs, by fire, sunstroke, cuts, burns, stabs, kicks from animals, bites, and fevers; in *watery* signs, by drowning, floods, dampness, etc.

In all cases, therefore, where the malefics occupy the third and ninth houses, or afflict the rulers of those houses, or the Moon or Sun, the travels are far from prosperous and in many cases are fatal.

As to the advisability of travelling, judgment is made as follows:—
If the benefics, or the Sun or Moon well aspected, occupy the first, tenth, ninth, or twelfth house, the native will do well abroad. If such be in the third or fourth house, it would be the height of folly for the native to leave the country of his birth.

Therefore, if the third and fourth houses are more favoured than the ninth and tenth, the native should not leave the country of his birth. The benefics, or the luminaries well aspected, in the ascendant, give the native free choice in the matter. He may go abroad or stay at home with equal success.

On the contrary, evil planets in the fourth house, or the Sun or Moon afflicted therein, are strong reasons for the native leaving his own country.

If by the foregoing rules it be found advisable for the native to go abroad, selection of the place or direction should be made as follows.

WHERE TO GO

Note the sign and house occupied by the benefics, Jupiter and Venus. Regulate the distance by the house, and the direction by the sign. In this respect the third and first houses denote places near to the birthplace; the second and sixth houses denote any place in the country of birth; the first and seventh denote adjoining countries; the twelfth and eighth show distant countries; the eleventh and ninth any distance in the world; the tenth, the antipodes.

The direction is judged by the house occupied by the benefics, or the luminaries well aspected.

Thus, the first house denotes the East, the tenth South, the seventh West, the fourth North; the quadrant between the first and tenth S.E., that between the tenth and seventh S.W., between the seventh and fourth N.W., and between the fourth and first N.E.

Thus, if Jupiter were in the ninth or tenth house of a London horoscope, and the horoscope favoured going abroad, the Cape would be a good place to go to, as that is in the right direction. This would be especially good if Jupiter were in good aspect to the Sun or Moon.

But should Jupiter be afflicting the Sun or Moon, it would not be advisable to take that direction, for it would be a significator of loss to the native. The place of Venus might then be taken, and if this were propitious, the direction its sign indicates should determine the *direction*, its house the *distance*.

If neither Jupiter nor Venus afford good influences, then take a planet which is in good aspect to the Sun or Moon, and if it be strong and well placed, take the judgment from its house. And this holds good even if that planet be Pluto, Neptune, Uranus, Saturn, or Mars, because its good aspect to the luminaries is of more value than an evil aspect from the benefics Jupiter and Venus. But always use these latter planets whenever possible.

If the fourth house is strongly favoured by the presence of the benefics, or by the luminaries well aspected, the native should never leave the country in which he was born whatever the indications of travelling may otherwise be. By doing so, he would infallibly leave behind him the best influences of his horoscope.

When a person goes to a foreign country, his destiny therein will be seen by referring the horoscope to the longitude and latitude of that country. This can readily be done by adding the longitude of the country to the mid-heaven of the horoscope if the place be east of the birthplace, or subtracting it if the place be west. Then, with this new mid-heaven, take out the cusps of the houses from the " Table of Houses " belonging to the latitude of the country. The planets will retain the same longitudes as at birth. While the native resides in that country, the " directions," " transits," and other influences, must be referred to this local horoscope. In the author's opinion, a person should travel to that place in which, by this method, the best influences of the natal horoscope are brought into prominence.

The old authors, however, have laid down rules as represented herein, and certainly we owe them much respect.

RESIDENCE

When it is determined, by the horoscope of birth, that a person shall remain in his native land, or that it is advisable so to do, it becomes a matter of some importance as to where he should reside.

Astrology offers some important information regarding the choice of a house, its aspect and locality.

Attention must be directed to the sign occupying the fourth angle, or cusp of the fourth house. If this be Aries, the house in which the native lives should face East; if Cancer, North; if Libra, West; if Capricorn, South. Taurus and Gemini, being between East and North, denote respectively N.E. by E. and N.E. by N., and so on. Then as to the locality. If a cardinal sign be rising, the house should be in a prominent position, on the top of a hill, or elevated above the sea level. If a common sign be rising, the house should be situated at sea level, and not in a conspicuous place, but between others. If a fixed sign ascend, then the residence should be in a valley. By this choice of aspect and locality it is believed that the native is put into magnetic conditions agreeable to his nature. The atmospheric conditions obtaining at the summit of a hill and at its foot are very different, and must have a differing effect upon the magnetic condition of the body. The difference of atmospheric pressure, saturation, etc., would alone cause a difference in the nervous condition of a person, and, therefore, harmonious surroundings can only be regulated by choice of habitation in regard both to locality and aspect.

CHAPTER XIV

THE KIND OF DEATH

MORTALITY is of two kinds—*natural*, arising from disease or old age; and *accidental*, arising from a variety of causes.

A natural death may be judged to ensue when there are no signs in the horoscope to the contrary.

A violent or accidental death occurs when the Sun and Moon are afflicted by a malefic, and when no assistance is given by Jupiter or Venus.

Again, when the Sun is afflicted by one malefic, and the Moon by another, or when the Moon alone is afflicted by more than one malefic, or the Sun alone by more than one, providing always that no assistance be given by Jupiter or Venus, then a violent death ensues.

The afflicting planets being in the violent signs—Aries, Scorpio, Capricorn—is an additional sign of violence; also if the Sun or Moon be in these signs.

The following aspects occurring in a horoscope, give warning of a violent death:—

1. Mars afflicting Sun and Moon by conjunction or aspect, or afflicting one of the luminaries only, and elevated above it.

2. The Sun or Moon afflicted by the malefics in the first, sixth, eighth, tenth, or fourth house.

3. A malefic in the first or eighth, or on the cusp of the seventh, if at the same time afflicting the luminaries, or one of them.

4. Malefics opposing one another from angles, particularly from violent signs or cardinal signs.

5. Both the Sun and Moon afflicted by one or more of the malefics, if one of the luminaries and one of the afflicting planets be in a violent sign.

6. Both luminaries afflicted by a malefic, one of the luminaries being oriental.

7. Two malefics attacking the same luminary.

8. Pluto and Neptune must both be considered as malefic planets if they are afflicted by adverse aspects, especially of the Sun, Moon, Mars or Saturn. If Pluto is in the eighth this will give indication of death occurring through being involved in some public catastrophe connected with the work that is being carried out, such as explosion, building collapse, or if in one of the National Services through such things as mines, torpedoes, submarine crash. If in

private life through such catastrophes as mine disasters, underground railway crashes. Neptune in the eighth will bring a danger of drowning, of poisoning or of death through wrong drugs being taken or administered or of overdoses of an anæsthetic.

If, with these indications, you find Jupiter or Venus in trine or sextile to the afflicted light, then danger is averted by strange interventions, or hairbreadth escapes will be made.

When the afflicting planets are in human signs—Gemini, Virgo, Sagittarius, Aquarius—the death will be by human means.

The eighth and fourth houses have chief signification in this matter, and the planets in them, together with their aspects, will indicate the nature of the death. Violent planets, such as Uranus and Mars, or Saturn and Neptune, when in violent signs, are testimonies of an untimely end.

When Neptune is the afflicting planet, he causes deaths by ambush and treachery, by drowning and by strange spiritual causes. There is danger of trance or simulated death, which must be carefully watched.

With Uranus as the cause of evil, death results in some extraordinary and remarkable manner. It inclines to suicide, especially if Mercury be found weak and badly afflicted, or Venus afflicted by Saturn or Uranus, and the luminaries also afflicted.

Saturn causes deaths by crushes, fractures, falls, drowning, etc., according to its sign and house.

Mars causes death by burns, cuts, loss of blood, scalds, ruptures, frenzy, and in battle. The exact nature is usually judged by the sign occupied by Mars, but the houses occupied by Saturn and Uranus must also be considered, in addition to the signs they are in.

The planet Mars has special signification of the cause of death according to the sign it occupies, whether human, animal, airy, fiery, earthy, etc. Observe always whether the malefics afflicting the Sun or Moon are elevated above the luminary or the reverse; for when you find the malefics so afflicting, and in elevation above the luminary, it is a sure sign of a violent end.

The lord of the eighth house being afflicted by malefic planets is an additional sign of a violent death.

Do not judge a violent death will happen, unless the positions are very striking and unmistakable.

When death is judged to ensue from *natural* causes, the sixth and eighth houses are taken into consideration, together with the signs in which the malefics may be placed.

Fixed signs show death by blood (Aquarius), disorders of the throat (Taurus), heart affections (Leo), and generative system (Scorpio).

Common signs show colds and affections of the lungs (Gemini), bowels (Virgo), and nervous system (Sagittarius and Pisces).

Movable signs denote death by affections of the head, brain fever, etc. (Aries), stomach (Cancer), the kidneys, liver (Libra), also erysipelas and disorders of the skin (Capricorn).

If Saturn be in the eighth, the death will be slow and tedious; Mars there, it will be quick and painful; Uranus, there, sudden and unexpected; Jupiter there, in comfort and order; Venus there, peaceful and without pang or throe of pain. The Moon and Mercury are passive, and act according to the nature of the planet in nearest aspect; but the Moon has a signification of death in the public streets, or in the presence of strangers, in public hospitals and other places of a public nature, when other testimonies point that way. Neptune in the eighth operates to produce trance, coma, and simulated death, ending in syncope.

CHAPTER XV
ILLUSTRATIONS

THE following examples will serve to illustrate the rules laid down in the preceding chapters.

THE BODILY FORM

Queen Victoria, the great Queen of England was born in London on 24th May, 1819 at 4.15 a.m. with Gemini rising and the Sun and Moon in the Ascendant; and Mercury, ruler of the Ascendant, in the sign Taurus. The fair blonde complexion of the Queen was due to the Sun and Moon rising, and she owed her short stature to Mercury in Taurus.

Her son, King Edward VII, was born on 9th November, 1841 at 10.48 a.m. in London. Jupiter was rising in Sagittarius and Saturn and Mars were intercepted in Capricorn in the Ascendant. King Edward's full florid physical body was due to the influence of Jupiter, and his fair complexion inherited through his mother the Queen was due to Sagittarius, while Saturn rising in Capricorn accounted for his shortness in height.

Mars in Capricorn gave the military regal bearing, and made him fond of pleasure and the company of the ladies of the day.

ACCIDENTS

H.R.H. Prince Leopold, Duke of Albany, born 7th April, 1853, at 1.10 p.m. Saturn in conjunction with Uranus in the mid-heaven; Moon in Aries, in conjunction with Mars, in the ninth house; five planets in a violent sign. Died from severe contusion of the head, the result of a fall. The truth of Astrology in general, and particularly of the rules contained in this work, is here admirably illustrated. Mars in conjunction with Moon in Aries, which rules the *head*, in the ninth house, *foreign countries*, and Saturn oriental, and in conjunction with Uranus, in the tenth house, in an earthy sign, show the fall, the cut on the head, the effusion of blood, and the danger of accidents abroad. Venus, in conjunction with the Moon, would have saved him, but Venus was retrograde, and in the sign of her debility, Aries.

The Duke, one of the sons of Queen Victoria, had inherited the full blooded way of life through his father Prince Albert of Saxe-Coburg-Gotha (The Prince Consort). He was fond of hard riding and the story goes that he met with his death as the result of a fall from a horse.

CHARACTER

The perfect example of a man of high character is shown in the horoscope of General Gordon of Khartoum, who was born on 28th January, 1833 at 9.50 a.m. Aries 13° rising, Capricorn 4° on mid-heaven, cardinal signs on angles; Mercury in tenth in Capricorn, sextile to Venus in Pisces; Moon in first in Taurus, square to Sun in Aquarius; Venus in conjunction with Jupiter in Pisces, dignified, in sextile to Neptune and Mars, but opposition to Saturn; four planets in fixed signs.

The description of the hero of Khartoum is in agreement with the rising sign, with Moon in Taurus in ascendant, and Mars in Taurus. Slight in figure, with a fair complexion; very clear, fearless, grey eyes, light curling hair and round head. He was unmarried, and this was often a source of self-gratulation. " You have wives and families," he wrote in one of his despatches, " I, thank God, have none: . . . to carry myself is enough for me, I want no other baggage." But what concerns us at this moment is the man's character. It has been unconsciously sketched by the hero himself in the despatch already quoted from. " Find me the man," he wrote, " and I will take him as my help, who utterly despises money, name, glory, honour; one who never wishes to see his home again; one who looks to God as the source of good, and the controller of evil; one who has a healthy body and energetic spirit, and one who looks on death as a release from misery. And if you cannot find him, then leave me alone!" Alas! Gordons were not too plentiful. The man, as measured by this saint and hero, was not within his reach.

His disregard of money is shown by Mars in Taurus occupying the second house, in exact sextile to Jupiter. Mercury in sextile to Venus in her exaltation, the near conjunction of the Sun to Uranus, the presence of the Moon in the ascendant; Mercury, Jupiter, and the Moon being the strongest planets in the horoscope: all these were signs of that inherent nobility of character, that " scorn of consequence " and disregard for life which characterised the man, and gave him his extraordinary faith throughout a career of restless activity, innumerable dangers, and severe privations. His honours were due to Mercury in mid-heaven, in sextile to Venus in Pisces, cardinal signs on angles, and the ruler of the horoscope in sextile to Jupiter, and trine to Saturn.

WEALTH

Another great character from history was the founder of Rhodesia, Cecil Rhodes who was born on 6th July, 1853. Time of birth unknown. At noon the Moon was in Cancer, 14° 46', and the Sun in Cancer, 14° 14'; Venus in Cancer, 28° 47'; Uranus in Taurus, 11° 52'; Saturn in Taurus, 27° 54'; Mars in Gemini, 9° 1'; Jupiter in Sagittarius, 16° 32' retrograde; Mercury in Leo, 6° 34'; and Neptune in 12th degree of Pisces. Here we find the Moon in its own sign with the Sun and Venus, and in sextile to Uranus, Venus sextile to Saturn, Sun and Moon trine to Neptune— all signs of success. Mars sextile to Mercury, and in opposition to Jupiter, gives recklessness and enterprise, keen judgment and ability to estimate the value of every opportunity which presents itself. It is well known that Cecil Rhodes used his money in no niggardly spirit. It is believed that the time of birth was 3.50 p.m., which gives the 20th degree of Scorpio rising. Jupiter on the cusp of second house, and Venus on cusp of ninth.

Horoscope of Kaiser Wilhelm II, born 27th January, 1859, 3 p.m. at Berlin.

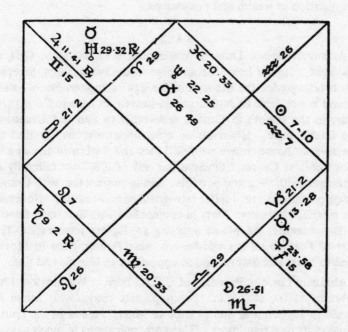

Here we find Saturn in the sign of its debility opposing the Sun in its weakest sign; Mars and Neptune conjoined in the meridian, and the Sun semisquare to both; the malefics—Neptune, Mars, and Uranus—elevated, and the Moon in opposition to Uranus.

The Emperor had a most fateful horoscope, and during his reign the German Empire suffered reversals of which it hitherto had had no shadow of experience. The destiny of Kaiser Wilhelm was such that he lost the whole of his possessions. He was never a popular monarch. Mars, in the meridian, caused him to engage in continual quarrels, and the Sun in opposition to Saturn denuded him of his power among the nations. He lost his royal spouse (the Moon in opposition to Uranus retrograde) suddenly. Nothing more adverse or less royal than this horoscope of the Kaiser, except, perhaps, that of the Sultan of Turkey, was to be found among the rulers of Europe. The Kaiser with his withered arm lived to a great age and died suddenly from a heart attack, as an outcast living in Doorn, Holland.

This horoscope is introduced to illustrate the rules in regard to the question of wealth and possessions.

RANK

Arthur Wellesley, Duke of Wellington, born 1st May, 1769, at midnight. Jupiter holds the meridian in the martial sign, Scorpio, but is retrograde; the Moon is in the sign of Jupiter, Pisces, in the second house, trine to Jupiter in mid-heaven, in trine to Saturn and Mars in the seventh in Cancer, and sextile to Sun and Uranus in the fourth angle. His rivals or open opponents are signified by the seventh house, where we find Mars and Saturn in the sign of their debility, Cancer. Observe the end of life, how faithfully in agreement with the astral portents: Sun in conjunction with Uranus on cusp of the fourth, Jupiter retrograde in mid-heaven. Note also the marriage portents: Mars in conjunction with Saturn in Cancer in the seventh; the Moon applying to Jupiter retrograde. The Part of Fortune on the mid-heaven, near Jupiter, trine to Moon, trine to Mars and Saturn, and in opposition to Uranus and Sun.

Abraham Lincoln, President of U.S.A., born at Washington, 12th February, 1809, at 2 a.m. Seven planets rising, with Moon in sextile to Jupiter, and Sun in trine to Mars; Jupiter in the fourth house in its own sign Pisces. These are indications of much success in life and rising fortunes. He died by the hand of an assassin. The malefics are all oriental, and Mars in Libra, square to the Moon in Capricorn, and elevated above all the other planets. Saturn and Neptune in conjunction with ascendant, and Uranus on the cusp of the twelfth house. The President died in the height of his political glory, when success and honours were wholly within his grasp, and Jupiter is found in the fourth house in sextile to the Moon in the second.

LOVE AND MARRIAGE

Lord Byron, the romantic poet, was born on 22nd January, 1788 at 1.18 a.m. (N.B.—The hour of birth is a matter of dispute, but this does not concern the author's purpose in bringing the horoscope forward under this head.) Venus is found in Aquarius, conjoined with Saturn; the Moon is with Mars in Cancer, opposed to Mercury; and the Sun in Aquarius is opposed by Uranus in Leo; four planets in fixed signs, and three in cardinal. The position of Venus, afflicted by Saturn, and the affliction of the Moon by Mars and Mercury, very aptly show the disappointment and trouble to which the Hellenic hero was born; the blighting of his love, the estrangement from his kindred and country, and the criticism to which he was subjected throughout his life, and even after his death, not only among his natural enemies, but also by the pen of his own sister.

King George VI was born on 14th December, 1897. His horoscope provides the perfect example of a quiet, kindly type of ruler who made a perfect marriage and was very much in love with his charming Queen until the end of his days. He had the sign Libra rising, the outstanding zodiacal sign which rules love, companionship and marriage. Being the sign of the " balance " it indicated a character well fitted to preside over both marital and national destinies. Venus, the ruling planet, together with the Moon and Uranus were in the sign Scorpio denoting his strength of will and personal firmness, and the splendid trine from Jupiter in Leo to Mars in Sagittarius indicated his geniality, natural charm of manner, good humour and generosity. The Sun and Mercury in Sagittarius rendered His Majesty democratic and philosophical and showed his great interest in all forms of social and philanthropic work. He did his work quietly and unobtrusively but was nevertheless thorough and efficient and in all these activities and interests he had the unstinted support of his beautiful queen who, by her devotion both to him and in the carrying out of national duties has endeared herself to all his subjects.

TRAVELLING

Commander Peary, the world famous explorer, who reached the North Pole, was born on 6th May, 1856 with his Moon and Saturn in the sign Gemini, and Jupiter and Neptune in the sign Pisces, both signs being very much connected with travel, and the combination showing travel of an unusual, adventurous and yet arduous nature, the latter being clearly signified by Saturn. He had his Sun in the sign Taurus applying to a sextile of Neptune, whilst his Moon was separating from a trine of Mars and applying to a square of Neptune, aspects showing travel that would stir the imagination and yet be associated with many strange vicissitudes

F

of life. Sun in conjunction with Uranus would also show un-expected events and unexpected honours.

KIND OF DEATH

President Garfield, born in America, 19th November, 1831, at 2 a.m. In this horoscope we find Saturn in the twelfth, denoting secret enemies; Mars in Scorpio, opposing the Moon, and Uranus in the fifth in square to the Moon, the Moon being in parallel to Mars. Mars ruling the eighth is afflicted by Uranus and Jupiter from the fifth house, which rules theatres. He met his death while in a theatre. Saturn ruling the fifth is in the twelfth: secret enemies. He was shot in the bowels, and Saturn is found in Virgo. The signs of this assassination are, therefore: Mars lord of eighth, in parallel and opposition to Moon in the eighth; the Moon in square to Uranus and Jupiter, from fifth house; Saturn lord of fifth in twelfth; ascendant sesquiquadrate to Uranus; Sun, Mars, and Mercury ruler of ascendant, in Scorpio.

Adolf Hitler provides the perfect example of one who through his own stupidity met a violent end. Throwing away the oppor-tunity of living and dying as one of the world's greatest characters in history, he came to a violent end in the ruins of Berlin. He was born on 20th April, 1889 and had the sign Libra rising with Venus, his ruling planet in the sign Taurus in conjunction with Mars, both within the eighth house sphere of influence, the house of death. His Sun was also in Taurus and the eighth house. Venus and Mars were in square to Saturn which was in Leo and elevated in his map showing a rise to power and a tremendous fall from power.

The student is advised to erect as many of the foregoing horo-scopes as may be practicable, and to study them in the light of the rules given in this section of our work. The mathematical and judicial aspects of the science of horoscopy will thereby be brought simultaneously to the knowledge of the student, progress being always in direct ratio to the amount of exercise given to the faculties employed.

END OF BOOK II

BOOK III

THE MEASURE OF TIME

CHAPTER I

THE PRE-NATAL EPOCH, AND
THE LAW OF SEX

THE general law controlling the Pre-natal Epoch is based upon the known relationship existing between the Moon and the ascendant of the horoscope. This relationship has been loosely formulated by Gadbury, and other writers, including Wilson, in his " Dictionary of Astrology "—wherein the idea is badly conceived and erroneously illustrated—and is generally known as the Trutine of Hermes. The theorem, however, is correctly stated by Coley. Its primary use is the correction of the time of birth, when the estimate time only is given. The Hindus have a theory, which is to be found in their ancient astrological writings, such as the *Brihat Jâtaka* and the *Brihat Samhitâ*, that the World-breath has definite and periodic pulsations, a systole and diastole action, whereby birth and death are controlled. This theory involves the concept of periodicity, which has been established by modern scientific research. It further employs the idea that births can only take place in respect to any single locality at intervals, that these intervals are in accordance with lunar motion, and that only every seventh impulse of the World-breath permits of human births. This theory, when referred to lunar action, a fact well within our knowledge and scrutiny, assumes the proportions of a scientific statement, from which the intelligent mind will not turn in a spirit of patronising contempt.

The author has been fortunate in having the collaboration of a trained and veteran scientist in the work of establishing the primary law designated as the Pre-natal Epoch. This law was first definitely formulated in June, 1886. It was published in 1890, and met with considerable comment and general approval. But every statement of a general law, of an idea in its incipience, is open to modification, and is only properly defined in the light of elaborate tests, which bring into array the many exceptions to which any general law is subject. Such tests have been made, and the variants have been reduced to a series of groups, all falling within the general statement of the law, capable of instant recognition and treatment.

If it can be shown, as we hold it can, that *all births are brought about in exact harmony with lunar laws, that intra-uterine life is in direct relations with the sidereal world without, that the great fact of maternity is capable of purely astronomical measurement*, we have good cause to claim the serious attention of all intelligent women, and more particularly that of physiologists and obstetricians, to whom this enquiry is of the most vital interest.

We may proceed, then, with a general statement of the law of the Pre-natal Epoch, as first formulated by the author. Afterwards it will be necessary to classify the exceptions to this law, and define their character.

GENERAL LAW OF THE PRE-NATAL EPOCH

1. The general period of intra-uterine life is nine *Solar*, or ten *Lunar* months.

2. This period is subject to an increase or decrease, according to the position of the Moon in regard to the Sun, and the horizon of the place of birth.

The law in regard to the period between the Pre-natal Epoch and the Natal day is thus defined:

THEOREM A

I. *When the Moon at birth is* INCREASING *in light, and* ABOVE *the horizon, the period is* LESS *than ten Lunar months.*

II. *When the Moon at birth is* DECREASING *in light, and* BELOW *the horizon, the period is* LESS *than ten Lunar months.*

III. *When the Moon at birth is* INCREASING *in light, and* BELOW *the horizon, the period is* MORE *than ten Lunar months.*

IV. *When the Moon at birth is* DECREASING *in light, and* ABOVE *the horizon, the period is* MORE *than ten Lunar months.*

The next question towards the determination of the exact epoch, is as to *how much* more or less than the average period any case may require. Therefore, note:—

THEOREM B

(a) *When the Moon is* BELOW *the horizon, the distance of the Moon from the* EASTERN *horizon is taken into account.*

(b) *When the Moon is* ABOVE *the horizon, the count is made from the Moon to the* WESTERN *horizon.*

(c) *The number of degrees between the Moon and the horizon will yield so many days, at the rate of 12 degrees for each day.*

(d) *These days, more or less than the Moon's tenth pre-natal revolution, will yield the day of the Epoch.*

Note.—It will be observed that the discussion of this problem of the Pre-Natal Epoch proceeds inductively from the birth, the known fact, to its presumptive ante-natal cause, which has to be established in the present argument. When the law governing the relations between the birth and the ante-natal cause is determined, it should not be impossible to reverse the operation, and argue from the Epoch to the Birth.

Theorems A and B contain the general statement of the law as to *time.* The following argument is advanced as a harmonious extension of what has been already stated:—

THEOREM C

1. *When the Moon is* INCREASING *at birth, it will be found at the Epoch in the sign which is* RISING *at birth, i.e., on the eastern horizon.*

2. *When the Moon is* DECREASING *at birth, it will be found at the Epoch in the sign which is* SETTING *at birth.*

Note.—Theorem A yields a general measure of the period. B and C determine it to an interval of two and a half days, the time the Moon is passing through any one sign.

THEOREM D

1. *That day on which the Moon transits the* EXACT *degree of the ascendant at birth (or its opposite), is the day of the Pre-natal Epoch.*

2. *If the Moon be* INCREASING *at birth, its place will be* RISING *at the Epoch.*

3. *If the Moon be* DECREASING *at birth, its place will be* SETTING *at the Epoch.*

Note.—Theorem D brings the argument for the *general law* to a close, inasmuch as it establishes the *exact moment* of the Pre-natal Epoch. Theorems A and B are in agreement with C and D, and make the ascendant at the Epoch and the Moon's place at birth interchangeable, either in direct or opposite terms, according to the Moon's increase or decrease at birth.

To summarise these theorems, and to formulate the general law in a succinct form, we say:—

I. *When the Moon at birth is increasing in light, and above the earth, or decreasing, and below the earth, the period is less than ten lunar revolutions by one day for every 12 degrees of the Moon's distance from the horizon to which it next comes after birth. But, when the Moon at birth is increasing and below the earth, or decreasing and above the earth, the period is by the same measure more than ten lunar revolutions, counted backwards from the day of birth.*

II. *When the Moon at birth is increasing in light, its place will be the ascendant at the Epoch, and the Moon's place at the Epoch will be the ascendant at birth. But, when the Moon at birth is decreasing in light, then its place will be setting at the Epoch, and the Moon's place at the Epoch will be the descendant at birth.*

To calculate the Pre-natal Epoch, take out from the horoscope of birth—The longitude (1) of the Sun; (2) of the Moon; (3) of the ascendant.

From these elements you will observe whether the Moon is above or below the earth, and whether increasing or decreasing in light. Then:

TO FIND THE DAY OF EPOCH

count nine months backwards, from the date of birth, and mark the date on which the Moon is in the sign it held at birth. [If the birth took place earlier than September, it will be necessary to procure an Ephemeris for the year preceding that of birth.] Having found the lunar place, count forward or backward, as the case may require, until you come to the day when the Moon is in the sign ascending or descending at birth, according to the rule. Take that day on which it transits the exact degree on the horizon at birth. Call this the *Day of Epoch.*

TO FIND THE HOUR OF EPOCH

1. Ascertain where the mother of the native was residing on the day of Epoch, and refer to the " Tables of Houses " for the latitude of that place, or, if none are available, calculate as directed on pages 48-49.

2. Bring the Moon's longitude at birth to the ascendant or descendant, as the case requires, and note the sidereal time, or right ascension of the meridian, in hours, minutes, and seconds. This will be the sidereal time at Epoch.

3. Take out of the Ephemeris the sidereal time at noon on the day of the Epoch. The difference between the sidereal time at noon, and the sidereal time at the Epoch will give the *time before* or *after* noon at which the Epoch occurred.

4. Find the Moon's longitude for this time on the day of Epoch, and this will give the ascendant or descendant at birth, as the case may be.

EXAMPLE

Male, born at Middlesbrough, Yorks., 6th June, 1892, at 7.40 a.m. The time of birth was taken by the accoucheur from a chronometer timed to Greenwich. The moment of birth, corrected to the longitude of birth is 7.35 a.m.

    Elements.—1. Moon in Libra, 28° 50'.
               2. Sun in Gemini, 16°.
               3. Asc. in Leo, 5° 23'.

The Moon is *increasing* in light and *below* the earth. The Epoch, therefore, will measure to *more* than ten lunar revolutions. (Theorem A.) The Moon being below the earth, the count is made from the Moon to the eastern horizon, *i.e.*, from Libra 28° 50' to Leo 5° 23'. (Theorem B, section *a*.) The distance from Leo 5° to Libra 29° is 84°, which, divided by 12, gives seven days as the excess of the period over ten lunar revolutions. (Theorem B, section *c*.) The measure of the nine solar or ten lunar months, backwards from the day of birth, measures to September 6th, and, by adding the seven days required by section *c*, we count to 30th August. The date on which the Moon transits the degree rising at birth is 31st August. (Theorem D, 1.)

The Moon at birth is in Libra 28° 50', and this degree of the Zodiac must rise at the Epoch. (Theorem D, 2.)

Then, to find the hour and minute at which this degree rises, refer to Tables of Houses for Middlesbrough. With Libra 28° 50', rising, we find the sidereal time of the meridian to be 8 hr. 50 min. (mid-heaven at Epoch), which we take from 10 hr. 41 min. (mid-heaven at noon), 31st August, 1891. This gives 1 hr. 51 min. as the time before noon at which the Epoch occurred, in *local time, viz.*—10.09 a.m., or G.M.T., 10.14 a.m.

Find the Moon's longitude for this time on the day of Epoch =
Leo, 5° 23', *which was the ascendant at birth.*

We have now to show that the case given in illustration of the
Law of the Pre-natal Epoch is not an isolated one. The following
births took place on their several dates in Middlesbrough, Yorks.,
the time being taken for the moment of the *first breath* of the child,
by the attendant physician.

EXAMPLES OF REGULAR EPOCHS

Births	*Epochs*
1.—Female, 11th June, 1892, at 11.21 p.m.	1.—31st August, 1891, at 11.22 p.m.
Asc. ♒ 11° 38'	☽ in ♌ 11° 52'
☽ in ♑ 7° 49'	Asc. ♋ 7° 49'
2.—Male, 22nd June, 1892, at 2.48 a.m.	2.—11th September, 1891, at 0.23 p.m.
Asc. ♊ 19° 15'	☽ in ♐ 19° 2'
☽ in ♉ 27° 49'	Asc. ♏ 27° 49'
3.—Female, 22nd June, 1892, at 6 a.m.	3.—14th September, 1891, at 0.22 p.m.
Asc. ♋ 28° 59'	☽ in ♑ 29° 38'
☽ in ♉ 29° 45'	Asc. ♏ 29° 45'
4.—Female, 23rd June, 1892, at 5.52 p.m.	4.—22nd September, 1891, at 1.43 p.m.
Asc. ♐ 0° 40'	☽ in ♉ 29° 33'
☽ in ♊ 21° 24'	Asc. ♐ 21° 24'
5.—Male, 10th July, 1892, at 11.36 p.m.	5.—3rd October, 1891, at 11.10 p.m.
Asc. ♉ 1° 51'	☽ in ♏ 2° 26'
☽ in ♒ 0° 16'	Asc. ♌ 0° 16'
6.—Female, 14th July, 1892, at 11.25 p.m.	6.—5th October, 1891, at 4.30 a.m.
Asc. ♉ 4° 55'	☽ in ♏ 5° 6'
☽ in ♓ 25° 17'	Asc. ♍ 25° 17'
7.—Male, 16th July, 1892, at 9.44 p.m.	7.—27th October, 1891, at 5.46 a.m.
Asc. ♓ 3° 29'	☽ in ♍ 3° 10'
☽ in ♈ 22° 29'	Asc. ♎ 22° 29'
8.—Male, 25th July, 1892, at 8.30 p.m.	8.—8th November, 1891, at 11.27 p.m.
Asc. ♒ 11° 56'	☽ in ♒ 11° 20'
☽ in ♌ 26° 13'	Asc. ♌ 26° 13'

Births	*Epochs*
9.—Male, 24th July, 1892, at 1.57 p.m. Asc. ♏ 10° 53′ ☽ in ♌ 9° 29′	9.—1st November, 1891, at 10.17 p.m. ☽ in ♏ 10° 57′ Asc. ♌ 9° 29′
10.—Male, 26th July, 1892, at 11.35 p.m. Asc. ♊ 1° 21′ ☽ in ♍ 10° 36′	10.—20th October, 1891, at 2.10 a.m. ☽ in ♊ 1° 2′ Asc. ♍ 10° 36′
11.—Male, 31st August, 1892, at 4.13 p.m. Asc. ♑ 4° 27′ ☽ in ♐ 21° 5′	11.—16th December, 1891, at 8.12 a.m. ☽ in ♋ 4° 22′ Asc. ♐ 21° 5′
12.—11th September, 1892, at 8.40 p.m. Asc. ♊ 6° 33′ ☽ in ♉ 27° 37′	12.—1st December, 1891, at 7.1 a.m. ☽ in ♐ 6° 33′ Asc. ♏ 27° 37′

Cases of Regular Epochs—that is, such as conform in all particulars with the law as already defined—might be adduced indefinitely. The above will, however, serve for examples of all the others.

It will be observed that they are all within the limits of an error of observation, and if referred to the latitude of birth, the apparent discrepancy of some minutes of space between the longitude of the ascendant at birth and the Moon at Epoch, will be found to yield a difference of *time* which is practically inconsiderable, owing to the oblique ascension of the signs in high North latitude. Thus, whereas on the equator the uniform rising of the signs is about one in every two hours, in the latitude of Middlesbrough we find the whole of Aries and Taurus, and the first five degrees of Gemini rising in the same interval of time. The " signs of short ascension " in northern latitudes are Capricorn, Aquarius, Pisces, Aries, Taurus, and Gemini; and hence the *apparent* discrepancy is likely to be greater when any one of these is the rising sign at birth, or its opposite.

Note.—In regard to Case 12 in the series above, the conditions of birth were somewhat remarkable, but, nevertheless, not such as to overthrow the Law of the Pre-natal Epoch. The right foot was extruded at 8.10 p.m., the left foot at 8.15 p.m., the head and arm at 8.19 p.m. The child was asphyxiated. Its first breath was taken at 8.23 p.m., the second at 8.25, the third at 8.27, etc. Regular breathing was established at 9 p.m. exactly. The mean between the first spasmodic breath and the establishing of regular breathing gives 8.41 p.m., and the Epoch, taken for this time, works out at 8.40 p.m. for the time of birth, a difference of one minute only.

IRREGULAR EPOCHS

are those wherein the Moon, although increasing at birth, is found at the epoch in the descending sign, or wherein the Moon, decreasing at birth, is found at the epoch in the ascending sign, or wherein the Moon's place at birth rises at the epoch, or sets, contrary to the rules laid down in the general statement of the law of the Pre-natal Epoch.

In all such cases, the count from the Moon to the ascendant or descendant at birth (Theorem B, section c) will not be in agreement with the other requirements of the law as set forth in Theorems A, C, and D, but exactly contrary. Examples:

Birth	*Epoch*
1.—Male, 21st May, 1892, at 12.54 a.m., London	1.—1st September, 1891, at 7 p.m.
Asc. ♒ 21° 55′	☽ in ♌ 21° 55′
☽ in ♓ 18° 53′	Asc. ♓ 18° 53′

In this case the Moon is decreasing at birth, and is found at epoch in the ascending sign Leo, instead of Aquarius, as required by the regular rule. The Moon being also below the earth, requires less than ten lunar revolutions, but not so much as ten days, being only twenty-seven degrees from the eastern horizon. But as the position of the Moon is reversed at the epoch, so must its count be as regards the horizon, and the Moon is found to be ten days' motion from the western horizon.

Birth	*Epoch*
2.—Male, 11th July, 1892, at 7.19 a.m., Middlesbrough	2.—13th October, 1891, at 2.52 p.m.
Asc. ♌ 25° 5′	☽ in ♒ 24° 32′
☽ in ♒ 4° 21′	Asc. ♒ 4° 21′

Here we find the Moon decreasing in light, and at epoch it is found in the sign descending at birth, according to rule; but instead of its place at birth setting at the epoch, we find it rising. The Moon being below the earth, the count should be made from the eastern horizon, instead of which we make it from the western, *viz.*: Aquarius, 25° 5', and find thereby about two days by which the period is to be reduced, since the Moon is below the earth and decreasing in light.

Birth	*Epoch*
3.—Female, 25th July, 1892, at 11.6 a.m., Middlesbrough	3.—30th October, 1891, at 2.25 p.m.
Asc. ♎ 13° 3'	☽ in ♎ 13° 2'
☽ in ♌ 21° 5'	Asc. ♒ 21° 5'

This was a case of *placenta prævia*. The Moon is seen to be increasing at birth, and above the earth. It is found at epoch in the rising sign Libra, but instead of its place at birth *rising* at epoch we make it set, and the count instead of being from the Moon to western horizon, is made in the contrary direction, as was found to be the case in Examples 1 and 2. This count gives us a matter of five days by which the period is to be curtailed, which accordingly is effected. The result is an epoch which differs from the birth by only one minute of space as regards the Moon's place at epoch and the ascendant at birth.

Birth	*Epoch*
4.—Male, 1st September, 1892, at 3.11 a.m., Middlesbrough	4.—6th December, 1891, at 4.14 p.m.
Asc. ♌ 17° 46'	☽ in ♒ 17° 53'
☽ in ♐ 26° 41'	Asc. ♊ 26° 41'

This is a case of *complete reversal* of the terms employed. Although the Moon is increasing and below the earth, the count is made from the Moon to the western horizon; it is then found in the descending sign of the birth, and its place at birth is setting at the epoch.

Birth	*Epoch*
5.—Female, 22nd Nov., 1862, at 11.42 p.m., London	5.—15th February, 1862, at 11.17 a.m.
Asc. ♍ 6° 12'	☽ in ♍ 6° 12'
☽ in ♐ 17° 50'	Asc. ♊ 17° 50'

Here the Moon is found at epoch in the sign which was rising at birth; but instead of its place rising at the epoch, it is found to be setting, and accordingly the count, instead of being from the eastern horizon, is made from the western, giving seven days in excess of the average period.

Birth	*Epoch*
6.—Female, 19th April, 1887, at	6.—13th July, 1886, at 9.52
11.37 p.m., London	a.m.
Asc. ♐ 20° 19′	☽ in ♐ 19° 57′
☽ in ♓ 22° 30′	Asc. ♍ 22° 30′

The generative act in this case is stated to have been effected on 11th July, 1886, at 11 p.m. We have the Moon at the epoch on the 13th, in the sign rising at birth, and the Moon's place at birth setting at the epoch. This irregularity makes the count from the western horizon, instead of the eastern, the Moon being below the earth at birth.

In 1892-93 our friend and collaborateur, E. S., to whom we have elsewhere referred as the discoverer of the septenary aspect (Book i, page 4), endeavoured to fathom the cause of this reversal of the terms in what we have called, for the sake of distinction, irregular epochs. On examining the series of degrees generated from the septenary division of the Zodiac, we found a wonderful harmony to exist in their several integers.

Primarily, we have seven points arising out of this septenary division of the Zodiac. They are—♈ 0°, ♉ 21⁴⁄₇°, ♋ 12⁵⁄₇°, ♍ 4⁴⁄₇°, ♎ 25⁵⁄₇°, ♐ 17⁴⁄₇°, and ♒ 8⁴⁄₇°. To these we add the opposite degrees of the Zodiac, taken from ♎ 0°; and again, dividing the Zodiac at seven points from the solstitial degrees, ♋ 0° and ♑ 0°, we get twenty-eight degrees in all.

It will be observed that the unit in the integer of each degree is the same as the unit of the fractional part multiplied by seven. Also, there are three whole degrees of even number, and three of odd number, with zero, from which they are generated.

Applying this observation to the question of sex distinction, we came to the conclusion that these degrees might be expressed by two trines or triangles, the upright being the male, the inverted the female, and the four sets of degrees generated from the four cardinal points would then stand in illustration as follows:—

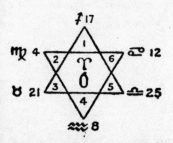

Generated from ♈0°

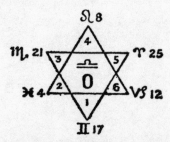

Generated from ♎0°

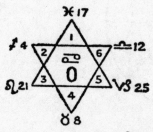

Generated from ♎0°

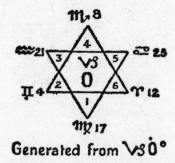

Generated from ♑0°

It will be observed that of the degrees generated from ♈ 0° and ♋ 0°, what are taken to be *female* degrees are attached to each of the reversed triangles, the *male* degrees being associated with the upright triangles; the reverse being the case in those generated from ♎ 0° and ♑ 0°. The fractional parts belonging to each whole degree are placed in the adjacent angles of the figure. Of the four cardinal points, ♈ 0° and ♋ 0° are here held to be *female*, and their opposites, ♎ 0° and ♑ 0°, *male*.

The segmentation of the embryonic cell is after the manner of the primary division suggested above, viz., firstly, vertically; and secondly, horizontally, making a circle and cross, thus—⊕.

The determination of sex in the fœtal life was considered to take place after the following manner:—The triangle of force represented by A B C, indicates the male-female potentiality, in which the line A B=male direction, and A C=female, B C being the plasmic substance on which these lines of force are acting.

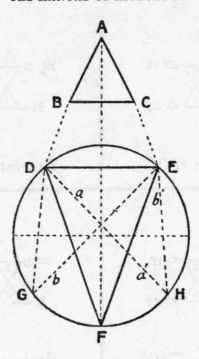

Potentiality is converted into active potency towards the fifth month after conception. The triangle, A B C, is then reflected in D E F, where D F is the male potency, and E F the female. All this takes place within the sphere of potentiality represented by the embryonic cell, and here illustrated by the circle whose quadrants, *a a'*, are *male*, and *b b' female*.

When the male potency, D F, overpowers the female, E F, the direction of the sex is determined to the quadrant *a'*, the line of force being deflected to H in the male quadrant. But when the female potency, E F, overpowers the male, D F, then the result is a female birth at G in the quadrant *b*.

And now we come to the statement of the Law of Sex in relation to the epoch, and in this connection the reader will please observe what has already been said regarding *Irregular Epochs*, because it will be found that the Law of Sex is the controlling factor. Many people have sent us epochs of a difficult nature, for which the general rules do not serve. In as many cases as our leisure would allow, we have returned the communication with a statement of the true epoch, but hitherto no statement of the *cause* of the irregularity has been given. The present publication will doubtless constitute sufficient apology for such denial.

THE LAW OF SEX

The epoch having been determined by the rules already laid down, the ascendant and the Moon's place in the epochal figure of the heavens must be observed. If the epoch be true, it will afford the following arguments:—

(1) The ascendant will be in or near one of the degrees already enumerated, and known as " critical " degrees.

(2) The Moon will be in or near one of such degrees.

(3) Both the ascendant and the Moon will be in such degrees.

(4) Neither the ascendant nor the Moon will be in or near a critical degree.

(5) The Moon will be in a male or female quadrant, of which the S.E. and N.W. are male, and the S.W. and N.E. female.

The agreement of the Law of Sex with the Law of the Pre-natal Epoch is here established. For observe:—

(1) If the ascendant of the epoch be in a male degree the sex of the birth will be male, and *vice versa.*

(2) If the Moon be in a " critical " degree, and the ascendant not in a critical degree at all, then the Moon's position controls the sex, according to whether its degree of longitude is male or female.

(3) When both the ascendant and Moon are in critical degrees of the same sex, the birth will be of that sex.

(4) When neither the Moon nor ascendant is in a " critical " degree, then the quadrant the Moon occupies will determine the sex.

(5) When the ascendant and the Moon are in " critical " degrees of opposite sexes, the quadrant the Moon occupies will determine the sex.

N.B.—The " orb of influence " of a critical degree is not as yet fully determined, but to be at all powerful the position must be close, *i.e.*, within three degrees.

The following diagrammatic table of the critical degrees and the quadrants is given for ready reference.

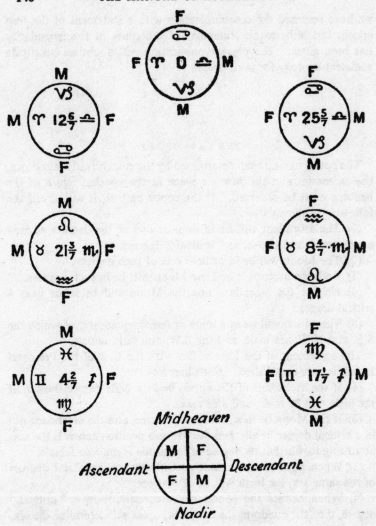

Irregular Epochs, therefore, may often be referred to the controlling influence of sex.

In practice, the safest way to find the epoch is to follow the rules for the regular epoch, and if these do not yield an epoch in agreement with the birth figure, then the count should be made in opposite direction to that stated in Theorem B, and an epoch tried for this measure of time, with the reversal of the factors, as shown in the examples of *Irregular Epochs*.

TO SET A FIGURE WITHOUT TABLES

The following method is employed in the calculation of horoscopical figures in latitudes for which no *Tables of Houses* exist.

To find the Ascending Degree

The right ascension of the mid-heaven, taken in hours, minutes, and seconds, is converted into degrees, minutes, and seconds of space at the rate of fifteen degrees for every hour, or one degree for every four minutes of time.   Then proceed:

(1) Add 90° to the mid-heaven.   This will give the oblique ascension of the ascendant.

(2) Find the distance in degrees, minutes, and seconds between the oblique ascension of the ascendant and the *nearest* equinoctial point.

(3) the *cosine*[1] of this distance plus the *cotangent* of the latitude of birth will give the *cotangent* of the FIRST ARC.

(4) If measured from Aries *add* 23° 28'; if measured from Libra *subtract* 23° 28'.   This will give the SECOND ARC.

(5) Add together the *tangent* of the distance of ascendant from equinoctial point (rule 2), and the *cosine* of the first arc. Subtract therefrom the *cosine* of the second arc.

(6) This will give the *tangent* of the longitude of the ascendant from the equinoctial point taken.   *Then, with this ascendant and the Moon's longitude, proceed*

To find the Epoch

I. When the Moon's place at birth is rising at the epoch.

(*a*) The *tangent* of latitude of epoch (*i.e.*, of the place where the mother of the native was residing at the time) plus the *tangent* of the declination of the Moon's longitude, equals the *sine* of the ascensional difference of the Moon's place.

(*b*) If the Moon's place falls between Aries 0° and Virgo 30°, the right ascension of the Moon's longitude minus this ascensional difference is equal to its oblique ascension.

---

[1] Consult Chambers's Mathematical Tables.

(c) This oblique ascension minus 90° is equal to the right ascension of the meridian.

(d) This meridian taken from, or added to, the sidereal time at noon on the day of epoch, will give the time, before or after noon, at which the epoch occurred.

Note.—If the Moon's place at birth falls between Libra 0° and Pisces 30°, then rule *b* is reversed, and its ascensional difference is *added* to its right ascension to get its oblique ascension. In other respects the procedure is the same as given above.

II.   When the Moon's place at birth is setting at the epoch.

Rule.—Take the opposite point of the Zodiac to that in which the Moon is placed at birth, consider the Moon there, and proceed exactly as shown above.

CHAPTER II

DIRECTIONS

THE period at which the different events promised by the horoscope of birth are brought into effect is determined by the process called Directing, wherein a day after birth, or a degree of the Zodiac, or again, a degree of the Equator equals one year of life. The system most in repute is that which regards the motions of the planets in the Zodiac, and the rising and culminating of the planets after birth.

In this system, the

PRIMARY DIRECTIONS

are of two kinds—Zodiacal and Mundane.

Zodiacal Directions are those formed in the Zodiac by the motion of the mid-heavens, ascendant, Sun, and Moon to the aspects of the planets. These directions may be divided into three classes, *viz.:* Direct Directions, Converse Directions, and Zodiacal Parallels. When the direction is made in the order of the signs, it is called a *Direct Direction;* when made against the order of signs, it is called a *Converse Direction.*

The Sun, Moon, mid-heaven, and ascendant are called " Significators." The planets to which they are directed are called " Promittors." But each of these significators becomes a promittor when any of the other significators are directed to it.   (See p. 161.)

The distance between any significator and the place where it forms its conjunction, parallel, or aspect with a promittor, is called the *Arc of Direction*, and is measured in degrees and minutes of the Equator, which degrees and minutes are turned into years and months at the rate of one degree for every year of life, and five minutes for every month.

The promittor, in each case, is supposed to stand still in the place it held at birth, while the significator is brought to its position or aspect.

Thus, in the specimen horoscope given on page 51 the longitude of the mid-heaven is Scorpio 1°, the right ascension of which is found to be 208° 33′, while Neptune in Virgo 23° 27′, has right ascension of 174° 5′.

$$
\begin{aligned}
\text{A.R., M.C.} &= 208° \ 33′ \\
\text{A.R., } \Psi &= 174° \ \ 5′ \\
\hline
\text{M.C., } \Psi &= \ \ 34° \ 28′ \text{ in zod. converse}
\end{aligned}
$$

This arc of direction, turned into time, equals 34 years, 5 months and 18 days, at which age the indication would be of an overseas and long distance journey by sea or air.

Again, in the same horoscope the mid-heaven is directed to the trine of Mercury by Direct Direction.

$$
\begin{aligned}
\text{A.R., } \ \ \ \ \mercury &= 353° \ 10′ \\
\text{A.R., M.C.} &= 208° \ 33′ \\
\hline
 &\ \ 144° \ 37′ \\
\text{Deduct } 120° \ \ &\ \ 120° \ \ \ 0′ \\
\hline
\text{M.C., } \ \mercury &= \ \ 24° \ 37′ \text{ in zod. direct}
\end{aligned}
$$

This arc of direction, turned into time, equals 24 years, 7 months and 12 days at which time some form of promotion in connection with vocational interests, together with the passing of examinations or tests of proficiency successfully would be signified.

The right ascension of a planet is its distance from Aries 0° measured on the Equator; and the latitude, or distance N. or S. of the ecliptic, that a planet has, is taken into account.

Rule.—To find the right ascension of a planet, take its longitudinal distance from the nearest cardinal point, Aries, Cancer, Libra, or Capricorn; take also the planet's latitude and declination at birth from the Ephemeris, and then say: *As* the cosine of the planet's declination *is to* the cosine of its longitudinal distance, *so is* the cosine of its latitude *to* the cosine of its right ascension.

When taken without latitude it is merely required to add the cosine of the planet's longitudinal distance to the arithmetical complement of the cosine of its declination in order to find the right ascension.

Note.—The arithmetical complement of a logarithm is what it lacks of 10·00000.

Direct and converse zodiacal directions are thus very easily calculated.

The *Zodiacal Parallel* has regard to the declination any planet may hold at the moment of a birth.

To direct the Sun to a zodiacal parallel, find the declination of the planet to which the Sun is directed. Next look in the Ephemeris for the day after birth on which the Sun attains that declination. Find the right ascension of the longitude of the Sun at the time, and subtract from it the Sun's right ascension at birth. The difference is the arc of direction.

The count may be made backwards (conversely) to any day before birth on which the Sun has the same parallel of declination as any planet at birth, and the space it has moved in the Zodiac from that time to the time of birth, measured by right ascension, is the arc of direction for the zodiacal parallel by converse motion.

The mid-heaven is moved or directed in the same way to the aspects and parallels of the planets, the Sun and Moon.

The ascendant is directed by oblique ascension under the latitude of the birthplace. An inspection of the Tables of Houses at the end of this work will show that the passage of the Zodiac over the meridian, or tenth house cusp, is uniform, while that over the ascendant, or cusp of the first house, is irregular. This oblique ascension of the Zodiac is due to the fact that the ecliptic and the circle of observation do not lie in the same plane.

Therefore, to direct the ascendant to a conjunction or aspect of a promittor, it is necessary to bring the longitude of that body or aspect to the horizon. This may be computed roughly from the Tables of Houses for the latitude of birth, but more accurately by trigonometry.

1. To the tangent of the latitude of the birthplace add the tangent of the declination of the required degree of the Zodiac, to find the sine of its ascensional difference. Add this ascensional difference to the right ascension of the said degree if the declination be south,

or subtract it if north. The result is the oblique ascension of the aspect or body to which direction is made.

2. Add 90° to the mid-heaven to find the oblique ascension of the ascendant.

3. The difference between the oblique ascension of the ascendant and that of the point directed to, will be the arc of direction.

Mundane Directions have no relation to the Zodiac whatever, but are based solely upon the axial rotation of the earth in relation to the circle of observation, by means of which the planets are carried from east to west through the several houses, forming thereby certain angular distances or aspects with the meridian, the horizon, and the radical positions of the Sun and Moon. Thus, if the Sun were on the cusp of the third house, it would be in mundane sextile to the ascendant, *i.e.*, the space of two houses; and if a planet were in the fourth house at birth, it would, after passing the lower meridian, rise to the cusp of the third house, when it would be in mundane sextile to the ascendant, and in mundane conjunction with the Sun.

Mundane directions, like zodiacal, are of three classes: the direct, the converse, and the mundane parallel.

When the meridian is moved in the order of the signs in order to form an aspect between a significator and promittor, the direction is called *direct*. When contrary to the order of the signs, the direction is called *converse*.

A mundane parallel is formed when a significator and a promittor come to an equal distance on opposite sides of any of the four angles; or, in other words, when the middle distance between the two bodies comes to either the mid-heaven, ascendant, descendant, or lower meridian.

CHAPTER III

SEPHARIAL'S METHOD OF DIRECTING

PRIMARY DIRECTIONS

THE Sun, by its diurnal motion in the Zodiac after birth, forms aspects and conjunctions with the positions of the celestial bodies in the horoscope of births, and also with the ascendant and mid-heaven.

It also forms such with the planets' places in the Zodiac after birth; and lastly, the planets in their motions after birth form aspects to the Sun, Moon, ascendant, and mid-heaven in the horoscope of birth.

These aspects and conjunctions are called *Primary Directions*.

SECONDARY DIRECTIONS

are those formed by the Moon in its motion through the Zodiac after birth, either to the radical positions of the planets, *i.e.*, their positions at birth, or to their progressive places, *i.e.*, the places they have attained at any given age, at the rate of one day after birth for each year of life.

Thus, the following table shows all the directions which can be formed, both primary and secondary, between the significators and promittors.

Primary

1. The Sun Radix and Planets Progressive.
2. The Moon Radix and Planets Progressive.
3. Ascendant Radix and Planets Progressive.
4. Mid-heaven Radix and Planets Progressive.
5. The Sun Progressive and Planets Radix.
6. The Sun Progressive and Planets Progressive.

Secondary

1. The Moon Progressive and Planets Radix.
2. The Moon Progressive and Planets Progressive.
3. The Moon Progressive and Ascendant Radix.
4. The Moon Progressive and Mid-heaven Radix.

The constitution and first principles of all mundane events are drawn from the Sun, and receive their special form through the vegetative power of the Moon. So Ptolemy writes:—" The Sun is the source of the vital power, the Moon of the natural power "; which is true in regard to events in the phenomenal world quite as much as in regard to the generation of natural bodies.

TIME-MEASURE

Years are measured by primary directions, accounting one day after birth as a year of life.

Months are measured by the secondary directions, accounting two hours, or one-twelfth of a day, as one month.

Primary directions are slow in their formation, extending sometimes over many days, which will measure so many years of the lifetime. Hence it is only necessary to note on what day after birth the aspects are complete. But the more a direction comes towards completion, the more powerful will be its action in the life of the native. The causative influences thus held in latency by the primary directions are brought into effect at such times as the secondary directions agree with them in nature.

TRANSITS

Transits produce effects when in aspect with important significators, and they should be neither ignored nor over-estimated. To form a just idea of their influence, the student should examine a few critical moments in the lives of persons known privately, or of celebrities, and should also read the published views of astrologers on such moments; *e.g.*, death, accident, promotion or succession to honour, termination of any matter whose beginning was accurately noted.

METHOD OF DIRECTING

The method of directing is extremely simple, and requires no more than a knowledge of the astrological aspects, and the use of simple proportion and addition.

Prepare a sheet with a column of figures from 1 to 70, or more, representing a scale of the years of life, or days after birth. Take the solar directions first.

1. Note the Sun's radical place. Run the eye down the columns marked Neptune, Uranus, Saturn, Jupiter, Mars, Venus, and Mercury in the Ephemeris, one at a time, and note the number of days *after birth* that each of these planets forms a *complete aspect* with the Sun's radical place. Set down the aspect in the " scale of years " opposite the day after birth on which it occurs.

2. The planets' aspects to the Moon's radical place are taken out next, and set down in the same manner. The Sun's aspects to the Moon's place at birth must be included under this head.

3. The aspects of the nine heavenly bodies to the ascendant and mid-heaven and the Part of Fortune, are taken next in their order, and set down in the scale of years.

4. Next, note the days after birth when the Sun in its progressive motion comes to an aspect with any of the planets in the horoscope of birth, and with the ascendant and mid-heaven. Set them down in their proper place in the scale of years.

5. Lastly, set down the aspects formed between the Sun in its

progress after birth, with the planets Neptune, Uranus, Saturn, Jupiter, Mars, Venus, and Mercury in their progressive motions.

N.B.—These are generally noted in the Ephemeris, but the student is warned that frequent omissions and printers' errors occur. It is therefore advisable to go through the process independently and with care.

The scale of primary directions will now be complete. It should be observed that when the progressive places of the planets are employed in the aspects noted, the letter P should be set against the symbol of the planet. The radical places, *i.e.*, those of the planets at birth, are denoted by the letter R against their respective symbols.

It should further be noted what *sign* the aspecting planet is in, and also the house, and if the planet be retrograde, that also should be marked ℞.

Example:—Suppose the Sun's radical place is attained by Venus thirty-three days after birth, the Sun being in Aquarius on the cusp of the eighth house. Against 33 in the scale of years we set down: ☉ R ☌ ♀ P ♒ 8.

The primary directions afford a general survey of the periods of good and evil throughout the life. A series of good aspects indicate a period of good fortune extending over the years embraced by them, and *vice versa* when evil aspects occur. When the influences are mixed, some good and some evil, the affairs of the native will be unsettled. The aspects falling out in any year of life are strongest at that age, but owing to the slow formation and distribution of the primary directions, the influence of any direction will be felt from two to three years in advance of its *exact* formation, and for an equal period afterwards, always coming into notable effect when the current lunar or secondary directions agree with it in nature.

It is now necessary to fill in the features of this general outline of the life, by calculating the secondary directions. These can be calculated for a single year or as many years in advance as the student may choose. One year will serve as an example for all others. Proceed then as follows:—

1. Subtract the year, month, and day of birth from the beginning of the year for which the secondary directions are required. Set the results down in years, months, and days.

2. Call the years *days;* multiply the months by two, and call them *hours;* the days by four, and call them *minutes.*

3. To this result add the hour and minute of birth. The result will be the *time of direction* for that year, and all others, on the 1st January.

4. Find the Moon's longitude on the day, hour, and minute thus obtained. This will be the Moon's progressive place for the beginning of the year required.

5. Find the Moon's motion in twenty-four hours; divide this by twelve. This will give the Moon's motion for each succeeding month of the year.

6. Add this monthly motion to the longitude of Moon for the 1st January, and this will give its longitude for the 1st of each succeeding month.

7. Now turn to the day after birth corresponding to the year of the direction, and note what aspects the Moon forms to the planets on that day. Set the aspects down opposite the month in which they are completed.

8. Then refer to the nativity, and note the aspects the progressive Moon forms to the radical places of the planets, ascendant, and mid-heaven therein. Set these down opposite the month in which they are completed.

Put R against the radical planets, and P against the progressive. Note also the sign and house in which the planets are situated in the radix or progress.

Example:—In the specimen horoscope (Book i), male, born 10th April, 1940, at 1 a.m. G.M.T. (2 a.m. B.S.T.). Required, the secondary directions for 1972.

	Year		Month		Day		
(1)	1972	..	1	..	0	=	1st January, 1972
	1940	..	4	..	10	=	10th April, 1940
	31		8		20	=	Age on 1st January, 1972
(2)		31 days			8	20	
		Multiply by			2	4	
					16 hrs.	80 mins.	
				Add 1		0 a.m.	
					18	20	
(3)			Subtract 12			0 to convert to secular time	
			Time of direction	6		20 p.m.	

(4) The Moon's longitude at 6.20 p.m. on the 31st day after birth, *viz.*, 11th May, 1940, = ♋ 11° 27′ = Moon's progressive longitude 1st January, 1972.

(5) The Moon's motion in the 12 hours from Noon to Midnight on 11th May, 1940, is 6° 39′, which divided by 6 gives 1° 6.5′ as the Moon's monthly progress for the first six months of the year.

(6) The Moon's motion in the 12 hours from Midnight on 11th May, 1940, to Noon on 12th May, 1940, is 6° 43′, which divided by 6 gives 1° 7′ as the Moon's monthly progression for the second six months of the year, plus 1′ extra, *i.e.*, 1° 8′ for the last month of the year.

(7, 8, 9) The Moon's monthly motion is added successively to ♋ 11° 27′, the Moon's longitude, 1st January, 1972, and the Moon's aspects to the radical and progressive planets' places are set out in order of formation. Thus—

1972				
January	11° ♋	27′		
February	12°	33′		
March	13°	40′	✳ ☽ *R*	Fourth House
April	14°	46′		
May	15°	53′		
June	16°	59′		
July	18°	6′	□ ♌ *P*	Ninth House
August	19°	13′	⅄♉ ⊕ *R*	First House
			□ ☉ *R*	Third House
September	20°	20′	□ ♌ *R*	Ninth House
			∠ ♀ *R*	Sixth House
			∠ ♂ *R*	Sixth House
			✳ ♅ *R*	Fifth House
October	21°	27′	□ ♃ *R*	Third House
			✳ ♅ *P*	Fifth House
			✳ ☉ *P*	Fifth House
November	22°	34′	△ ☿ *R*	Third House
			✳ ♆ *R & P*	Ninth House
December	23°	42′		

As will be seen by the above table there are no lunar aspects formed during the months of January, February, April, May, June and December. When this occurs the lunar aspects in force during the previous month, if any, will overlap as it were into the following month.

It will usually be found however that even when no lunar aspects are in force, some part of the month will be affected by one or more transits (described in Chap. iv, under the heading of Transits) or by the New Moon (Lunation) of the month.

PRIMARY CONSIDERATIONS

The effects of directions are to be judged according to the interplay of the primary and secondary forces. The following rules will serve to guide the judgment in this matter:—

I. If the primary and secondary directions agree in nature, both being either good or evil, the secondary directions will produce marked results of the nature denoted by the planet to which the Moon is directed, considered with the sign, and *particularly* the house in which it is placed.

II. When the primary and secondary disagree in nature, the effects denoted by the secondary will not be lasting, and the affairs of the native generally will be unsettled at that period.

N.B.—The *nature* of the direction is judged by the *aspect*, not by the planet. A square is *bad*, whether from Jupiter or Saturn, from Uranus or Venus; and a trine or sextile is always good, whatever may be the planet throwing the aspect.

III. When the primary directions are of a mixed nature, partly good and partly bad, then both the good and evil secondary directions will have force at that time.

IV. When a period of two or more years elapses between the formation of primary directions of an *opposite* nature, a *critical* epoch is formed midway between the two directions. Until that point is reached, the secondary directions act in abeyance to the primary last formed, and during the *critical* year they are free to act either for good or evil as they are formed.

V. When a period of two or more years intervenes between primary directions of the *same* nature, then the *whole interval* will be good or bad, according to the nature of the aspects. In such case the secondary directions will act in accord therewith.

These considerations will serve to indicate why, at certain times, good secondary directions fail to compass those benefits and emoluments which might be anticipated from them, and again, why certain evil directions fortunately pass without leaving their scars upon the native.

CHAPTER IV

EFFECTS OF DIRECTIONS

Primary directions have a general signification extending over the period of their operation. Although their influence is brought to a climax whenever the secondary directions agree with them in nature, yet they will be found to exercise a continuous influence for good or evil as long as they are in operation; when evil, suppressing the good effects of secondaries and increasing the evil ones, and when good, suppressing the evil and augmenting the good.

Secondary directions have a particular significance in regard to the exact time and nature of events. They operate in harmony with the primaries, as already stated. They always produce results when complete, but in a variable degree of good or evil, according to the primaries which control them.

The house and sign in which a planet is situated when directed to the Sun, Moon, ascendant, or mid-heaven, are the chief keys to interpretation of effects of directions.

When a planet is within five degrees of the cusp of a house, it generally operates as if it were *in* that house, owing to its orb of influence.

Mercury's nature is interchangeable, and always acts in the same manner as the planet to which it is in nearest aspect, either in the progress or the radix, as the case may be, or if not in aspect to any planet, the sign it is in must be taken.

Primary directions are judged in a general way, according to the aspects and the planets forming them.

Secondary directions are judged more exactly by the house and sign occupied by the planet to which the Moon is directed and the nature of the aspect formed.

The following general observations will prove of service:—

1. Never lose sight of the radix and its potentialities. It is the root in earth from which the tree of life grows.

2. Have regard to the environment of the native. What would be true prediction in regard to a person born in fortunate circumstances, would not hold good to the same extent in the case of one born under the very lash of tyranny and oppression. These are disparities which must be referred to ante-natal causes reaching back one cannot say how far.

3. If the radix does not promise fortune, no directions will permanently secure it to the native.

4. If the constitution be a good one, do not conclude the first attacks made upon it will be fatal.

5. Consider first the promise of the radix, next that of the primaries in operation, and judge of the secondary directions in accord with these.

6. Do not founder on the rock of fatalism. Remember that Astrology supports the idea of continual causation, and whereas the future is only the past unfolded, new causes are continually being evolved, and these will have their effects in all future years, and for all time.

The Sun, Moon, ascendant, meridian, and Pars Fortuna are called " Significators." The planets Pluto, Neptune, Uranus, Saturn, Jupiter, Mars, Venus, and Mercury (together with the Sun and Moon when these are directed to the ascendant, mid-heaven, or Pars Fortuna) are called " Promittors." They have a general signification according to their several natures, and a particular signification according to the house and sign they are in, and those houses over which they rule in the nativity.

The SUN has signification of the life, constitution, and honour of the native; also the trade, profession, and credit of the native, and the male relatives.

The MOON governs the health, general changes in life, and the female relatives.

The ASCENDANT has relation to the body and person of the native; the health, life, and fortunes in a general sense.

The MID-HEAVEN has relation to honour, credit, business, and worldly standing. It is associated with the Sun in this respect, just as the Moon is with the Ascendant in others.

The PART OF FORTUNE has relation to the possessions of the native, his money and effects. In general practice it is not directed, but the progressive aspects of the planets to its position in the radical figure are taken as primary directions. We would, however, advise the student to calculate its position for each month, taking the radical Ascendant, the progressive Moon, and progressive Sun as the factors for the calculation, the method being similar to that for the calculation of its place in the radix. The reason for suggesting this method of directing the Part of Fortune is, that as the radical position has a signification in regard to the general possessions of the native, so the progress of the Sun and Moon in relation to the ascendant of the horoscope must throw the Part of Fortune continually and successively from one point of the Zodiac to another, and its aspects and conjunctions with the progressive and radical planets must have a temporary signification of the same general nature. We have repeatedly found this to be the case, and recommend independent research.

SECONDARY DIRECTIONS

☽ ☌ Asc. or M.C. produces *changes*, attended with honour or ill fame as the *primary* influences may indicate. If in a *watery sign* it brings voyages. The period is restless and unsettled. The ☽ ☌ M.C. causes benefits and honours from women, or the reverse. Its conjunction with the ascendant often causes illness of a cold or watery nature affecting the head and the part ruled by the sign ascending.

☽ ⚹ △ Asc. or M.C., benefits from women; advantageous changes; popularity and preferments; success with public bodies, and general prosperity.

☽ □ ∠ ⚿ or ☍ Asc. or M.C. brings losses through women and public functionaries; loss of fame, troubles, annoyances, and a restless anxious time. It is an ill time to travel or make changes in home or business affairs.

☽ ⚹ △ ♅ produces benefits of a sudden and unexpected nature from such persons and things as are shown by the house Uranus is in. It makes the mind curious and enquiring, yet fanciful and eccentric. The disposition bears strongly towards romance and adventure. The magnetic power is increased, and a man is inclined to company and the friendship of women. It produces *changes* and unexpected events generally.

☽ ☌ ∠ □ etc. ♅ denotes a critical time, when all the affairs go wrong unexpectedly. Accidents are frequent. The native is likely to suffer from public bodies and powerful enemies. He is criticised or slandered. It makes the mind hypercritical, bitter, sarcastic, and stubborn. It brings disgrace, loss of office, and changes of an unpleasant nature. Travelling is dangerous. The society of the opposite sex should be avoided. The mind is troubled and anxious, and destructively or aggressively inclined. Its effects are sudden and extraordinary.

☽ ⚹ △ ♄ indicates success in business, especially through aged persons and saturnine things. A steady, prosperous time. The mind is industrious, patient, contemplative, and soberly inclined. If the body is feverish, the health will improve under this direction. If Saturn is in good aspect to Jupiter at birth, it frequently brings legacies under these directions.

☽ ☌ ∠ □ etc. ♄ produces serious evils in the life. Dishonour, failure in business, losses, grief, disappointment, and bereavement are among the effects of the evil direction of Saturn. The mind is melancholy and morbid; the health suffers from cold, want of tone, lingering diseases, and aches and pains, according to the sign Saturn is in. The disposition is cramped and constrained; the native is suspecting, nervous, and misanthropic. It is an ill time to begin any new concern, and much care is needed in all the affairs of life.

☽ ☌ ✳ △ ♃. These are very good directions, and produce gain, prosperity, fame, and success in all affairs. The mind is jovial, frank, generous, and free from all care. The body is healthy and in good tone. Jupiter acts chiefly on the arterial blood, which at this time is replenished and in a healthy condition. In business, affairs go very successfully, and profits accumulate. Many advantages accrue from these directions, and honourable attachments and friendships are made.

☽ ∠ □ etc. ♃. This is a bad time for business affairs. Losses occur. There is trouble through the law or church. Speculations should be avoided, and thrift should be exercised. The disposition is free, extravagant, and profligate, and friends or associates impose upon the goodwill of the native at this time. The blood is gross or corrupted, and the body afflicted with congestion, etc., in parts governed by the sign Jupiter is in. The period generally brings many expenses and few receipts, and leaves the native in an impecunious condition.

☽ ✳ △ ♂ denotes a brisk, busy, and active time. Some new enterprise is generally begun. The affairs succeed through the industry of the native. Journeys and business activities are frequent. The mind is courageous, demonstrative, dauntless, and free, and the native is disposed to exercise and sports. Gain is shown by military men, doctors, surgeons, etc., as denoted by Mars. With females this direction inclines to marriage or courtship, but it is usually of an impulsive nature.

☽ ☌ ∠ □ etc. ♂. Danger of accidents and loss of blood. Fevers are produced. The native suffers discredit, slander, and dishonour. He acts impulsively, and so falls into dangers. He is extravagant and reckless, and his judgment is hasty, so that he loses money. In *fiery* signs there is danger of high fever, loss or hurt by fire; in *airy* signs, fevers, accidents by gunshot, hurts by human hands; in *watery* signs, scalds, danger of drowning, evils from drink and excess; in *earthy* signs, falls, hurts from animals, bites, etc. The native rarely escapes without loss of blood, if the primaries are evil, and especially if Mars be angular. With women it produces slander and discredit, and inclines to impulsive actions. The opposite sex ought to be avoided at this time, or entertained with due discretion.

☽ ☌ ☉. This is productive of *changes;* it brings honours to men, and some success in public affairs and business, but it frequently afflicts the health in a manner somewhat after the nature of Mars, to which planet the Sun closely corresponds. Generally, very important changes in the affairs of life result from this direction: it often produces marriage with both sexes.

With women, the direction is not so good, and induces many anxieties upon the mind, affects the health, and produces feverish symptoms as the result of cold or chills. If the primary influences are bad, it may cause death. In all cases a *change* in life.

☽ ⚹ △ ☉. This is a good direction for both sexes, producing honours, success, credit, and renown. The favour of dignified persons is conferred upon the native; new friends are made; success with superiors and parents is experienced; the health is good; the mind dignified, lofty, and ambitious of honour and esteem, which generally is attained to a large degree. These influences tend strongly to a successful and happy marriage in both sexes.

☽ ∠ □ etc. ☉. Brings ill health, loss of fame, dignity, and honour; troubles through the parents, and bereavement in many cases. It is an ill time for all affairs. The mind is prone to be overbearing and haughty, and troubles through superiors arise; loss of employment or office is to be feared; troubles from the opposite sex, and, in some cases, bereavement. It is a bad time for all concerns. The native loses friends and supporters.

☽ ☌ ⚹ △ ♀. This produces a happy, prosperous, and peaceful time, with events of a domestic nature which are pleasurable or advantageous. It is a frequent testimony of courtship or marriage. The health is good; the mind temperate, but given to the pleasures of company; the disposition is peaceful, happy, and joyous.

☽ ∠ □ etc. ♀. This brings disappointments, grief, losses, and bereavement; domestic affairs go badly. The relations of the native with the opposite sex are not productive of happiness at this time. It creates intemperate tendencies and irregular habits. The native is inclined to excesses of the nature denoted by the sign Venus is in at the time of direction; troubles through females, servants, and relatives are experienced.

☽ ☌ ✶ △ ☿. If Mercury at birth is dignified and well aspected, it brings results attaching to the nature of the planet to which it is in closest relationship. [This must be a matter of judgment with the student.] This rule applies chiefly to the conjunction, as the sextile and trine are both good in their effects by whatever planet the aspect is thrown.

The general nature of Mercury is to produce changes, journeys, new business affairs; scholastic honours and success through writings, etc., when in good aspect. It renders the mind industrious, active and restless; but much attention must be paid to the nature of the sign and house Mercury is in at the *time of direction*.

☽ ☌ ∠ ☐ etc. ☿. If Mercury is not well placed at birth, it will produce evil effects by its conjunction. The mind is restless and anxious, and a multitude of small worries attend the native's affairs. The body is afflicted according to the nature of the sign Mercury is in at the time. Nervous disorders and brain affections are frequent under these directions. It is a bad time to sign any agreements or to frame contracts; and in business, generally, little success attends the efforts of the native; he is criticised, slandered, and meets with disgrace.

☽ ☌ ☐ ☍ etc. ♆. Produces serious complications in the affairs of the native. Ambushes and deceptions are experienced. The native is the subject of plots and schemes designed to bring him into discredit. Secret enemies become active and dangerous. The mind is troubled and harassed with fears; the health suffers from wasting disease, or a depletion of the vital forces; lassitude and indifference follow as a consequence. The native may give way to unhealthy desires. The influence of Neptune is seductive, and the moral nature suffers under its evil aspects.

☽ ✶ △ ♆. Gain and credit accrue to the native from works of an artistic or inspirational nature. He has success with the opposite sex and in society. He gains by schemes and combinations, overthrows his enemies, and discovers evils existing around him. The mind is changeful and disposed to pleasures.

☽ ✶ △ ♇. Will give an excellent opportunity for the reviving or furthering of what has appeared to be a lost cause, a fading romance, a receding business or financial opportunity. Personal initiative will find new ways of bringing interests to fruition and completion in all important avenues of life. The mental inspiration will be enhanced, new ideas will be born, activities will move ahead on a wave of progress and many benefits will be derived.

G

☽ ☌ ☐ ☍ etc. ♇. Brings disappointments and setbacks. The objective that has been aimed at and worked for, probably for many months, will seem to recede just when it is anticipated that it will be achieved. Friends, helpers and supporters will seem to be taken out of the life as a result of their circumstances changing and in some instances will never really come back into it again. Difficulties of a business and financial nature will be experienced and there will be a disturbing of matters to do with the affections, with the marital or partnership sides of life if the latter apply.

Note.—These rules are necessarily only of a general nature. To enumerate the various results attaching to the directions of each planet when posited in the different signs and houses, would require a volume in itself; and even then certain considerations necessary to be made would have to be left out. But for general guidance the student should take the following points into consideration:—

1. The nature of the aspect, whether good or evil.
2. The strength of the aspect.
3. The radical power of the planet to which the Moon is directed.
4. The sign that planet is in at the time of direction.
5. The house it is in at the time.
6. The general nature of the planet.

CHAPTER V

OTHER TIME MEASURES—LUNATIONS

The New Moons falling on important places in the horoscope, or progress, such as the mid-heaven, ascendant, Sun, Moon, or the planets' places, have much signification of events happening within the month following upon the conjunction of the luminaries.

When no secondary influences are in operation, the New Moons will be found to have an equal influence in the production of events by development of the primary directions.

A table of the places of New Moons will be found in the Appendix to this volume. By means of it, the past and future lunations can be examined in the light of the following general rules.

1. A New Moon falling out coincident with a secondary direction,

and of the same general nature, will bring that direction into activity within fourteen days, and most frequently at the full of the Moon.

2. A New Moon falling out coincident with a secondary direction, and of opposite nature, will delay the effects of that direction, and will even nullify it, if the direction be weak, or contrary to the primaries in force at the time.

3. A succession (two or three) of New Moons falling on important places in the nativity or progress, will constitute an epoch of great good or evil, according to the natures of the planets which the lunations excite to action.

4. A New Moon falling on a malefic will produce evil results; and the reverse of this when falling on the place of good planets, or those which favour the horoscope by position at the nativity, or by aspect in direction.

5. New Moons produce good when in good aspect to the planets in the radix or progress. The events will be of the nature indicated by the position of the planets in aspect to the New Moon. Contrary results will be manifest when the New Moon falls in evil aspect to any of the planets. Eclipses particularly should be noticed.

Examples:—In the specimen horoscope (Book i) ♄ is in ♉ 2°. The New Moon of 23rd October, 1957, was a solar eclipse and fell in 0° of ♏ (see Table of Lunations in Appendix, under October 1957). This is within 2° of the opposition of Saturn which is in ♉ 2° in the fourth house of the map and the signification of this opposition would be the danger of a severe illness affecting the bladder (ruled by ♏) with a reaction upon the throat (ruled by ♉).

The New Moon of 9th May, 1948, which was also a solar eclipse, fell in 18° ♉, within 2° of Uranus which is in 20° ♉, near the cusp of the fifth house and this would indicate that interests of an educational and an artistic nature would become very prominent and would increase both the capacity and the expressing of ability in these directions.

The Full Moon of 24th May, 1956, which was an eclipse of the Moon fell in 3° ♐, within 2° of the opposition to Venus and Mars which were both in 5° of ♊, near to the cusp of the sixth house. The eclipse fell in the twelfth house of the map and the dual indication from the twelfth to the sixth houses would signify a period in hospital as a result of shock and a feverish condition resulting from an accident, the twelfth house showing hospital treatment and the position of Venus and Mars in ♊, showing the accident.

These examples will help to serve as illustrations of the working powers of lunations (New Moon's) and of Full Moon's, particularly when a solar or lunar eclipse occurs, as an eclipse accentuates the power of the New or Full Moon. The power will naturally be enhanced should there be no monthly lunar aspect in force during that particular month.

The *Table of Lunations* in the Appendix gives the approximate longitudes of the New Moons in each month. It should be remembered that the first of each month corresponds approximately to the 11th degree of the sign beneath it in the same column. Thus 1st January corresponds to ♑ 11°, and any lunation falling in degrees before the 11th of Capricorn would take place in December of the preceding year, and within the last ten days thereof. Its influence, however, would be felt at the full of the Moon, more particularly in the month of January following.

TRANSITS

The transits of planets over the places of the Sun, Moon, ascendant, and mid-heaven of the radix, or the progressive mid-heaven, ascendant, Sun and Moon, have marked influence in the affairs of life. The benefic planets produce good, and the malefics evil. A transit is the ephemeral passage of a planet over the place of a significator in the horoscope, or the place to which it has progressed by direction after birth. The *aspects* of the planets have not the same influence. The transits must be taken out of the ephemeris for the current year.

Raphael has published a book entitled *The Geocentric Longitudes of the Planets* 1900 *to* 2001, which gives the longitudes of the superior planets Neptune, Uranus, Saturn, Jupiter and Mars for the 1st of each month, together with their Declinations for this period.

Observe that the transits are subsidiary to the lunations and secondary directions, and act freely only when these latter are in agreement or not in force at the time of a transit.

ECLIPSES

The eclipses, whether of the Sun or Moon, should be noticed in conjunction with the current directions. They are very significant, and will produce striking events when in agreement with the directions, or when no directions are in force at the time. Their full effect, or climax, is often delayed for some time, though they have their current effects, like New Moons, during the month following their formation.

In order to obtain the date of their climax, observe the following rule:—The distance from the eastern horizon of the luminary which last rose before an ecliptic conjunction or opposition, will give the number of months and days, from the day of the eclipse to its climax, at the rate of 30° for each month.

1. Take the time of the last rising of the luminary which is above the earth at the eclipse, and subtract it from the hour and minute of the eclipse. Result = ×.

2. Then say—As 24 hours is to 12 months, so is × to the answer.

3. Add this result to the date of the eclipse, to obtain the date of the climax.

Note that events pre-signified by the eclipse in its bearing on the horoscope of birth, will transpire at the time of the climax.

A *Table of Eclipses* with their approximate dates will be found in the Appendix. By reference to any solar calendar, the longitude of the eclipse can be found by the Sun's longitude on the given date. The lunar eclipses, of course, fall in the opposite points of the Zodiac.

It is generally believed that eclipses are uniformly evil. Nothing can be more erroneous. What is one man's loss is another's gain, and an eclipse that falls in good aspect to the benefic planets in a horoscope, will produce good to the native. Only when falling on the mid-heaven, ascendant, or the places of the Sun, Moon, and the malefic planets in the horoscope, will the eclipses produce evil.

PROPORTIONAL ARCS

Proportional arcs are of the nature of *longitudinal parallels* in the Zodiac. They first came under the observation of the author in 1895. A proportional arc is measured from the ascendant, mid-heaven, Sun and Moon (in the horoscope of birth) in relation to any of the celestial bodies. Thus, a planet that is fourteen degrees away from the Sun throws its proportional arc to the same distance on the other side of the Sun. It is as if the Sun became the centre of a circle whose circumference is traced by a planet moving round the Sun.

So if the Sun were in ♈ 5°, and Venus in ♈ 19°, the balance of influence would be thrown to ♓ 21°, and in that point of the Zodiac the influence of Venus would be felt, whenever a New Moon fell thereon, or when the Moon by direction came thereto. Also a transit over that point would act upon the Venus affairs of the native as if the planet were actually there.

As there are nine planets (including as such the Sun and Moon), the ascendant and mid-heaven, taken as centres of action, will produce eighteen such points of influence by their proportional arcs. The Sun will produce eight, and the Moon as many more; altogether thirty-four points in the Zodiac which hitherto have escaped attention among students of Astrology.

The observation is entirely original, and was first made by the writer while endeavouring to fill in one of those ugly blanks which are within the experience of every practical astrologer: an event of great importance and no direction, either Ptolemaic, Placidian, primary, or secondary, and a lunation that fell apparently nowhere! We say " apparently," because not only did the lunation fall on a proportional point, but the Moon by direction also fell upon a proportional point at the exact time of the event. This and subsequent investigations have fully established the Proportional Arcs in the author's consideration.

By these proportional arcs, measured from the ascendant, mid-heaven, the Sun and Moon to any planet, and thence to the same distance on the opposite side of the significator, each of the planets is thrown into four distinct points of the Zodiac, in addition to its actual longitude at birth. Thus the influence of a planet may be strongly felt at a time when no direction to that planet's radical or progressive longitude is in force, or when no lunation occurs thereon. Then it will often be found that a direction or lunation falls on a proportional point.

In all cases where this occurs, the influence of the house in which the radical planet is actually situated will be brought into activity, together with the full influence of that planet according to its signification in the horoscope.

PLANETARY PERIODS

Ptolemy has referred to the chronocrators, or time-measurers, as producing notable events in their periodic revolutions. Raphael, in his " Manual of Astrology," has elaborated the system of planetary periods or " periodic directions."

In this connection, we would observe that the periods of the planets are stated to be—Moon, four years; Mercury, ten years; Venus, eight years; Sun, nineteen years; Mars, fifteen years; Jupiter, twelve years; Saturn, thirty years. In regard to these, it should be noted that the " least years " of the planets are observed in most cases; but, to be uniform, the periods ascribed to Mercury and Moon should be altered to their shortest years, *viz.*, twenty and twenty-five years respectively, as given by Lilly in his " Christian Astrology." Raphael makes the error of ascribing to Mars the same period as the Sun, thus making impossible any aspect between them after birth. With the above comments in view, the reader is referred to Raphael's " Manual of Astrology " for a statement of the system of periodic directions.

PLANETARY GEOCENTRIC LONGITUDES

The author has completed some important researches in the matter of planetary cycles, and believes that an excerpt therefrom in regard to the longitudes of the planets, will be of assistance to the student. A set of ephemerides for eighty-five years, such as that published by Raphael, is all that is required in order to obtain all past or future positions of the planets.

The Sun's place in the Zodiac is approximately the same from year to year, owing to the equation of the calendaric and solar year by the leap-year addition and other adjustments. It has a very close period of thirty-three years, at the end of which it returns to the same minute of longitude on the same day of the year at noon.

Neptune has a period of nearly one hundred and sixty-five years, its yearly increment being about 2° 15′ between each solar conjunction.

Uranus has a period of eighty-four years. It returns to the same longitude in the Zodiac at the end of eighty-four years, but is 40′ further advanced. Thus, on 4th May, 1564, its longitude was ♐ 7° 40′ ℞; same date, 1648 (eighty-four years later), ♐ 8° 20′ ℞; same date, 1732, ♐ 9° ℞; same date, 1816, ♐ 9° 40′ ℞; same date, 1900, ♐ 10° 20′ ℞.

Saturn has a period of fifty-nine years. It comes to the same longitude in the Zodiac on the same date every fifty-nine years, but is about 1° 45′ further advanced.

Jupiter's period is exactly eighty-three years.

Mars and Mercury have both a period of seventy-nine years, but Mars gains 1° in that period.

Venus has a period of eight years nearly.

The Moon forms its conjunction with the Sun on the same day every nineteen years.

The Moon's longitude can be approximately ascertained by reference to its place at the New Moon preceding the epoch required.

By means of these periods the planetary places can be approximately ascertained for any day in any year from observations made during the present century.

Note on Venus' Period

Venus has a mean period of eight years, in which it returns to the same geocentric longitude on the same day of the year. But this period is inconstant, having a *plus* and *minus* increment of variable quantity. Thus, taking its position at the end of several periods of eight years, we find a *plus* increment of from 10′ to 18′, which is within 1° of the same longitude.

Epoch		♀ Longitude		Increment
1st January, 1842	..	6° ♐ 19′	..	—
„ 1850	..	6° 37′	..	+ 18′
„ 1858	..	6° 54′	..	+ 17′
„ 1866	..	7° 9′	..	+ 15′
„ 1874	..	7° 24′	..	+ 15′
„ 1882	..	7° 37′	..	+ 13′
„ 1890	..	7° 47′	..	+ 10′

In forty-eight years the longitudinal *plus* increment amounts to 1° 28′, which is at the mean rate of 15′ per cycle of eight years. But this mean advance of Venus' longitude is not true for any other similar period of time. Thus:

Epoch		♀ Longitude		Increment
1st January, 1840	..	24° ♏ 6′	..	—
„ 1848	..	24° 22′	..	+ 16′
„ 1856	..	24° 40′	..	+ 18′
„ 1864	..	25° 0′	..	+ 20′
„ 1872	..	25° 21′	..	+ 21′
„ 1880	..	25° 43′	..	+ 22′
„ 1888	..	26° 6′	..	+ 23′

Here we find increase of longitude in forty-eight years equal to 2°. Mean periodical increment equal to 20′.

Taking another equal period we find a *minus* difference of longitude, instead of *plus* as in the former cases.

Epoch		♀ Longitude		Increment
1st January, 1843	..	20° ♐ 18′	..	—
„ 1851	..	17° 14′	..	— 3° 4′
„ 1859	..	14° 22′	..	— 2° 52′
„ 1867	..	11° 51′	..	— 2° 31′
„ 1875	..	9° 32′	..	— 2° 19′
„ 1883	..	7° 27′	..	— 2° 5′
„ 1891	..	5° 35′	..	— 1° 52′

The difference in this instance is very great, amounting to 14° 43′ in a period of forty-eight years, the mean periodical deficit being 2° 27′.

Yet the mean geocentric period of Venus is established by the following and other observations.

2nd October, 1842	..	♀ longitude	..	25° ♍ 26′
„ 1850	..	„	..	25° 33′
„ 1858	..	„	..	25° 37′
„ 1866	..	„	..	25° 38′
„ 1874	..	„	..	25° 38′

After which there is a decrease in the periodical difference of longitude thus:—

2nd October, 1882	..	♀ longitude	..	25° ♍ 32′
„ 1890	..	„	..	25° 27′

Again,

17th February, 1867	..	♀ longitude	..	11° ♑ 44′
„ 1875	..	„	..	11° 44′
10th May, 1868	..	„	..	5° ♋ 27′
„ 1876	..	„	..	5° 27′

Further research will probably show that after a period which is a multiple of eight years, these irregularities of Venus become constant and sequential.

SOLAR REVOLUTIONS

The return of the Sun to its radical longitude is considered to be of importance in Astrology. From the aspects to the Sun, Moon, ascendant, and mid-heaven of the figure for the revolution of the Sun, much can be inferred in regard to the fortunes, etc., of the

REVOLUTIONAL ADDITIVES

YEARS.	H.	M.	YEARS.	H.	M.	YEARS.	H.	M.
1	5	49	31	12	28	61	19	5
2	11	38	32	18	17	62	0	54
3	17	28	33	0	6	63	6	44
4	23	17	34	5	55	64	12	33
5	5	6	35	11	45	65	18	22
6	10	55	36	17	34	66	0	11
7	16	45	37	23	23	67	6	1
8	22	34	38	5	12	68	11	50
9	4	23	39	11	2	69	17	39
10	10	12	40	16	51	70	23	28
11	16	2	41	22	40	71	5	18
12	21	51	42	4	29	72	11	7
13	3	40	43	10	19	73	16	56
14	9	29	44	16	8	74	22	45
15	15	19	45	21	57	75	4	35
16	21	8	46	3	46	76	10	24
17	2	57	47	9	36	77	16	13
18	8	46	48	15	25	78	22	2
19	14	36	49	21	14	79	3	52
20	20	25	50	3	3	80	9	41
21	2	14	51	8	53	81	15	30
22	8	3	52	14	42	82	21	19
23	13	53	53	20	31	83	3	9
24	19	43	54	2	20	84	8	59
25	1	32	55	8	10	85	14	48
26	7	21	56	13	59	86	20	37
27	13	11	57	19	48	87	2	27
28	19	0	58	1	37	88	8	16
29	0	49	59	7	27	89	14	5
30	6	38	60	13	16	90	19	54

native during the succeeding year. It is further to be noted that transits made over the places of the planets at the solar return have important effects.

To this we would add that the dates when the Sun comes to the place of any of the planets in the solar figure are *important* dates, productive of events in accordance with the promise and potency of such planets in the horoscope of the solar return.

For the more ready calculation of the solar figure, the preceding table is added. (See previous page.) In the column marked " years," the age at the birthday return will be found, and opposite this will be found certain hours and minutes which must be added to the meridian of the radical or birth horoscope. The result will be the meridian for the solar return. By referring this mid-heaven to the sidereal time at noon on the birthday anniversary, the time before or after noon, for which the figure is to be erected, will be readily known. Calculate the planets' places for this time, and set them in the figure of the solar horoscope.

The judgment is to be made in all points as for a nativity, only respect must be had to the age and condition of the native, and to the fact that the prognostic extends only to the following year of the native's life.

The planets, the houses, and the signs retain, as ever, their primary significations.

The positions of the planets in the solar figure as regards those at birth are of importance, as, if the Moon in the solar figure were on Mars at birth, the year would be ominous of accidents, more particularly that date when the Sun comes to the place of Mars in the radix, and the Moon in the solar figure, or the opposition thereof.

The progressive solar revolution is of great importance in practical astrology. It is found by adding to the day of birth as many days as the native has attained in years. Then with the longitude of the Sun on that date, reference is made to the Ephemeris for the current year, and the positions, aspects, etc., of the planets calculated as shown above. The transits, eclipses, and lunations occurring in important places of the progressive revolution, have great significance.

LUNAR MANSIONS

The critical degrees already referred to in connection with the law of sex are the initial degrees of the twenty-eight lunar mansions so much in repute among the old Arabian astrologers. It is our intention to introduce them here in a light not hitherto familiar to the modern astrologer.

It has been found by continual experience that whenever the Moon by progressive direction enters upon one of these degrees, whether in aspect to any planet or not, a critical and important epoch in the life is reached. Events of a striking nature occur, and always agree with the sign the Moon is in by direction. In this connection, the reason of the variety of events and relations attributed to each of the signs will become apparent.

Thus, Libra does not only rule marriage, but also contracts of all sorts, and enemies or rivals, denoted by the seventh house, with which it is associated. In the same way Gemini denotes not only relatives, such as brothers and sisters, but journeys and writings. The points of demarcation are those coincident with the " critical " degrees, or Lunar Mansions set forth in chapter i of this book.

Thus, Libra, 0° to 13°, refers to enemies; 13° to 26° to marriage; 26° to 30° to contracts. Similar divisions of other signs and their corresponding houses are made, according to the influence of the mansions. When the Moon enters the gate of a mansion, *i.e.*, the " critical " degree commencing it, the trend of affairs takes a turn from events of one order to those of another, the good or evil results being shown by the Moon's aspects. Each mansion comprises $12\frac{4}{9}°$, which practically may be taken as 13°.

Much research will be required in order to establish the exact dominion of the several mansions over the various affairs of life, but it may be taken as true that the Moon's ingress by direction to any " critical " degree will produce a change in the trend of events, and the time will be a critical one in many ways.

The presence of planets at birth in the " critical " degrees brings such planets into prominence in the life of the native, and a number of planets so placed produces a marked individuality, particularly if the ascendant and mid-heaven also occupy such degrees.

END OF BOOK III

BOOK IV

HINDU ASTROLOGY

AFTER PARÂSHARA

THE applicability of Hindu Astrology to European and Western
conditions of life has ever been a subject of great interest, and as
the result of considerable research and experience in the matter,
we venture to bring the subject to the test in the following pages.
The first point that presents itself to the student of Jyotisha (the
name for Hindu Astrology), is one that has already been canvassed
to some considerable extent, *viz.*, the relation of the Hindu Zodiac
to our own. This question comes up in relation to the " Dignities "
of the Planets. Ever since the days of Ptolemy, the writer of the
Tetrabiblos, the dignities of the planets have been received by
Western astrologers exactly as given by him in that famous work.
But there is every reason to believe that Ptolemy received his initial
instruction in the celestial science from one of the Alexandrian
teachers, and that primarily the teaching was derived from India.
At all events, it is well known that the science had attained considerable excellence in that country many centuries prior to the
time of Ptolemy. Now, in Ptolemy's days the *Natural* Zodiac,
consisting of the constellations Aries, etc., and the *Intellectual*
Zodiac, commencing from the shifting Vernal Equinox, were so
nearly identical as to justify his statement of the " Dignities,"
whether he referred them to one or the other of these aforesaid
zodiacs. It is certain, however, that Hindus referred them to the
Natural Zodiac, and Varaha Mihira only perpetuates and carries on
the teachings of his far more ancient predecessors, in marking the
distinction between the two zodiacs, and referring all his astrological

observations to that which we have called the "Natural." By reference to various Sanskrit and vernacular works, we have decided, in common with many competent Pandits that the two zodiacs exactly coincided in the year of the *Kali Yuga*, 3600. And this agrees with the observation of Mihira in his *Samhitâ*, where, commenting on the phenomenon of the Precession of the Equinoxes, he states that in his day the Summer Solstice coincided with the first degree of *Kâtakam* (*i.e.*, Cancer of the Hindu Zodiac), and the Winter Solstice with the first degree of *Makaram:* whereas at one time, he observes, quoting from his predecessors (Parâshara and others), " the Summer Solstice coincided with the middle of *Aslesha*" (Leo of the Hindu Zodiac). Hence we know that those from whom he quotes must have made their observation about 1,080 years previous to the time of Mihira, which extended from A.D. 416 to 572. Let us bring this into line with our own researches, which supply the date, K.Y. 3600. The *Kali Yuga* began in February, B.C. 3102. Therefore, to obtain the date of the coinciding of the zodiacs, we say, 3600 – 3102 = A.D. 498, which falls well within the limits of the period ascribed to Mihira, and thus supports his independent statement and observation.

This point being settled to our satisfaction, and it being understood that Mihira and all his ancestors, Nârada, Garga, Parâshara, etc., refer to the Natural Zodiac when speaking of the planets' places, dignities, etc., let us see to what extent we are justified in continuing to refer those statements to our own Zodiac. The present year, 1898 less 498 = 1,400, the time elapsed since the coinciding of the two zodiacs. The Precession of the Equinoxes is taken in India at 50″ per year, and 1,400 × 50″ = 70,000″ = 19° 26′ 40″. This increment is referred to in the Hindu books as the *Ayanâmsha*, or interval between the beginning of their Zodiac and the Equinox. Consequently, the Sun does not reach the first degree of the Hindu Zodiac until about the twentieth day after the Vernal Equinox, when the solar month of *Mesham* commences. According to the European Zodiac, however, the Sun will then have reached the twentieth degree of Aries, and will continue to be in that sign for ten days more. Hence, it follows that (1) if the exaltation of the planets were known to the Hindus before the days of Ptolemy, and (2) if they referred those exaltations to the Natural Zodiac, then we, who have taken our cue from Ptolemy, do wrong to maintain the dignities of the planets as given by him, except when, in modern times, the planets fall in *the last ten degrees of their respective exaltation signs in our Zodiac.*

EUROPEAN ZODIAC

Date of entry of the Sun into the first point of { ♈ Mar. 20. ♉ Apr. 20. ♊ May 21. ♋ June 21. ♌ July 23. ♍ Aug. 23. } etc.

♈ Apr. 11. ♉ May 12. ♊ June 12. ♋ July 14. ♌ Aug. 14.

HINDU ZODIAC

Ptolemy seems to have taken his astrological knowledge from the East, and applied it to the zodiac instituted by Hipparchus in the second century B.C.   This was putting old wine into new bottles, a perfectly safe but inadvisable proceeding. Who can say how much the *wine* may not have suffered in consequence? At all events, the two hypotheses presented above have been proved to the satisfaction of all who have studied the *Jyotisha Shâstras*, or astrological writings of the Hindus, and the conclusion is of some consequence to modern astrologers.

The distinction between the Natural (Hindu) Zodiac and the Intellectual (European) Zodiac being understood from the above comments, we may at once proceed to indicate the practical use of the *Ayanâmsha* in the system of Hindu Astrology we are about to place before European readers.

THE AYANAMSHA

Having the horoscope of birth in hand, made in the usual European manner, the first thing is to convert it into terms of the Hindu Zodiac.   This is done as follows:—

1. From the year of birth subtract 498.   This will give the *Ayanâmsha* period.
2. Multiply the *Ayanâmsha* period by 50⅓″, and reduce to degrees, minutes, and seconds of space.
3. Uniformly subtract this number of degrees, minutes, and seconds from
   (a) The cusps of the houses in the European figure of birth;
   (b) The planets' places.

The figure thus obtained is the figure of birth according to the Hindu system.

N.B.—A serious error, which may not be at first apparent, will occur in the event of the student subtracting the *Ayanâmsha* from the mid-heaven only, and then erecting the figure, with this new mid-heaven, from the Tables of Houses; for the oblique ascension of the signs and planets will be falsified.

To avert this possibility, observe that if, in the original European figure, a planet holds a certain place, distant, say, 5° from the cusp of the second house, it ought to be in the same relative position in the Hindu figure derived by the above rules. The only difference will be that the planet may have changed its sign, which is the case when the degrees held by it in any sign are less than the *Ayanâmsha*.

THE ASTERISMS

The Asterisms, or *Nakshatrams*—as they are called in Sanskrit— are twenty-seven in number. A twenty-eighth asterism, falling in Capricorn, is sometimes used in Hindu Astrology for the purpose of some branches of *Prashna*, or Horary Astrology; but with this we are not concerned. Its name is *Abhijit*.

The asterisms count from the beginning of the Hindu Zodiac for purposes of the present system, and are each exactly 13° 20′ in extent. Each asterism is divided into four parts, called *Padams*, or quarters, but for simplicity we may call them merely " parts."

As there are 30° in each sign, and 13° 20′ in each asterism, it follows that a sign contains just 2¼ asterisms, *i.e.*, two whole asterisms and one " part." The following table shows the asterisms contained in each of the signs; a separate column indicates the planet ruling each asterism, and another, the period through which it is said to rule:—

♈		♌	♐		
4	Ashvini	Magha	Mula	☊	7
4	Bharani	Purva Phalguni	Purvashadha	♀	20
1	Krittika	Uttara Phalguni	Uttara Shadha	☉	6
	♉	♍	♑		
3	Krittika	Uttara Phalguni	Uttara Shadha		do.
4	Rohini	Hasta	Shravana	☽	10
2	Mrigashirsha	Chitra	Dhanistha	♂	7
	♊	♎	♒		
2	Mrigashirsha	Chitra	Dhanistha		do.
4	Ardra	Svati	Satabhisha	♌	18
3	Punarvasu	Vishaka	Purvabhadra	♃	16
	♋	♏	♓		
1	Punarvasu	Vishaka	Purvabhadra		do.
4	Pushya	Anuradha	Uttarabhadra	♄	19
4	Ashlesha	Jyeshta	Revati	☿	17

If attention be paid to the following explanation, the table will soon be understood. In the first column we find Aries, and underneath it four Ashvini, four Bharani, one Krittika, which means that in the sign Aries there are four parts of Ashvini, four of Bharani, and one of Krittika. Under Taurus we find the remaining three parts of Krittika, the whole of Rohini, and half of Mrigashirsha. In the same line with Ashvini we find, in the second column, the asterism Magha under Leo, and Mula in the third column under Sagittarius; while still further in the same line we find the Dragon's Tail (called *Ketu* by the Hindus) and the figure seven, which means that Ashvini, Magha, and Mula are all ruled by Ketu, and that Ketu's period is seven years.

In order to overcome the difficulty of introducing Sanskrit words into this dissertation upon Hindu Astrology, we propose to call the asterisms by their numbers, Ashvini being one, Bharani two, and so on to Revati, which is twenty-seven. The names of the planets in use among us will be preserved, but for the purposes of reference, their Hindu equivalents are given in this place: The Sun is *Surya;* the Moon, *Chandra;* Mars, *Kuja;* Mercury, *Budhan;* Jupiter, *Guru;* Venus, *Shukra;* Saturn, *Shani;* the Dragon's Head, or Moon's Ascending Node, *Rahu;* the Dragon's Tail, or Moon's Descending Node, *Ketu.*

THE PLANETS' PERIODS

We have made very careful and prolonged enquiries among the native Jyoshis of southern India, to find out upon what principle the various periods are allotted to the several planets, but without success; and the books we have consulted are silent upon the matter. Upon study of the subject, however, it is seen that the total of the different periods is one hundred and twenty years, which the Hindus regard as the natural life-period. This period, therefore, in some way corresponds to the complete circle of 360°, which is three times one hundred and twenty. The zodiacal circle we have found to be divided into twenty-seven asterisms, each of 13° 20′, and the life-period of one hundred and twenty years, when divided by nine, the number of the significators employed, gives thirteen years four months; so that there is a proportion of 1° for each year of life, as in our own systéms. It will be readily seen, moreover, that the basis of the system lies in the Triad—

$$360 = 3 \text{ times } 120$$
$$120 = 3 \quad ,, \quad 40$$
$$40 = 3 \quad ,, \quad 13\tfrac{1}{3}$$
$$9 = 3 \quad ,, \quad 3$$

Let us grant, for the purpose of investigation, that the periods of the planets are the result of experience, and at once the intelligent astrologer would be prepared to find that there is some underlying numerical harmony, by which this apparently arbitrary division of the life-period is brought into line with all we know of the Astral science; and although we are quite prepared to find it so, at the present time we are not in a position to state that the said harmony actually exists. Experience is the great test, and had not experience proved to us the truth of the deductions of Hindu astrologers, we should not deem this exposition worth writing.

THE SIGNS OF THE ZODIAC

From what has already been said, it will be seen that the Hindu Zodiac is similar to our own, having twelve divisions of equal degrees to one another. The order of the signs is the same, and the natures of both the signs and their rulers are, in all essentials, the same as those obtaining among Western astrologers.

These signs have no symbols among the Hindus, who always suppose Aries to be in the first house, and merely mark the ascendant (*Lagnam*) either by a line, or by the letter L. In the north of India, another system is in vogue; but all tends to the same end, *viz.*, to determine the rising sign. From this, as a starting point, the rest of the signs are equally and uniformly distributed through the twelve houses, though there are no symbols to indicate the fact. At the present day, there are many astrologers in the north of India who use Tables of Houses, and indicate oblique ascension of signs, but these are only copyists of the more mathematical systems of the West. In the famous and most ancient of all Nâdis, the *Brighu Samhita*, numerous figures are given, but in none of them is any attention paid to oblique ascension.

The names of the zodiacal signs corresponding to ours are:—

Aries	..	*Mesham*	Libra	..	*Tulâm*
Taurus	..	*Vrishabham*	Scorpio	..	*Vrishchika*
Gemini	..	*Mithuna*	Sagittarius	..	*Dhanus*
Cancer	..	*Kâtakam*	Capricorn	..	*Makaram*
Leo	..	*Simha*	Aquarius	..	*Kumbha*
Virgo	..	*Kanya*	Pisces	..	*Minam*

The meanings of the Sanskrit words are the same as imported by the Latin names in use among ourselves.

THE HOUSES

It is at this point that the Hindu system of Astrology really becomes perplexing to the European student. The great variety of seemingly unconnected things, attributed to the several houses by the Jyoshis, renders anything like a systematic statement of the rulership of the houses a matter of great difficulty.

It will simplify matters if, in this place, we draw out into prominence some of the points of contradiction between the two systems.

Among the elements of the first house, then, we find, among other things, the *Memory* is under its dominion. This would probably fall, in the European system, to the third or ninth house, or perhaps the fourth or tenth, as being the second (wealth) of the third and ninth. And truly, the things of the memory may be regarded as the *acquired property* of the mind, just as the second house denotes the acquired property of the physical man.

The five physical senses (*Gnanendriyas*) are attributed to this, the first, house also. But, observe, the *eyes* are ruled in the same system by the second house, the *ears* by the third house, and how the senses can be dissociated from their respective organs, we know not! In the same way, the Religion is said to be ruled by the first house, while all that constitutes it, and from which it is built up, comes under the ninth house, *e.g.*, education, temples, religious instruction, the " thread ceremony " (*upadesha*), the occult, or spiritual powers (*siddhis*), etc.

From these illustrations, it is quite evident that the modern writers have disturbed the original harmony and simplicity of the system, and we would therefore point out at once the remarkable and assuring fact that, with four exceptions, the system of Garga, Parâshara, and Brighu—the more ancient Eastern astrologers—is identical with that followed by ourselves. These exceptions we shall now deal with.

The first exception of our system is the fourth house. This all Hindu astrologers uniformly attribute to the *mother*, and not the father, as we do. To our own mind, there is every evidence of the correctness of this arrangement, for the fourth house is the " angle of the earth," and the earth is the symbol of the *mother* in all mythologies. The connection of the gods with Gaia (earth) and the birth of the Heroes of the Greek Pantheon will recur to the reader in this connection. Then, again, the sign Cancer, identified with the fourth, is the sign of the Moon (Juno-Lucina, Hevah, Eve, and Parvati), the universal symbol of the mother-principle in nature. The fourth house is, further, associated with the night, over which the Moon is said to rule, and the Night, as contra-distinguished from the Day, is feminine, e.g., *Delilah* (ruler of the night) is the wife of *Samson* (the Sun). For these reasons, and others which will suggest themselves to the student, the fourth house more naturally signifies the mother than the father, and the Hindu system in this instance appears to be more consonant with nature than our own; at least, as regards a male horoscope.

The second exception is the tenth house, which, while indicating honour, fame, the family titles, and the profession, also denotes in the Hindu system, the *father*. This latter conclusion naturally follows upon what has been said concerning the fourth house; and assuredly the tenth house, as identified with the noon-day and the mid-heaven, and with the Sun, the maker of the day, seems more naturally to signify the father than the mother, especially when it is remembered that the family titles—the *Dharma* (special occupa-tion or magistery)—and the honour of the native, follow the ancestral line on the father's side, and that none of these come through the mother, whose name changes with marriage, and from whom no titles descend. Moreover, the mid-heaven is mythically identified with Ouranos, the First of all the Gods, and father of Saturn (Kronos) the significator of Time itself. Surely, then, there is every reason to think that the Hindus, in giving the tenth house to *Shiva*, and the fourth to his divine spouse *Parvati*, indicated once for all the mundane relations of these houses from " the pattern of things in the Heavens ;" and rightly denoted the father by the tenth house and the mother by the fourth, in the typal male horoscope.

The third exception falls in the sixth house, the ruler of enemies, which we attribute to the seventh house. But the seventh house is the house of partnerships, and such persons as we form alliances and contracts with; and chiefly the wife, the friend of our adversity, the protector of our children, our partner in joy and woe, our best friend, and life-long confidant. Such is the true wife. How, then, does the seventh come to denote enemies? It is the result, probably, of the astrologers having failed to take into consideration the corrupting influence of a malefic in the seventh. When those whom we have drawn nearest to us come to be corrupted by the evil planet, then assuredly they are our worst enemies. Then, too, the seventh house denotes such as are capable of afflicting us physically, and hence hurts and injuries result from the affliction of the significators by planets in the seventh house. The argument for the seventh house being that ruling " open enemies," would be: since the first house represents in a particular and special sense the personality of the native, the seventh, *which is opposed to it*, would denote his enemies.

But on the same lines one might argue that all the houses have their respective seventh, or opposition; and hence the " relatives " signified by the third would have their open enemies in the ninth, and so on all round the circle. But when we come to the sixth house, we have a position in which even good planets are debilitated, a house of disease and sickness, of servitude and obscurity. This is far more fitting as a place of " enemies " than the seventh, which latter satisfies the law of polarity in nature, and brings about harmonious alliances and unions.

The next exception, and the last, is that of the twelfth house, which, in common with ourselves, the Hindus regard as an *evil* house; but they likewise give *monetary losses* as ruled by this house, in connection with other things, whereas we should judge both gain and loss from the second. We must leave these points to the investigation of the student so far as they may apply to European systems of astrology, and merely state here that they must be taken as principles of the Eastern system, and judgment must be made according to the statements above, *viz.*, the fourth house for the mother, tenth for father, the sixth for enemies, and the twelfth for losses. All other affairs may be safely taken as ruled by the same houses as ascribed to them in the standard European works on the subject.

Note.—The Hindu *Trimurti*, or Deific Trinity, are astrologically denoted by the planets Saturn, Jupiter, and Mars. Brahma, from the root *Brih* " to expand," is the name for the Creator, or Deity, in the act of manifestation. Our words *Breath*, *Breathe*, express the same idea, and the act of manifestation in the Divine impulse is often referred to as the Mahâ-Swara, or Great Breath. Jupiter is called in Sanskrit *Brihaspati*, or the " Lord of Expansion." He it is who brings all things to fruition, and perfects every work of man. The wife of Brahma is *Saraswati*, the goddess of arts and sciences, of knowledge and education, represented by the planet Mercury in its female aspect. But Jupiter is also called *Guru*, the " Preceptor " and spiritual teacher, and in this sense is related to the sign Sagittarius and the ninth house, which rules over religion and spiritual things, being Kabalistically the significator of the Spirit of Man, as the fifth house denotes the soul, and the first house the body. The image of Sagittarius in this capacity is faithfully depicted in the *Apocalypse*, chap. iv, verse 11. It is well known that in the old institutes of the Aryans, the father was invariably the spiritual preceptor, or *guru*, of the eldest son, to whom he transmitted his *mamtram* and spiritual heirloom at the time of death, and, as some believe, his *siddhis*, or psychic powers, also. This is why we have the anomaly of the ninth house ruling the " father " in the works of Varaha Mihira, who followed the ancient teachings of the more spiritual system of his predecessors. Observe also that the " joint family system," which constitutes the eldest son the head of the family and its branches in India to-day, is a relic of the ancient system of spiritual heredity; and as the fortunes of the family are merged in the horoscope of the eldest born son, it follows that the *guru* and the *father* came to be judged of from the condition of the same house, *viz.*, the ninth, and Jupiter was the natural significator. In the name of Jupiter we have the *Deva-pitri* or *Deo-pitar* of the Hindus, the *Deus-pater* of the Latins, the Jovah, or Jehovah, of the Semites, and the " God-father " of the Christian baptism.

ASPECTS

The aspects in Hindu Astrology are counted from sign to sign. There are no half signs employed, as in the semisquare and sesquiquadrate of our system. The *trikonam*, or trine aspect, is the chief aspect, and the half trikonam, or sextile, belongs to the same order. Both these are good. The *kendra*, or square aspect, gives good results when good planets are so placed, and evil when the planets are evil. The method of signifying aspects is to refer to the number of signs from the significator which the aspecting body may hold. Thus: if the Sun be in the second house, and Venus in the third house of the figure, Venus is spoken of as in the second from the Sun, and third from *lagnam* or ascendant.

In the judgment of a figure the condition of the planets are taken by sign and house, *i.e.*, by essential and accidental dignities or debilities. The signs and their rulers we have already seen to be the same as with ourselves. The houses are also the same: *Kendra* (angular) first, fourth, seventh, and tenth; *Panapara* (succedent) second, fifth, eighth, and eleventh; *Apokalima* (cadent) third, sixth, ninth, twelfth.

Of these houses, the third, fifth, ninth, and eleventh are uniformly good; and the sixth, eighth, twelfth, evil. The first, second, fourth, seventh, and tenth depend upon the planets occupying them. These aspects may be counted from any significator, and must not be restricted to the houses bearing those numerals in the figure itself. *Example:* Ascendant, Aquarius; Saturn in the eighth house of figure in the sign Virgo, the Sun in Taurus in the fourth of the figure. Here Saturn is evil in regard to the first house; but accidentally in good aspect to Sun, being in the fifth from that luminary. So that in judging of the things ruled by the fourth house, Saturn would be taken as favourable; but in relation to the things of the first house, unfavourable.

The planets Jupiter and Venus, Sun and Moon, in the fourth from a significator are friendly, unless in their *neecham* or " fall ;" while Saturn and Mars, Rahu and Ketu, are evil, unless in their dignities.

It may be mentioned here that the sign Scorpio is identified with Rahu, and Taurus with Ketu, in which signs they are respectively strong.

The above remarks have reference to judgment from the radix only.

In judging the general effects of the combination of the planets by period and sub-period (a measure of time which will presently be given), the general rule in regard to the planetary relations is that of *temporal* position. Thus: all planets in the tenth, eleventh, twelfth, second, third, and fourth houses from the significator, and those also which (being themselves *good*) are in the same sign as the significator, are *benefic;* all other are *evil.* This is the simplest and surest rule that is known in all the books, and, if due allowance be made for the accidental and essential *strength* of the planets, a sure judgment can be given. Yet the essential or natural sympathies and antipathies of the planets among themselves must not be lost sight of, for a temporal relationship cannot entirely prevail against a natural and inherent one that is contrary to it. Nevertheless, experience will show that the radical affections are often swayed into temporal service that is contrary to their free or unconditional nature; so that even Saturn may confer some benefits when in temporal benefic relations with its natural enemy, the Moon.

ILLUSTRATION

In order to properly set out the system under notice, we shall have recourse to an example, which we find ready to hand in the horoscope of Her Majesty Queen Victoria. The Ayanâms'a, or difference between the Vernal Equinox and the star Revati, is thus determined: 1819—498 A.D. = 1,321 years, × 50⅓″ = 66,490″ = 18° 28′ 10″.

This amount must be subtracted from the ascendant and the planets' places, and the signs must be set in the figure without regard to oblique ascension, as in the example given below. The subtraction of the Ayanâms'a is not for the purpose of marking the exact degrees held by the planets in the Hindu Zodiac, but to determine merely what change of sign, if any, is due to them by the conversion from one Zodiac to another. And in the example given, we find that the ascendant falls in Taurus (*Vrishabham*), the Sun and Moon are in the same sign of the Hindu Zodiac, Mercury passes into Aries, Jupiter into Capricorn, and Mars into Pisces. Uranus, not being included in the system of Parâshara and of the Hindu writers generally, is left out of the figure, while the Moon's Nodes, ☊ and ☋, are included therein. The signs, too, are differently placed in regard to the houses, being equally distributed throughout. Shorn of all the elements which properly belong to the European figure, and which are not required by the Hindu Jyoshi, the result would be as follows:—

Saturn Mars		Jupiter	
Venus Mercury Dragon's Head	EMPRESS		
Taurus Sun Moon	OF INDIA		Dragon's Tail

There are different methods of drawing the figures among the
Dravidians in the south of India and the Aryans in the north; and
the first house is placed indifferently in various parts of the figure
by the several schools of astrologers; but all would agree in placing
the planets and signs in the same relative positions as above. It will
be remarked that the ascending sign only is given; the rest are understood as being identified with the several successive houses of the
figure. Reading this figure we say: Taurus rising, with Sun and
Moon; Dragon's Tail in Libra in the sixth; Jupiter in Capricornus
in the ninth; Saturn and Mars in Pisces in the eleventh; Venus,
Mercury, and Dragon's Head in Aries in the twelfth. A Southern
Hindu would say: Vrishabha Lagnam, Surya and Chandra ;
Ketu in sixth; Guru in ninth; S'ani, Kuja in eleventh; S'ukra,
Budhan and Râhu in twelfth; and with these elements he would go
to work, remarking that Chandra (Moon) is in " Svocham " (its
exaltation), and S'ukra in " svaneecham " (its debility).

The accidental relations of the planets are as follows:—Dragon's
Tail is an " enemy " to all the planets except Jupiter; Jupiter is
friendly to Dragon's Tail, Saturn, Mars, Venus, Mercury, and
Dragon's Head, and also to the Sun and Moon; Saturn, Mars,
Venus, Mercury, and Dragon's Head are friendly to all except the
Dragon's Tail; and the Sun and Moon are friendly to all except the
Dragon's Tail. Now, to determine the asterism of birth, observe
the *exact* longitude of the Moon in the Hindu Zodiac. The
longitude given in the European figure of birth is ♊ 3° 39', and that,
being reduced by the Ayanâms'a 18° 28', gives ♉ 15° 11'. Reference
to the table on page 180 will show that in the sign ♉ there are three
parts of Krittika, four of Rohini, and two of Mrigas'irsha. Each
of these parts we know to be 3° 20' in extent; therefore, three of
Krittika = 10°; and 15° 11' − 10° leaves 5° 11' to be accounted for.
These 5° 11' form part of the next asterism—Rohini. Therefore
we say that at the Queen's birth the Moon was in Rohini, having
passed through 5° 11' of that asterism, and being in the " second "
part thereof. Looking at the table again, we see that Rohini is
ruled by the Moon, whose period is ten years. We have therefore
to find how much of the ten years is due to 5° 11' of Rohini, through
which the Moon has passed up to the birth-time. Each asterism
being 13° 20' in extent, we say, in this case: If 13° 20' gives ten
years, what will 5° 11' give?

13° 20' (800') : 5° 11' (311') :: 10 : 3 years 10 months 19 days

Then, with this expired portion of the Moon's period of ten years, we are able to determine under what sub-period in the Moon's period the Queen was born.

THE SUB-PERIODS

The sub-periods are obtained by multiplying together the years due to the planet ruling the period and sub-period; then, cutting off the last figure in the product, multiply it by 3, and call the result *days*, the first figure in the product being so many *months*. Thus, to find the sub-period due to the Moon in its own period:—The period of the Moon is ten years—10 × 10 = 100 = 10 months. There is a cipher for the last figure of the product, and therefore the sub-period has no odd days. Take another example:—

Find the sub-period due to Mars in the period of the Sun, the Sun's period being six years, and that of Mars seven years.

7 × 6 = 42 = 4 months 6 days. These sub-periods are called in Sanskrit *Bukthi*.

They are further divided into *antaram* periods. The rule for determining their duration is as follows:—

1. Divide the *months* of the Bukthi period by 4; this will give so many *days, hours,* etc.

2. Divide the *days* of the Bukthi period by 5; this will give so many *hours, minutes,* etc.

3. The days, hours, and minutes thus produced must be multiplied by the total period (Das'â) of the planet whose *antaram* period is required.

Example.—Required the (*antaram*) inter-period of Jupiter in the sub-period (*Bukthi*) of Saturn, and the period (*Das' â*) of Dragon's Tail (*Ketu*).

☋ Period = 7 years
♄ Sub-period = 13 months 9 days
♃ Inter-period, or *Antaram* = ?
By Rule 1, 13 ÷ 4 = 3 days 6 hours
By Rule 2, 9 ÷ 5 = 1 hour 48 minutes
Total = 3 days 7 hours 48 minutes

This period, multiplied by 16, the total period of Jupiter whose *antaram,* or inter-period, is required = 1 month 25 days 9 hours 48 minutes, which is Jupiter's inter-period in the sub-period of

Saturn and the period of Dragon's Tail, or, as the Hindus would say, *Ketu Das'â, S'ani Bukthi, Guru Antaram.*

It is stated that the ancient Hindu astrologers sub-divided these periods into most minute fractions, and stayed only at the *Swara*, or breath, a period of a few seconds. Whether or not they were able to determine the *phalam*, or effects, due to these minute periods is a matter of question. For all practical purposes, the inter-periods of the planets will be found sufficient.

The order of the planets in the successive subdivisions of the periods is as follows:—

In all cases the planet whose period is subdivided takes the first place, and the rest follow on in the order observed in the Table of Asterisms, *viz.*, ☋ ♀ ☉ ☽ ♂ ☊ ♃ ♄ ☿.

So, if the period belongs to ☽, then ☽ will rule the first sub-period, and the first inter-period of that sub-period. Then follows the sub-period of Mars in the period of the Moon, and the first inter-period of the sub-period will likewise be ruled by Mars; ☊, ♃, ♄, etc., following in their order.

EXAMPLE OF PLANETARY SUBDIVISIONS

Moon's Period

Sub-Periods		Inter-Periods								
1. Moon	☽	♂	☊	♃	♄	☿	☋	♀	☉
2. Mars	♂	☊	♃	♄	☿	☋	♀	☉	☽
3. Dragon's Head	☊	♃	♄	☿	☋	♀	☉	☽	♂
4. Jupiter	♃	♄	☿	☋	♀	☉	☽	♂	☊
5. Saturn	♄	☿	☋	♀	☉	☽	♂	☊	♃
6. Mercury	☿	☋	♀	☉	☽	♂	☊	♃	♄
7. Dragon's Tail	☋	♀	☉	☽	♂	☊	♃	♄	☿
8. Venus	♀	☉	☽	♂	☊	♃	♄	☿	☋
9. Sun	☉	☽	♂	☊	♃	♄	☿	☋	♀

The above example will, no doubt, make the preceding chapter intelligible to all. In subsequent chapters the letters P., S.P., and I.P. will stand for period, sub-period, and inter-period.

The Birth-Period

We have seen that, in the case of the Queen, the period in force at the time of birth was that of the Moon; but it was also seen that of the ten years due to the Moon as its full period, 3 years 10 months 19 days had expired at the moment of birth. We need, therefore, to determine the sub-period which is operating at the time of birth, and to set out the scale of periods and sub-periods for the whole term of life.

Moon's Period—10 years

					Years	Months	Days
Moon's sub-period	..	..	..	..	0	10	0
Mars' „	..	..	..	..	0	7	0
Dragon's Head's sub-period	..	..	..	1	6	0
Jupiter's „	..	..	..	1	4	0
Saturn's „	..	..	..	1	7	0
Mercury's „	..	..	..	1	5	0
Dragon's Tail's „	..	..	..	0	7	0
Venus' „	..	..	..	1	8	0
Sun's „	..	..	..	0	6	0
			Total	10	0	0

Of these sub-periods, the whole of the Moon's, the whole of Mars', the whole of the Dragon's Head's, and 11 months and 19 days of that of Jupiter, in all amounting to 3 years 10 months 19 days, had expired at the time of birth, thus leaving 4 months 11 days of Jupiter's sub-period to be worked out.

The ages at which the various sub-periods of the Moon's period will expire can thus be set out in order:

Moon's Period

				Years	Months	Days	
Moon's sub-period	..	..	..	0	10	0	expired
Mars' „	..	..	..	0	7	0	„
Dragon's Head's sub-period	..	..	1	6	0	„
Jupiter's „	..	..	0	11	19	„
		Total	3	10	19	„

					Years	Months	Days
Jupiter's sub-period expires at the age of	..	0	4	11
Saturn's „ „ „ „	..	1	11	11
Mercury's „ „ „ „	..	3	4	11
Dragon's Tail's „ „ „	..	3	11	11
Venus' „ „ „ „	..	5	7	11
Sun's „ „ „ „	..	6	1	11

It will thus be seen that the Queen's age at the expiry of the Moon's period was 6 years 1 month 11 days.

The next period is that of Mars, which rules for seven years. Add this to the above age and we get 13 years 1 month 11 days, the age at expiry of Mars' period. After Mars comes the Dragon's Head, which rules for eighteen years, bringing us to the age of 31 years 1 month 11 days. Then Jupiter, with a period of sixteen years, reaching to the age of 47 years 1 month 11 days. Next Saturn, with nineteen years for its period, rules to the age of 66 years 1 month 11 days. Next Mercury, whose period is seventeen years, brings us up to the age of 83 years 1 month 11 days.

These periods can be set out according to the example given in the Moon's period, and the age progressively shown at the expiry of each sub-period.

It will now be more or less clear to the student of Hindu Astrology upon what basis the Zodiac rests; how the Nakshatrams (or asterisms) are counted, and what planets rule over each of them, together with the periods of their rule. It will further be clear after what manner the periods, sub-periods, and inter-periods (the Hindu method of computing the time of events, corresponding to our directions) are to be calculated. To this part of the work a complete set of all necessary tables will be appended, so that it is only necessary here that the *methods* should be known in order for the student to use those tables intelligently.

A good deal of controversy has been raised in regard to this system by Hindus who have received a European education, and who consequently wish to appear in all matters to be " up to date ;" such persons claiming for the East a common use of Tables of Houses, the computation of horoscopes by oblique ascension under the latitude of birth, and a full knowledge of the Zodiac which begins with the equinoctial point. Despite the efforts of these gentlemen to improve their credit for intelligence at the expense of their Jyotish Shâstra, we maintain that, although Mihira knew of the Precession of the Equinoxes, and quoted Parâshara and Garga to the same effect in his *Brihat Samhitâ*, he nevertheless used the Equinox beginning from Revati, and referred all his rules and horoscopes to a fixed Zodiac, which is now (1898) 19° 34′ 26″ East of the vernal equinox. In proof of this, and to silence the contention that the system of Parâshara was confined to the South of India, where it is yet in vogue, we refer critics to the *Bhrigu Samhitâ*, which is in the possession of Pandit Nandkishor of Meerut, N.W. Province. We have in our possession over a hundred horoscopes from that colossal work, and in none of them is there any observance of oblique ascension, while the planets' places are referred to the fixed Zodiac, and not to the Vernal Equinox. Can any further, more reliable, or more ancient authority be adduced to the contrary?

JUDGMENT BY PLANETARY POSITION

In judging the effects due to the planets in the horoscope and their successive combinations in the P., S.P., and I.P. after birth, the following general dominion of the planets must be taken into account:—

The Sun governs honour, fame, nobles, advancement, profession, father, health.

The Moon governs females, marriage, travelling, change of residence, wealth, health, the mother, the house of residence, and native place.

Mars governs, fire, fever, madness, quarrels, ambitions, energy, prowess, courage, adventures, poison, hurts, passions, and health.

Jupiter governs the religion (*dharma*), religious duties, the law, the father's brothers and sisters, teachers and preceptors, journeys to foreign lands, devotion, religious ceremonies, good fortune, increase.

Saturn governs the father, disease, wasting, chronic affections, ill health, poverty, condition of the family.

Mercury governs the mind, the memory, hearing, brothers and sisters, mother's relatives, sickness, servants, food, journeys in one's own country, pilgrimages, and messages of all kinds.

Venus governs money, apparel, wealth in kind or specie; trinkets, jewellery, articles of value; the speech, learning, the wife, marriage, alliances, pleasures, arts and sciences.

Râhu and Ketu (Dragon's Head and Tail) govern such things as are denoted by the houses occupied by them at the time of birth.

In general, it is necessary to take into consideration, when judging the effects of a planet, (1) its natural rulership in the order of the signs; (2) the house (*bhâva*) occupied by it; (3) the house, or houses, over which it rules in the horoscope.

Râhu has affinity with the sign Scorpio where it is strong, and

Ketu with Taurus. These signs are called their *uchha*, or exaltations.

From these descriptions, it will be seen that judgment concerning any planet is derived from a consideration of its rulership in the signs and the houses occupied by those signs, in addition to the place of the planet itself, its general nature, and its sympathies and antipathies in the natural world and in man.

For this reason, the Moon is strong in the second and fourth houses; the Sun in the fifth and first; Mars in the first and eighth; Saturn in the tenth and seventh, etc., irrespective of the signs in which they are found; for they have affinity with these several houses by their affinities in the world-soul, the horoscope of which is *Meshalagnam* (Aries for rising sign), during the whole of *Kali Yuga* (the present age), *i.e.*, the Dark, or Iron Age.

PERIODS

As the general *phalam* (effects) of the horoscope is derived from the configurations and conditions of all the planets, taken as significators for the whole life, so, in judging of the effects of any *period* of the life, attention must be paid to the condition (by position and configuration) of the planet ruling that period as determined by the calculation called *Kâlachakradashâphalakathna*, *i.e.*, the dividing of time (the life-period) into its periodical effects. This calculation was set forth in the chapter upon periods, sub-periods, and interperiods. Its basis is the Moon's place at birth. According to the condition of the planets ruling the required period, the life and fortunes of the native will be affected.

SUB-PERIODS

These are considered in relation to the general effects due to the planets governing the period in which they fall, and they are subsidiary to the fortunes promised by the period planet. In this respect they may be considered in the same manner as lunar and solar directions, which will, perhaps, simplify matters. Then, if the period planet shows *good* effects, it does so from its position and aspects at birth, and an *evil* sub-period planet cannot counteract its effect wholly, but some good will remain behind. The result is similar when, *mutatis mutandis*, the P. planet is evil and the S.P.

planet good. But when both agree in nature and point to the same end, then the effects are forcible and decided, either for good or evil, as the case may be.

INTER-PERIODS

These are taken as subsidiary to the sub-periods in the same manner that transits or lunations are considered in relation to lunar or secondary directions in our European methods. The longest of these reaches over a period of 6 months 20 days, viz., the ♀ I.P. of the ♀ S.P. in the ♀ P.; the shortest inter-period is that of the Sun in its own sub-period and period; it lasts only 5 days 9 hours 36 minutes. The condition of the I.P. planet must be taken into account, and its relations to the sub-period planet properly estimated. Its effects may then be accurately known.

A few straightforward rules are necessary in order to bring the above observations into systematic form.

RULES TO JUDGE OF PLANETARY PERIODS

I. Consider well the positions and affections of the period planet, for even a good planet will not bear good fruit during its period if it be ill affected by sign or position, or afflicted by the majority of planets.

II. The sub-period planet must be considered in the same way as the period planet, but in addition thereto its *relations* with the period planet must be taken carefully into account; for though the planets have a natural enmity and friendship existing between them, and due to their respective natures, yet when the sub-period planet is in good aspect to the period planet it will produce good, even though these planets be natural enemies. Similarly, friendly and benefic planets will not produce good fruits if weak or afflicted, or themselves afflicting (by position) the period planet to which they are related.

III. The effects of the ruling planets are intensified at such time as the Sun may be passing through the signs occupied by them or the signs over which they rule.

N.B.—The Sun does not enter the Hindu signs until twenty days after its entry into the European signs bearing the same name.

IV. The inter-period planets are considered in the same manner, in regard to the sub-period planets to which they are related, as these latter are to the period planets. It thus happens that even when the period is a good one, as shown by the position and affections of the period planet, yet there are sub-periods, and again inter-periods, when evils may naturally arise.

V. The general effects of the planets thus related must be taken into account, and their natural relations, as well as their temporary relations in the horoscope, must be well considered. Thus, Saturn and Sun, although natural enemies by sign and exaltation, may be respectively in Libra and Leo, in which case they are in temporary good relations, occupying the third and eleventh signs respectively from one another. Judgment is made accordingly, but it is to be understood that a temporary friendship will not entirely overcome a radical and constitutional enmity.

VI. The effects will further have relation to the nature of the house corresponding to the sign occupied by the sub-planet, in the period under consideration. Thus if the period be that of Sun, and the sub-period be that of Venus, and Venus be in the sign Aquarius, the effects will fall out in relation to the eleventh house affairs; if Venus be in Libra, then seventh house affairs will be affected.

VII. The sign, counted from the rising sign, will give a further element of interpretation. Thus, if, in the sub-period of any planet, that planet occupies Leo, and Scorpio be rising, the effects will fall on the tenth house affairs.

VIII. The number of the signs counted from the period to the sub-period planet will give the house corresponding thereto, over which the effects will hold sway. Thus: Sun in Virgo and Venus as sub-period planet in Scorpio will show the third house affairs to be affected.

IX. The houses in the horoscope ruled by the planet whose

H

period, sub-period, or inter-period is considered must also be regarded as affecting.

N.B.—Rahu and Ketu (Dragon's Head and Tail) have no houses, but transmit the influence of the signs they are in, and of the planets to which they are conjoined. The Dragon's Head has affinity with the sign Scorpio, and the Dragon's Tail with the sign Taurus.

LOCALITY

In judging of the direction in which a person will travel, when such is shown in the horoscope, or again in the P., S.P., and I.P. effects, the following rule is usually taken:—The first house, with its complements twelfth and second, governs the *South*. The tenth, with ninth and eleventh, governs the *East*. The seventh, with fifth and eighth, governs the *West*; and the fourth, with third and fifth, governs the *North*

So in the signs: ♓ ♈ ♉ = South; ♊ ♋ ♌ = North; ♍ ♎ ♏ = West; and ♐ ♑ ♒ = East.

Therefore, Mars rules the East; the Moon rules the North; Venus governs the West; and Saturn the South.

Judgment is chiefly to be made from the *houses*, and next, but subserviently, from the signs occupied by the planets.

THE KALAMRITAM

The effects of periods and sub-periods, measured from the asterism held by the Moon at birth, and known as the *Dasâ Bukthi Phala*, are given variously in different Sanskrit and vernacular works current in India. But that which seems to be held most in esteem among the astrologers of Southern India is the *Kâlâmritam*, a small but explicit treatise upon the system of Parâshara. The following statement of the effects of the periods and sub-periods of life (measured according to the rules already given in this exposition) are taken from its pages. Like most treatises of its kind, the original takes the form of a *Kavita* or poem.

In making this translation, respect has been had to the customs of European life, and this fact alone draws it away from the domain of scholastic criticism which would only be concerned with a work of scholarly pretensions. The sense and import of the text have been chiefly considered, and the ideas embodied have been put into simple English. Thus, instead of enumerating the " gold, pearls, granaries, carriages, soft cushions, sunshades, rich cloths, and turbans " that certain periods and sub-periods will confer upon the native, it is quite English enough to state that his " wealth and property will increase." With these reservations, and bearing in mind what has been said in regard to the radical relations of the different planets, the following may be accepted as the general.

EFFECTS OF PERIODS AND SUB-PERIODS

PERIOD OF SUN

Sun's Sub-period.—There will be trouble among relatives, quarrelling and difficulties with superiors and those in office above the native. Anxieties, headaches, pains in the ears, some tendency to urinary or kidney affections. Sickness is to be expected between 12th April and 12th May (if included in this period) or again between 12th August and 12th September, *i.e.*, when the Sun is in *Mesham* (Aries) or *Simha* (Leo).

Moon's Sub-period.—Benefits from superiors or patrons, gain and success in business, new enterprises, troubles through women, pains in the eyes. (This will be augmented in the month of *Katakam*, 12th July to 12th August, and on those days when the Moon passes through Cancer.)

Mars' Sub-period.—Rheumatic or other sharp pains, feverishness, quarrelling, some danger of enteric fever, dysentery, or other wasting disease; troubles fall on the relatives; the native wastes his money, or may lose it by theft or carelessness. His efforts will not be very successful.

Dragon's Head Sub-period—A great many troubles and fears, crosses and changes, according to the condition and place of the Dragon's Head. Entire break-up of the family. The native will be away from his home at the time.

Jupiter's Sub-period.—Friends will benefit him. He will increase in knowledge and will give evidence of his powers in some form or other. Employment among people of good position;

association with people of high rank. Will overcome all obstacles, and, if married, may have the birth of a child.

Saturn's Sub-period.—Sickness of children, much anxiety, trouble on account of the wife or children. Enemies will be made. Loss of property. Bodily sickness; much unhappiness. He may leave his home or country. Accidental or enforced estrangement.

Mercury's Sub-period.—Even his own friends will be against him; many will become his enemies; and there will be cause for grave anxiety and fear. The health will be afflicted; children will cause trouble. He will be involved in disputes and trouble by a superior, a ruler or a judge. He will suffer some disgrace. Irregular meals and sleep. Many short journeys, wanderings, etc.; a predominance of mental and physical pain in this sub-period.

Dragon's Tail Sub-period.—Memory will decrease; the mind will be afflicted with troubles; there will be fainting or nervous exhaustion, and the mind will be filled with doubts and misgivings. He will go to a distant country or place. Owing to disputes he will live in a different house. Troubles among relatives and associates. There will be no benefits in this sub-period unless Dragon's Tail is well placed and in good aspect to the Sun.

Venus' Sub-period.—A possibility of marriage. Increase of prosperity. Some bodily sickness. The eyes may be affected. This will be cured. He will do good actions in this period, and will reap their reward.

MOON'S PERIOD

Sub-Periods

Moon.—Marriage frequently occurs during the rule of this sub-period, and is fortunate. The native does heroic actions and noble deeds. He inclines to public life. He will have changes of residence. All his wishes will be fulfilled. A child may be born to him.

Mars.—Useless quarrels and litigation; disputes of all kinds; rashness; impetuosity; loss of property; cutaneous affections;

danger of fire in the month from 12th April to 12th May.
Danger of disputes between husband and wife, or between
lovers, or in regard to marital affairs.

Dragon's Head.—Loss of money; danger of stirring up enemies,
sickness, according to the sign the Dragon's Head occupies.
Anxiety on account of friends; enmity of superiors or those
in power. Anxiety or trouble through the wife or lover.

Jupiter.—Property will increase; food and comforts will be plentiful;
there will be prosperity. Benefits from persons in good
position, masters, governors, the father, or the ruling powers.
The native may beget a child at this time.

Saturn.—The partner (wife or lover) may die or be separated from
the native. Much mental trouble. Loss of wealth, or a
state of impecuniosity. Dishonour or slander will be experienced. Loss of friends; some ill health.

Mercury.—Disputes will cease. The native will have pleasure
through children or love affairs. Wealth will increase. All
intentions will be accomplished. In the month of Virgo,
12th September to 12th October, he will give evidence of some
intellectual achievements.

Dragon's Tail.—There will be sickness of a feverish nature, or hurt
by fire. The body will be subject to some eruptions or swellings.
The eyes may suffer. The mind will be filled with cares, and the
native will experience some trouble. He may incur some
public criticism or displeasure; may meet with dishonour or
be the means of his own undoing.

Venus.—According to the position of Venus in regard to the Moon
and rising sign, there will be sickness, pain, loss of property,
enmity, and loss through enemies—or, the reverse of this.

Sun.—Biliousness and feverish complaints. Some change in the
bodily appearance. Severe pain in the eyes. Success, or the
reverse, according to the relative positions of the Sun and
Moon.

MARS' PERIOD

Sub-Periods

Mars.—Danger of hurts according to the sign held by Mars. In
the month of Aries or Scorpio (if included) he will have trouble

with superiors, and some anxiety through strangers, foreigners or people abroad, and through Mars men generally. In the month of Cancer, *i.e.*, 12th July to 12th August, there will be danger of open violence.

Dragon's Head.—He will suffer from poisonous complaints, according to the sign held by Dragon's Head. Loss of relatives. Danger of scrofulous or skin affections. Change of residence. Some severe form of cutaneous disease.

Jupiter.—Loss of property. Enmity of superiors. Enemies will be created in the place of residence and beyond it. But the end of this sub-period will be more fortunate; and favours from superiors and persons in position may be looked for.

Saturn.—Quarrels, disputes, litigation, loss of property, cutaneous affections; loss of office or position; much anxiety.

Mercury.—He will be inclined to marry at this time, and if so will be fortunately wedded. Knowledge and the fruits of knowledge will increase. Wealth will increase. Existing evils in body and mind will disappear. But in the month of Gemini or Virgo (if included) he will be subject to slander, or may be poisoned in his body by hurts from animals, or insects, or by abrasions.

Dragon's Tail.—Family disputes; troubles with his own kindred. Disease. Poisonous complaints threaten him; trouble through women. Many enemies.

Venus.—He will acquire property or gain money. Will have domestic happiness and successful love affairs. He may feel more inclination to religious observances and festivities. His associations are beneficial. He is influenced by churchmen or sectaries. Skin eruptions, boils, or sloughings may be expected. Travelling will give him pleasure at this time.

Sun.—Anxieties. Fever or other inflammatory affection. Danger of fire. Troubles through persons in position. The wife is likely to be afflicted with disease. He will have many enemies.

Moon.—Profit; gain of property, and the acquision of valuables. There is likely to be renovation of the house or improvements made therein. But in the end of this sub-period there will be a decrease of all these good effects.

DRAGON'S HEAD PERIOD

Sub-Periods

Dragon's Head.—Death of the king, superiors, senior partner, master, or the head of the family. Mental anxiety. Danger of blood poisoning. The wife is afflicted. The native will have some removals. All sorts of quarrels and scandals will take place in regard to him.

Jupiter.—Pleasure will increase. Gain through nobles or persons of position. Benefits and comforts through his superiors. All his efforts will succeed. He will be married, engaged, or if married will be re-united to his wife.

Saturn.—Enemies will arise. There will be cause for mental anxiety. Disease will appear. Incessant disputes and contests. Rheumatism, biliousness, etc., will attack his health. Trouble will prevail.

Mercury.—Of the thirty months ruled by this sub-period planet, the first eighteen will be very busy. The native will thrive well. He will be seriously inclined, and will gain money. In the last twelve he will experience enmity through his own actions.

Dragon's Tail.—Danger of physical hurts and poison. Ill health to his children. Some swellings in the body. Troubles on account of the wife. Danger from superiors.

Venus.—Acquisition of money and other advantages. Friendly alliances will be formed. The wife will be fortunate and a source of happiness. Benefits from superiors or those in office above the native. Some trouble will happen through deceit being practised upon the native. False friends will come to light in their true colours. But all evils will pass away.

Sun.—Quarrels on account of the family. Benefits from persons in good position. Fear and suspicion will arise in connection with the wife, children, and relatives. Changes of position or residence will occur.

Moon.—Loss of relatives. Loss of money through the wife. Pains in the limbs. He will leave his native place or his present residence. There will be danger of personal hurts. The health will be unstable.

Mars.—Danger of fire, burns, and other physical hurts. Dangers to the person through the malice of enemies. A tendency to lax or dissolute habits will show itself. Danger of loss by theft. Disputes and mental anxiety.

JUPITER'S PERIOD

Sub-Periods

Jupiter.—Much prosperity. Fame, good position. Property will increase. There will be domestic plenty and happiness. Benefits from the employment or occupation. Lawyers, priests (clergy), and superiors favour the native.

Saturn.—There will be an increase of wealth and property. After this, pains in the body will be experienced, rheumatic pains in the limbs. Troubles through the wife or partner. A falling off of profit and credit in the place of abode. But these troubles will pass away.

Mercury.—Gain by knowledge in the fine arts. Birth of a well-favoured child, in the case of married people. Wealth increases and advantages from superiors fall to the native.

Dragon's Tail.—The partner, although strong, will die. The native will change his place of abode. He will be separated from his relatives and friends, and he may leave his business or forsake his occupation because of all this.

Venus.—There will be a reunion in the family. Good success in the profession or business. He will gain land in the month of Taurus or Libra (*i.e.*, when the Sun is in these signs). Much enjoyment. Relatives are friendly, and he will live in peace.

Sun.—Gain. Good actions are performed or the fruits of past good action come to the native at this time. Loss of bodily strength may be experienced. Some disease will appear according to the sign held by the Sun. But these evils will not endure.

Moon.—Prosperity increases. He gains honour and fame. Acquires property. Benefits through children and happiness to them. All good efforts in the past will collectively render their fruits to the native.

Mars.—Annoyances and troubles of various kinds. Danger of loss by theft. Loss of a friend, elder brother, or parent.

Some inflammatory disease arises in the system. He will move from his present place, and will fail to accomplish his engagements.

Dragon's Head.—Relatives give trouble. Small quarrels are numerous. There is some loss of property. Troubles to the wife or through her. The native becomes the object of deception, which occasions some loss or trouble.

SATURN'S PERIOD

Sub-Periods

Saturn.—Disease appears, and the body languishes. Loss of children and money is to be feared. Serious enmities arise; relatives cause disputes. Troubles come upon the native through his relatives.

Mercury.—Knowledge in some particular direction will increase. The native will be wise and discreet. Children will prosper. Relatives will meet with success. The native will prosper and receive favours and approbation from superiors.

Dragon's Tail.—Rheumatism in the right leg. Some biliousness, or sickness. Danger of poisonous elements in the system. Danger from the native's own son. Loss of money. Contentions and quarrels. A bad time generally.

Venus.—Attentions and favours from others. Gifts. Profit in business. Increase in the family circle by a birth or marriage. Victory over enemies and the overcoming of obstacles.

Sun.—Danger of blood-poisoning. Hæmorrhage of the generative system. Chronic poisoning. Intestinal swellings. Affections of the eyes. Even healthy children and wives come to the sick-bed under this influence. The body is full of pains and disorders. Danger of death.

Moon.—Trouble and sickness fall upon the native. There are family disputes. Losses both of money and property. The native will be reduced to great need, and will sell or mortgage his property, and will recover it only after a lapse of time.

Mars.—Some disgrace will fall upon the family. Very serious enmity and strife will ensue. Much blame will attach to the native. He will go from one place to another, and will lead an unsettled life at this period. He will have many enemies; will be deprived of money by fraud or theft. He will leave his home and kindred.

Dragon's Head.—Loss of money. Will be in danger of physical hurts. Various physical troubles will ensue. Even foreigners will become his enemies. Troubles increase under this influence.

Jupiter.—He will find favour and refuge with good men or clergy. Will have some increase in his bodily comforts. Through the aid of superiors he will accomplish his intentions. He will abide happily in one place, and have an increase of family.

MERCURY'S PERIOD

Sub-Periods

Mercury.—The native gains a brother or sister, either by marriage or birth. An increase of the family is shown. He gains in business, and receives advancement. Learning will attract his attention and engage his efforts.

Dragon's Tail.—The native leaves his place of abode. He experiences some sickness, loss of property, misfortune to his relatives, etc. He has some trouble through doctors, and danger in regard to his medicine. Mental anxiety.

Venus.—The native has good children born to him. Happiness in the married state. Relatives prosper. Trade increases. Knowledge is gained. He returns from a long journey. If not already married, he will form an alliance at this time.

Sun.—Danger of fire. Anxieties. Sickness of the wife. Enemies give trouble. Many obstacles in all his affairs. Troubles through superiors.

Moon.—Loss of health. Some swellings or hurts in the limbs. Quarrels and troubles through females. Many difficulties will arise. Will have troubles through women, and will consequently try to avoid them.

Mars.—Some danger of jaundice or bilious fever. Affections of the blood. Neuralgic pains and severe headaches. Neighbours cause troubles. Sickness due to trouble; wounds or hurts. This period will end in quarrels.

Dragon's Head.—The native is removed from his present position.

Fear and danger through foreigners. Disputes concerning property, in which the native loses. Evil dreams, headaches, sickness, and loss of appetite.

Jupiter.—Will have a fair degree of happiness; some renown or esteem; good credit; advancement through superiors. Birth of a child, or marriage (if not already married). Good fortune generally.

Saturn.—Bad fortune. He becomes a stranger to success and happiness. Severe reversal. Enmity is incurred. Some disease or pain in the part governed by Saturn. Relatives suffer a downfall or some disgrace. The native suffers in consequence. The mind is filled with gloomy forebodings and grief.

DRAGON'S TAIL PERIOD

Sub-Periods

Dragon's Tail.—The native has some mental troubles. Will be separated from his relatives. Will be subject to some estrangement, restraint, or detention.

Venus.—A child may be born to the native. Wealth increases. All his efforts are crowned with success. In the end of this period, however, he will have sickness. His wife also will be ill. But these troubles will pass away.

Sun.—He will have a long journey, and will return. Some disease or sickness will disfigure the body. Anxiety on account of the partner in marriage.

Moon.—Disputes on account of the actions of the other sex. Trouble through the children or on account of them. Gain and financial success. All troubles will vanish.

Mars.—Obstacles bar the path of progress. There is cause for fear and anxiety. Disputes and contests of different kinds. Enemies arise. Danger of destruction through one of the opposite sex. Danger of fire, fever, or an operation.

Dragon's Head.—Danger of blood-poisoning will come and go. Females will suffer. The native is in danger of ruin. Loss of property, fame and honour is to be feared.

Jupiter.—Profitable transactions. Association with people of good position. Danger of poison. The wife becomes the cause

of pleasure. If unmarried, his love affairs progress well.
Wealth will increase considerably.

Saturn.—All properties will be in danger of ruin. The native will
suffer heavy losses in different ways. He will change his place
of abode. Some cutaneous disease is to be feared. Anxiety
owing to the sickness of the wife or partner.

Mercury.—Changes will occur. Danger from relatives. Anxiety
on account of children. His plans will not succeed.

VENUS' PERIOD

Sub-Periods

Venus.—Financial success. Good servants and the accessories of
good fortune. Many pleasures. Money will be plentiful,
but in the month of Libra (12th October to 12th November)
there will be cause for sorrow.

Sun.—He will have cause for anxiety and fear. Prosperity will
decline. This will be caused by superiors. There will be
disputes with the wife or partner, with children and others.
Family and domestic troubles. Even in sacred places or in
regard to spiritual matters he will be involved in disputes and
quarrels.

Moon.—He will accomplish all his intentions. There will be
troubles through the wife, but they will pass away, and domestic
happiness will ensue in full measure.

Mars.—Property will increase. Through the influence of women
he will not perform his duties and will become lax in his efforts,
neglecting his duties. His mind will be upon earthly things,
bent upon pleasure and neglecting religion. Some affection
of the eyes and skin will appear and pass away.

Dragon's Head.—" Like a perfect *mouni* (one under a vow of
silence), he will perform Tapas (religious austerity). Fore-
seeing quarrels among his people or relations, and between
them and himself, by a very rare medicine he will withdraw
himself from them, and become as distant as possible."
This is a difficult passage to render into astrologic parlance.
It may mean that he will retire (if he be wise) from his family
or circle of acquaintances and seclude himself. In some

cases it may have a more sinister meaning. In all cases, an entire change of surroundings may be expected to happen.

Jupiter.—Means of livelihood will increase. Profit through the occupation. Many benefits through superiors or employers, or persons ruled by Jupiter. He will gain fame, but will experience some anxiety in the end.

Saturn.—Affections of the excretory system, piles, etc. Sciatica or rheumatic pains in the legs and hands. Disease in the system. Danger of the eyesight being affected at this time. Distaste for food, loss of appetite. The physical condition of the native will be in a very poor way.

Mercury.—Pleasure through the wife and children. Increase of wealth. Gain of knowledge in the arts and sciences. Successful period.

Dragon's Tail.—Troubles in love affairs or through the wife. Danger from quadrupeds. The partner will be ill. Someone in the house will come by an accident and may have blood-poisoning, but it will be cured.

(*End of Extract from " Kâlâmritam."*)

NOTE UPON THE ABOVE EXTRACT

In going through the various effects of the periods and sub-periods in our own life and others, we have been not only convinced of the truth of the Hindu system of *Das'â bukthi phala*, but actually surprised at the literal exactness of the predictions. If the inter-periods of the different sub-periods be taken into account, the above " effects " will apply equally well to those also, by counting the sub-period planet as a *period* planet, and the inter-period planet as a *sub-period* planet. In this way the prognostics serve for every period of life, from the greatest to the least, allowance being made for the relations of the significators in the minor periods. In all cases the effects due to the " period " planet are of prior importance, the sub-periods and inter-periods following in subsidiary order.

APPENDIX

APPENDIX

Containing Tables of Lunations, Proportional Logarithms, Neptune's Approximate Longitudes, Eclipses Past and Future; Tables of Houses for Central England, etc.

LUNATIONS

Years of the Metonic Cycle						Jan. ♑	Feb. ♒	Mar. ♓	April ♈	May ♉	June ♊	July ♋	Aug. ♌	Sept. ♍	Oct. ♎	Nov. ♏	Dec. ♐
1857	1876*	1895	1914	1933	1952*	6	5	5	5	4	3	1 29	27	25	25	24	24
1858	1877	1896*	1915	1934	1953	24	24	24	23	21	20	19	17	16	15	14	13
1859	1878	1897	1916*	1935	1954	14	13	13	12	11	10	8	6	5	3	3	3
1860*	1879	1898	1917	1936*	1955	3	3	2	2	1 28	27	25	24	22	22	22	22
1861	1880*	1899	1918	1937	1956*	21	22	21	21	19	18	15	13	12	11	10	11
1862	1881	1900	1919	1938	1957	11	11	11	10	9	7	5	3	1 29	29	29	29
1863	1882	1901	1920*	1939	1958	29	30	29	28	27	25	23	22	19	18	18	18
1864*	1883	1902	1921	1940*	1959	18	18	18	18	16	15	14	12	10	8	7	7
1865	1884*	1903	1922	1941	1960*	7	7	7	7	6	5	3	1 29	28	26	26	25
1866	1885	1904*	1923	1942	1961	26	25	26	24	24	22	20	19	17	16	15	15
1867	1886	1905	1924*	1943	1962	15	15	15	14	13	12	9	8	6	5	5	5
1868*	1887	1906	1925	1944*	1963	4	4	4	3	3	1 29	27	26	24	24	23	23
1869	1888*	1907	1926	1945	1964*	24	23	23	22	20	19	17	15	14	12	12	12
1870	1889	1908*	1927	1946	1965	12	12	12	12	10	9	7	4	3	1	1	0
1871	1890	1909	1928*	1947	1966	1	1	1	1	0 28	26	25	22	21	20	20	19
1872*	1891	1910	1929	1948*	1967	20	20	20	19	18	17	15	13	10	9	9	8
1873	1892*	1911	1930	1949	1968*	8	9	9	8	8	6	4	3	0 29	27	27	27
1874	1893	1912*	1931	1950	1969	28	27	27	26	25	23	22	20	19	17	17	16
1875	1894	1913	1932*	1951	1970	16	17	16	16	15	14	11	10	8	7	6	6

The years marked with an asterisk (*) are Leap years.

Note.—A lunation falling in one to ten degrees of a sign actually takes place in the last ten days of the month preceding that to which it is referred in this table. But, as its influence extends to the following month, the reason for this departure will be obvious. Where two lunations fall in one sign they are put together under that sign, as under ♉, ♊, ♋, ♌, and ♍.

PROPORTIONAL LOGARITHMS FOR FINDING THE PLANETS' PLACES

Min.	0	1	2	3	4	5	6	7	8	9	10	11	12	13	14	15	Min.
0	3.1584	1.3802	1.0792	9031	7781	6812	6021	5351	4771	4260	3802	3388	3010	2663	2341	2041	0
1	3.1584	1.3730	1.0756	9007	7763	6798	6009	5341	4762	4252	3795	3382	3004	2657	2336	2036	1
2	2.8573	1.3660	1.0720	8983	7745	6784	5997	5330	4753	4244	3798	3375	2998	2652	2330	2032	2
3	2.6812	1.3590	1.0685	8959	7728	6769	5985	5320	4744	4236	3730	3368	2992	2646	2325	2027	3
4	2.5563	1.3522	1.0649	8935	7710	6755	5973	5310	4735	4228	3773	3362	2986	2640	2320	2022	4
5	2.4594	1.3454	1.0614	8912	7692	6741	5961	5300	4726	4220	3766	3355	2980	2635	2315	2017	5
6	2.3802	1.3388	1.0580	8888	7674	6726	5949	5289	4717	4212	3759	3349	2974	2629	2310	2012	6
7	2.3133	1.3323	1.0546	8865	7657	6712	5937	5279	4708	4204	3752	3342	2968	2624	2305	2008	7
8	2.2553	1.3258	1.0511	8842	7639	6698	5925	5269	4699	4196	3745	3336	2962	2618	2300	2003	8
9	2.2041	1.3195	1.0478	8819	7622	6684	5913	5259	4690	4188	3737	3329	2956	2613	2295	1998	9
10	2.1584	1.3133	1.0444	8796	7604	6670	5902	5249	4682	4180	3730	3323	2950	2607	2289	1993	10
11	2.1170	1.3071	1.0411	8773	7587	6656	5890	5239	4673	4172	3723	3316	2944	2602	2284	1988	11
12	2.0792	1.3010	1.0378	8751	7570	6642	5878	5229	4664	4164	3716	3310	2938	2596	2279	1984	12
13	2.0444	1.2950	1.0345	8728	7552	6628	5866	5219	4655	4156	3709	3303	2933	2591	2274	1979	13
14	2.0122	1.2891	1.0313	8706	7535	6614	5855	5209	4646	4148	3702	3297	2927	2585	2269	1974	14
15	1.9823	1.2833	1.0280	8683	7518	6600	5843	5199	4638	4141	3695	3291	2921	2580	2264	1969	15
16	1.9542	1.2775	1.0248	8661	7501	6587	5832	5189	4629	4133	3688	3284	2915	2574	2259	1965	16
17	1.9279	1.2719	1.0216	8639	7484	6573	5820	5179	4620	4125	3681	3278	2909	2569	2254	1960	17
18	1.9031	1.2663	1.0185	8617	7467	6559	5809	5169	4611	4117	3674	3271	2903	2564	2249	1955	18
19	1.8796	1.2607	1.0153	8595	7451	6546	5797	5159	4603	4109	3667	3265	2897	2558	2244	1950	19
20	1.8573	1.2553	1.0122	8573	7434	6532	5786	5149	4594	4102	3660	3258	2891	2553	2239	1946	20
21	1.8361	1.2499	1.0091	8552	7417	6519	5774	5139	4585	4094	3653	3252	2885	2547	2234	1941	21
22	1.8159	1.2445	1.0061	8530	7401	6505	5763	5129	4577	4086	3646	3246	2880	2542	2229	1936	22
23	1.7966	1.2393	1.0030	8509	7384	6492	5752	5120	4568	4079	3639	3239	2874	2536	2223	1932	23
24	1.7781	1.2341	1.0000	8487	7368	6478	5740	5110	4559	4071	3632	3233	2868	2531	2218	1927	24
25	1.7604	1.2289	0.9970	8466	7351	6465	5729	5100	4551	4063	3625	3227	2862	2526	2213	1922	25
26	1.7434	1.2239	0.9940	8445	7335	6451	5718	5090	4542	4055	3618	3220	2856	2520	2208	1917	26
27	1.7270	1.2188	0.9910	8424	7318	6438	5706	5081	4534	4048	3611	3214	2850	2515	2203	1913	27
28	1.7112	1.2139	0.9881	8403	7302	6425	5695	5071	4525	4040	3604	3208	2845	2509	2198	1908	28
29	1.6960	1.2090	0.9852	8382	7286	6412	5684	5061	4516	4032	3597	3201	2839	2504	2193	1903	29
30	1.6812	1.2041	0.9823	8361	7270	6398	5673	5051	4508	4025	3590	3195	2833	2499	2188	1899	30
31	1.6670	1.1993	0.9794	8341	7254	6385	5662	5042	4499	4017	3583	3189	2827	2493	2183	1894	31
32	1.6532	1.1946	0.9765	8320	7238	6372	5651	5032	4491	4010	3576	3183	2821	2488	2178	1889	32
33	1.6398	1.1899	0.9737	8300	7222	6359	5640	5023	4482	4002	3570	3176	2816	2483	2173	1885	33
34	1.6269	1.1852	0.9708	8279	7206	6346	5629	5013	4474	3994	3563	3170	2810	2477	2168	1880	34
35	1.6143	1.1806	0.9680	8259	7190	6333	5618	5003	4466	3987	3556	3164	2804	2472	2164	1875	35
36	1.6021	1.1761	0.9652	8239	7174	6320	5607	4994	4457	3979	3549	3157	2798	2467	2159	1871	36
37	1.5902	1.1716	0.9625	8219	7159	6307	5596	4984	4449	3972	3542	3151	2793	2461	2154	1866	37
38	1.5786	1.1671	0.9597	8199	7143	6294	5585	4975	4440	3964	3535	3145	2787	2456	2149	1862	38
39	1.5673	1.1627	0.9570	8179	7128	6282	5574	4965	4432	3957	3529	3139	2781	2451	2144	1857	39
40	1.5563	1.1584	0.9542	8159	7112	6269	5563	4956	4424	3949	3522	3133	2775	2445	2139	1852	40
41	1.5456	1.1540	0.9515	8140	7097	6256	5552	4947	4415	3942	3515	3126	2770	2440	2134	1848	41
42	1.5351	1.1498	0.9488	8120	7081	6243	5541	4937	4407	3934	3508	3120	2764	2435	2129	1843	42
43	1.5249	1.1455	0.9462	8101	7066	6231	5531	4928	4399	3927	3501	3114	2758	2430	2124	1838	43
44	1.5149	1.1413	0.9435	8081	7050	6218	5520	4918	4390	3919	3495	3108	2753	2424	2119	1834	44
45	1.5051	1.1372	0.9409	8062	7035	6205	5509	4909	4382	3912	3488	3102	2747	2419	2114	1829	45
46	1.4956	1.1331	0.9383	8043	7020	6193	5498	4900	4374	3905	3481	3096	2741	2414	2109	1825	46
47	1.4863	1.1290	0.9356	8023	7005	6180	5488	4890	4365	3897	3475	3089	2736	2409	2104	1820	47
48	1.4771	1.1249	0.9330	8004	6990	6168	5477	4881	4357	3890	3468	3083	2730	2403	2099	1816	48
49	1.4682	1.1209	0.9305	7985	6975	6155	5466	4872	4349	3882	3461	3077	2724	2398	2095	1811	49
50	1.4594	1.1170	0.9279	7966	6960	6143	5456	4863	4341	3875	3454	3071	2719	2393	2090	1806	50
51	1.4508	1.1130	0.9254	7947	6945	6131	5445	4853	4333	3868	3448	3065	2713	2388	2085	1802	51
52	1.4424	1.1091	0.9228	7929	6930	6118	5435	4844	4324	3860	3441	3059	2707	2382	2080	1797	52
53	1.4341	1.1053	0.9203	7910	6915	6106	5424	4835	4316	3853	3434	3053	2702	2377	2075	1793	53
54	1.4260	1.1015	0.9178	7891	6900	6094	5414	4826	4308	3846	3428	3047	2696	2372	2070	1788	54
55	1.4180	1.0977	0.9153	7873	6885	6081	5403	4817	4300	3838	3421	3041	2691	2367	2065	1784	55
56	1.4102	1.0939	0.9128	7854	6871	6069	5393	4808	4292	3831	3415	3034	2685	2362	2061	1779	56
57	1.4025	1.0902	0.9104	7836	6856	6057	5382	4798	4284	3824	3408	3028	2679	2356	2056	1774	57
58	1.3949	1.0865	0.9079	7818	6841	6045	5372	4789	4276	3817	3401	3022	2674	2351	2051	1770	58
59	1.3875	1.0828	0.9055	7800	6827	6033	5361	4780	4268	3809	3395	3016	2668	2346	2046	1765	59
	0	1	2	3	4	5	6	7	8	9	10	11	12	13	14	15	

The following formula should be used to obtain the correct position of the Sun, Moon and the planets for any time of day apart from noon.

RULE.—Add proportional log. of planet's daily motion to log. of time from noon, and the sum will be the log. of the motion required. Add this to planet's place at noon, if time be p.m., but subtract if a.m. and the sum will be planet's true place. If Retrograde, subtract for p.m., but add for a.m.

TABLE OF BRITISH SUMMER TIMES

(COMMENCING FROM 1916)

1916	May	21st,	2.0 a.m.	G.M.T.	to	October	1st	3.0 a.m.	B.S.T.
1917	April	8th	„	„	„	September	17th	„	„
1918	March	24th	„	„	„	September	30th	„	„
1919	March	30th	„	„	„	October	5th	„	„
1920	March	28th,	„	„	„	October	25th,	„	„
1921	April	3rd,	„	„	„	October	3rd,	„	„
1922	March	26th,	„	„	„	October	8th,	„	„
1923	April	28th,	„	„	„	September	16th,	„	„
1924	April	13th,	„	„	„	September	21st,	„	„
1925	April	19th	„	„	„	October	4th,	„	„
1926	April	18th,	„	„	„	October	3rd,	„	„
1927	April	10th,	„	„	„	October	2nd,	„	„
1928	April	22nd,	„	„	„	October	7th,	„	„
1929	April	21st,	„	„	„	October	6th,	„	„
1930	April	13th,	„	„	„	October	5th,	„	„
1931	April	19th,	„	„	„	October	4th,	„	„
1932	April	17th,	„	„	„	October	2nd,	„	„
1933	April	9th,	„	„	„	October	8th,	„	„
1934	April	22nd,	„	„	„	October	7th,	,	„
1935	April	14th,	„	„	„	October	6th,	„	„
1936	April	19th,	„	„	„	October	4th,	„	„
1937	April	18th,	„	„	„	October	3rd,	„	„
1938	April	10th,	„	„	„	October	2nd,	„	„
1939	April	16th,	„	„	„	November	19th,	„	„
1940	February	25th,	„	„	„	December	31st,	„	„
1941	January	1st,	„	„	„	December	31st,	„	„

(But Double Summer Time, 2 hrs. advance from May 4th to August 10th)

1942 January 1st, 2.0 a.m. G.M.T. to December 31st, 3.0 a.m. B.S.T.
(But Double Summer Time April 5th to August 9th)

1943 January 1st, 2.0 a.m. G.M.T. to December 31st, 3.0 a.m. B.S.T.
(But Double Summer Time April 4th to August 15th)

1944 January 1st, 2.0 a.m. G.M.T. to December 31st, 3.0 a.m. B.S.T.
(But Double Summer Time April 2nd to September 17th)

1945 January 1st 2.0 a.m. G.M.T. to December 31st, 3.0 a.m. B.S.T.
(But Double Summer Time April 2nd to July 15th)

1946 April 14th, 2.0 a.m. G.M.T. to October 6th, 3.0 a.m. B.S.T.
(Double Summer Time discontinued)

1947 March 16th, 2.0 a.m. G.M.T. to November 2nd, 3.0 a.m. B.S.T.
(But Double Summer Time April 13th to August 10th)

1948 March 14th, 2.0 a.m. G.M.T. to October 31st, 3.0 a.m. B.S.T.
(Double Summer Time discontinued)

TABLE OF BRITISH SUMMER TIMES (Continued)

1949 April	3rd, 2.0 a.m. G.M.T. to				October	30th, 3.0 a.m. B.S.T.			
1950 April	16th,	,,	,,	,,	October	22nd,	,,	,,	
1951 April	15th,	,,	,,	,,	October	21st,	,,	,,	
1952 April	20th,	,,	,,	,,	October	26th,	,,	,,	
1953 April	19th,	,,	,,	,,	October	4th,	,,	,,	
1954 April	11th,	,,	,,	,,	October	3rd,	,,	,,	
1955 April	17th,	,,	,,	,,	October	2nd,	,,	,,	
1956 April	22nd,	,,	,,	,,	October	7th,	,,	,,	
1957 April	14th,	,,	,,	,,	October	6th,	,,	,,	
1958 April	20th	,,	,,	,,	October	5th,	,,	,,	
1959 April	19th,	,,	,,	,,	October	4th,	,,	,,	
1960 April	10th,	,,	,,	,,	October	2nd,	,,	,,	
1961 April	2nd,	,,	,,	,,	October	22nd,	,,	,,	
1962 April	15th,	,,	,,	,,	October	7th,	,,	,,	

(For 1962 liable to be extended by Order in Council)

TABLE OF ECLIPSES 1856 to 1964

	Y	M	D	Y	M	D	Y	M	D	Y	M	D	Y	M	D		Y	M	D
●	1856	4	5	1874	4	16	1892	4	26	1910	5	9	1928	5	19	●	1946	5	30
☽		4	20		5	1		5	11		5	22		6	2	●		6	14
●		9	29		10	10		10	20		10	1		10	12	●		6	29
●		10	14		10	25		11	4		11	15		11	26	●		11	23
●	1857	3	25	1875	4	6	1893	4	16	1911	4	28	1929	5	9	☽	1947	5	20
☽		9	18		9	29		10	10		10	20		10	31	●		6	3
☽	1858	2	27	1876	3	10	1894	3	21	1912	4	1	1930	4	12	●		11	12
☽		3	15		3	25		4	5		4	16		4	27	●	1948	4	23
●		8	24		9	3		9	14		9	25		10	6	☽		5	9
☽		9	7		9	17		9	29		10	10		10	21	●	1949	11	1
●	1859	2	17	1877	2	27	1895	3	10	1913	3	21	1931	4	1	●		4	13
●		3	4		3	15		3	25		4	5		4	16	☽		4	28
●		7	29		8	8		8	19		8	30		9	25	☽		10	7
☽		8	13		8	23		9	3		9	14		9	25	●		10	21
●		8	28		9	7		9	17		9	28		10	9	●	1950	3	18
●	1860	1	22	1878	2	2	1896	2	13	1914	2	24	1932	3	7	☽		4	2
☽		2	7		2	17		2	27		3	9		3	20	●		9	12
☽		7	18		7	29		8	9		8	21		8	31	●		9	26
●		8	1		8	12		8	23		9	3		9	14	●	1951	3	7
●	1861	1	11	1879	1	22	1897	2	2	1915	2	13	1933	2	24	●		9	1
☽		7	8		7	19		7	29		8	9		8	20	☽	1952	2	11
●		12	17		12	28	1898	1	8	1916	1	18	1934	1	29	●		8	25
●		12	31	1880	1	11		1	22		2	3		2	14	☽		8	20
☽	1862	6	12		6	12		7	3		7	14		7	25	●	1953	2	14
●		6	27		6	27		7	18		7	29		8	9	●		7	11
●		11	21		12	2		12	13		12	23	1935	1	3	●		8	5
●		12	6		12	16		12	27	1917	1	7		1	18	☽	1954	1	14
●		12	21		12	31	1899	1	11		1	22		2	2	☽		6	29
●	1863	5	17	1881	5	27		6	7		6	18		6	29	●		7	14
☽		6	1		6	1		6	22		7	3		7	14	●		12	9
☽		11	11		11	11		12	2		12	13		12	24	☽	1955	6	20
☽		11	25		12	5		12	16		12	27	1936	1	7	●		11	29
●	1864	5	6	1882	5	17	1900	5	28	1918	6	8		6	19	☽	1956	5	24
☽		10	30		11	11		11	21		12	2		12	13	●		6	8
●	1865	4	11	1883	4	22	1901	5	3	1919	5	14	1937	5	25	☽		11	18
☽		4	25		5	6		5	18		5	29		6	8	●		12	2
☽		10	4		10	16		10	26		11	6		11	17	☽	1957	4	29
●		10	19		10	30		11	11		11	21		12	2	☽		5	13
●	1866	3	16	1884	3	27	1902	4	6	1920	4	17	1938	4	28	●		10	23
☽		3	31		4	10		4	21		5	1		5	12	●		11	7
●		4	15		4	25		5	6		5	17		5	28	●	1958	4	19
☽		9	24		10	4		10	15		10	26		11	6	☽		5	3
●		10	8		10	19		10	30		11	10		11	21	●		10	12
●	1867	3	6	1885	3	16	1903	3	27	1921	4	6	1939	4	17	☽	1959	4	8
●		3	20		3	30		4	10		4	21		5	2	●		4	24
●		8	29		9	8		9	21		10	1		10	11	●		10	2
●		9	13		9	24		10	4		10	15		10	26	●	1960	3	13
☽	1868	2	23	1886	3	6	1904	3	16	1922	3	27	1940	4	7	☽		3	27
●		8	18		8	29		9	9		9	21		9	30	☽		9	5
●	1869	1	28	1887	2	8	1905	2	18	1923	3	1	1941	3	12	●		9	20
☽		2	11		2	22		3	5		3	16		3	27	●	1961	2	15
☽		7	23		8	3		8	14		8	25		9	5	●		3	2
☽		8	7		8	19		8	30		9	10		9	20	☽		8	11
●	1870	1	17	1888	1	28	1906	2	8	1924	2	19	1942	2	30	☽		8	26
☽		1	31		2	11		2	22		3	3		3	16	☽	1962	2	5
●		6	28		7	7		7	20		7	31		8	11	●		2	19
●		7	12		7	23		8	2		8	14		8	25	☽		7	17
●		7	28		8	7		8	18		8	29		9	9	●		7	31
●		12	22	1889	1	1	1907	1	14	1925	1	24	1943	2	3	●		8	14
☽	1871	1	6		1	17		1	28		7	9		2	19	☽	1963	1	25
☽		6	17		6	17		7	23		7	23		7	31	●		7	6
☽		7	2		7	12		7	12		8	8		8	14	●		7	20
●		12	12		12	22	1908	1	3	1926	1	14	1944	1	23	☽		12	30
●	1872	6	6	1890	6	6		6	28		7	9		7	20	☽	1964	1	14
☽		11	15		11	26		12	7		7	18		12	29	●		6	10
☽		11	30		12	12		12	22	1927	12	22	1945	1	13				
☽	1873	5	12	1891	5	23	1909	6	3		6	13		6	24				
☽		5	26		6	6		6	6		7	9		7	9				
☽		11	4		11	15		11	17		12	7		12	18				
●		11	20		12	1		12	12		12	23	1946	1	3				

TABLES OF HOUSES FOR LIVERPOOL, Latitude 53° 25' N.

Upper table — Block 1

Sidereal Time (H. M. S.)	10 ♈	11 ♉	12 ♊	Ascen ♋ °	Ascen '	2 ♌	3 ♍
0 0 0	0	9	24	28	12	14	3
0 3 40	1	10	25	28	51	14	4
0 7 20	2	12	25	29	30	15	4
0 11 0	3	13	26	0♋	9	16	5
0 14 41	4	14	27	0	48	17	6
0 18 21	5	15	28	1	27	17	7
0 22 2	6	16	29	2	6	18	8
0 25 42	7	17	♋	2	44	19	9
0 29 23	8	18	1	3	22	19	10
0 33 4	9	19	1	4	1	20	10
0 36 45	10	20	2	4	39	21	11
0 40 26	11	21	3	5	18	22	12
0 44 8	12	22	4	5	56	22	13
0 47 50	13	23	5	6	34	23	14
0 51 32	14	24	6	7	13	24	14
0 55 14	15	25	6	7	51	24	15
0 58 57	16	26	7	8	30	25	16
1 2 40	17	27	8	9	8	26	17
1 6 23	18	28	9	9	47	26	18
1 10 7	19	29	10	10	25	27	19
1 13 51	20	♋	11	11	4	28	19
1 17 35	21	1	11	11	43	28	20
1 21 20	22	2	12	12	21	29	21
1 25 6	23	3	13	13	0	♍	22
1 28 52	24	4	14	13	39	1	23
1 32 38	25	5	15	14	17	1	24
1 36 25	26	6	15	14	56	2	25
1 40 12	27	7	16	15	35	3	25
1 44 0	28	8	17	16	14	3	26
1 47 48	29	9	18	16	58	4	27
1 51 37	30	10	18	17	32	5	28

Upper table — Block 2

Sidereal Time (H. M. S.)	10 ♉	11 ♊	12 ♋	Ascen ♌ °	Ascen '	2 ♍	3 ♍
1 51 37	0	10	18	17	32	5	28
1 55 27	1	11	19	18	11	6	29
1 59 17	2	12	20	18	51	6	♎
2 3 8	3	13	21	19	30	7	1
2 6 59	4	14	22	20	9	8	2
2 10 51	5	15	22	20	49	9	2
2 14 44	6	16	23	21	28	9	3
2 18 37	7	17	24	22	8	10	4
2 22 31	8	18	25	22	48	11	5
2 26 25	9	19	25	23	28	12	6
2 30 20	10	20	26	24	8	12	7
2 34 16	11	21	27	24	48	13	8
2 38 13	12	22	28	25	28	14	9
2 42 10	13	23	29	26	8	15	10
2 46 8	14	24	29	26	49	15	10
2 50 7	15	25	♌	27	29	16	11
2 54 7	16	26	1	28	10	17	12
2 58 7	17	27	2	28	51	18	13
3 2 8	18	28	2	29	32	19	14
3 6 9	19	29	3	0♍	13	19	15
3 10 12	20	29	4	0	54	20	16
3 14 15	21	♋	5	1	35	21	16
3 18 19	22	1	5	2	17	22	17
3 22 23	23	2	6	2	59	23	19
3 26 29	24	3	7	3	41	23	20
3 30 35	25	4	8	4	23	24	21
3 34 41	26	5	9	5	5	25	22
3 38 49	27	6	10	5	47	26	22
3 42 57	28	7	10	6	29	27	23
3 47 6	29	8	11	7	12	27	24
3 51 15	30	9	12	7	55	28	25

Upper table — Block 3

Sidereal Time (H. M. S.)	10 ♊	11 ♋	12 ♌	Ascen ♍ °	Ascen '	2 ♍	3 ♎
3 51 15	0	9	12	7	55	28	25
3 55 25	1	10	13	8	37	29	26
3 59 36	2	11	13	9	20	♎	27
4 3 48	3	12	14	10	3	1	28
4 8 0	4	12	15	10	46	2	29
4 12 13	5	13	16	11	30	2	♏
4 16 26	6	14	17	12	13	3	1
4 20 40	7	15	18	12	56	4	2
4 24 55	8	16	18	13	40	5	3
4 29 10	9	17	19	14	24	6	4
4 33 26	10	18	20	15	8	7	5
4 37 42	11	19	21	15	52	7	6
4 41 59	12	20	21	16	36	8	7
4 46 16	13	21	22	17	20	9	8
4 50 34	14	22	23	18	4	10	9
4 54 52	15	23	24	18	48	11	9
4 59 10	16	24	25	19	32	12	10
5 3 29	17	24	26	20	17	12	11
5 7 49	18	25	26	21	1	13	12
5 12 9	19	26	27	21	46	14	13
5 16 29	20	27	28	22	31	15	14
5 20 49	21	28	29	23	16	16	15
5 25 9	22	29	♍	24	0	17	16
5 29 30	23	♌	1	24	45	18	17
5 33 51	24	1	1	25	30	18	18
5 38 12	25	2	2	26	15	19	19
5 42 34	26	3	3	27	0	20	20
5 46 55	27	4	4	27	45	21	21
5 51 17	28	5	5	28	30	22	21
5 55 38	29	6	6	29	15	23	22
6 0 0	30	7	7	30	0	23	23

Lower table — Block 1

Sidereal Time (H. M. S.)	10 ♋	11 ♌	12 ♍	Ascen ♎ °	Ascen '	2 ♎	3 ♏
6 0 0	0	7	0	0	0	23	23
6 4 22	1	8	7	0	45	24	24
6 8 43	2	9	8	1	30	25	25
6 13 5	3	9	9	2	15	26	26
6 17 26	4	10	10	3	0	27	27
6 21 48	5	11	11	3	45	28	28
6 26 9	6	12	12	4	30	29	29
6 30 30	7	13	12	5	15	29	♐
6 34 51	8	14	13	6	0	♏	1
6 39 11	9	15	14	6	44	1	2
6 43 31	10	16	15	7	29	2	3
6 47 51	11	17	16	8	14	3	4
6 52 11	12	18	17	8	59	4	5
6 56 31	13	19	18	9	43	4	6
7 0 50	14	20	18	10	27	5	6
7 5 8	15	21	19	11	11	6	7
7 9 26	16	22	20	11	56	7	8
7 13 44	17	23	21	12	40	8	9
7 18 1	18	24	22	13	24	8	10
7 22 18	19	24	23	14	8	9	11
7 26 34	20	25	23	14	52	10	12
7 30 50	21	26	24	15	36	11	13
7 35 5	22	27	25	16	20	12	14
7 39 20	23	28	26	17	4	13	15
7 43 34	24	29	27	17	48	13	16
7 47 47	25	♍	28	18	30	14	17
7 52 0	26	1	28	19	13	15	18
7 56 12	27	2	29	19	57	16	18
8 0 24	28	3	♎	20	40	17	19
8 4 35	29	4	1	21	23	17	20
8 8 45	30	5	2	22	5	18	21

Lower table — Block 2

Sidereal Time (H. M. S.)	10 ♌	11 ♍	12 ♎	Ascen ♎ °	Ascen '	2 ♏	3 ♐
8 8 45	0	5	2	22	5	18	21
8 12 54	1	6	2	22	48	19	22
8 17 3	2	7	3	23	30	20	23
8 21 11	3	8	4	24	13	20	24
8 25 19	4	8	5	24	55	21	25
8 29 26	5	9	6	25	37	22	26
8 33 31	6	10	7	26	19	23	27
8 37 37	7	11	7	27	1	24	28
8 41 41	8	12	8	27	43	25	29
8 45 45	9	13	9	28	25	25	♑
8 49 48	10	14	10	29	8	26	1
8 53 51	11	15	11	29	50	27	2
8 57 52	12	16	11	0♏	33	28	3
9 1 53	13	17	12	1	16	28	4
9 5 53	14	18	13	1	59	29	4
9 9 53	15	19	14	2	41	♐	5
9 13 52	16	19	15	3	23	1	6
9 17 50	17	20	15	4	6	1	7
9 21 47	18	21	16	4	48	2	8
9 25 44	19	22	17	5	30	3	9
9 29 40	20	23	18	6	12	4	10
9 33 35	21	24	18	6	54	5	11
9 37 29	22	25	19	7	36	5	12
9 41 23	23	26	20	8	18	6	13
9 45 16	24	27	21	8	59	7	14
9 49 9	25	27	21	9	41	8	16
9 53 1	26	28	22	10	23	8	17
9 56 52	27	29	23	11	4	9	18
10 0 43	28	♎	24	11	46	10	19
10 4 33	29	1	24	12	25	11	20
10 8 23	30	2	25	12	28	11	19

Lower table — Block 3

Sidereal Time (H. M. S.)	10 ♍	11 ♎	12 ♎	Ascen ♏ °	Ascen '	2 ♐	3 ♑
10 8 23	0	0	25	12	28	11	19
10 12 12	1	1	26	13	6	12	20
10 16 0	2	2	27	13	45	13	21
10 19 48	3	4	27	14	24	14	22
10 23 35	4	5	28	15	4	15	23
10 27 22	5	6	29	15	42	15	24
10 31 8	6	7	29	16	21	16	25
10 34 54	7	8	♏	17	0	17	26
10 38 40	8	9	1	17	39	18	27
10 42 25	9	10	2	18	17	18	28
10 46 9	10	11	2	18	55	19	29
10 49 53	11	11	3	19	34	20	♒
10 53 37	12	12	4	20	13	21	1
10 57 20	13	13	4	20	52	22	2
11 1 3	14	14	5	21	31	22	3
11 4 46	15	15	6	22	8	23	5
11 8 28	16	16	7	22	46	24	6
11 12 10	17	16	7	23	25	25	7
11 15 52	18	17	8	24	4	26	8
11 19 34	19	18	9	24	42	26	9
11 23 15	20	19	9	25	21	27	10
11 26 56	21	20	10	25	59	28	11
11 30 37	22	20	11	26	38	28	12
11 34 18	23	21	12	27	16	♑	13
11 37 58	24	22	12	27	54	1	14
11 41 39	25	23	13	28	33	1	15
11 45 19	26	24	14	29	11	2	16
11 49 0	27	25	14	29	50	3	17
11 52 40	28	26	15	0♐	30	4	18
11 56 20	29	26	16	1	9	5	20
12 0 0	30	0♏	16	2	0	6	21

TABLES OF HOUSES FOR LIVERPOOL, Latitude 53° 25' N.

Upper table

Block 1

Sidereal Time (H.M.S.)	10 ♎	11 ♎	12 ♏	Ascen ♐	2 ♑	3 ♒
12 0 0	0	27	16	1 48	6	21
12 3 40	1	28	17	2 27	7	22
12 7 20	2	29	18	3 6	8	23
12 11 0	3	♏	18	3 46	9	24
12 14 41	4	0	19	4 25	10	25
12 18 21	5	1	20	5 6	10	26
12 22 2	6	2	21	5 46	11	28
12 25 42	7	3	21	6 26	12	29
12 29 23	8	4	22	7 6	13	♓
12 33 4	9	4	23	7 46	14	1
12 36 45	10	5	24	8 27	15	2
12 40 26	11	6	24	9 8	16	3
12 44 8	12	7	25	9 49	17	5
12 47 50	13	8	26	10 30	18	6
12 51 32	14	9	26	11 12	19	7
12 55 14	15	9	27	11 54	20	8
12 58 57	16	10	28	12 36	21	10
13 2 40	17	11	28	13 19	22	11
13 6 23	18	12	29	14 2	23	12
13 10 7	19	13	♐	14 45	25	13
13 13 51	20	13	1	15 28	26	15
13 17 35	21	14	1	16 12	27	16
13 21 20	22	15	2	16 56	28	17
13 25 6	23	16	3	17 41	29	18
13 28 52	24	17	4	18 26	♒	19
13 32 38	25	17	4	19 11	1	21
13 36 25	26	18	5	19 57	3	22
13 40 12	27	19	6	20 44	4	23
13 44 0	28	20	7	21 31	5	24
13 47 48	29	21	7	22 18	6	26
13 51 37	30	21	8	23 6	8	27

Block 2

Sidereal Time (H.M.S.)	10 ♏	11 ♏	12 ♐	Ascen ♐	2 ♒	3 ♓
13 51 37	0	21	8	23 6	8	27
13 55 27	1	22	9	23 55	9	28
13 59 17	2	23	10	24 43	10	♈
14 3 8	3	24	10	25 33	12	1
14 6 59	4	25	11	26 23	13	2
14 10 51	5	26	12	27 14	15	4
14 14 44	6	26	13	28 6	16	5
14 18 37	7	27	13	28 59	18	6
14 22 31	8	28	14	29 52	19	8
14 26 25	9	29	15	0 ♑ 46	20	9
14 30 20	10	♐	16	1 41	22	10
14 34 16	11	1	16	2 36	23	11
14 38 13	12	2	18	3 33	25	13
14 42 10	13	2	18	4 30	26	14
14 46 8	14	3	19	5 29	28	16
14 50 16	15	4	20	6 29	29 ♓	17
14 54 7	16	5	21	7 30	♓	18
14 58 7	17	6	21	8 32	1	20
15 2 7	18	7	22	9 35	3	21
15 6 8	19	8	23	10 40	4	22
15 10 12	20	9	24	11 46	6	24
15 14 15	21	10	25	12 54	7	25
15 18 19	22	11	26	14 3	9	26
15 22 23	23	11	27	15 13	11	27
15 26 29	24	12	28	16 25	12	28
15 30 35	25	13	29	17 38	13	♈
15 34 41	26	14	♑	18 53	15	1
15 38 49	27	15	1	20 10	16	2
15 42 57	28	16	2	21 28	18	3
15 47 6	29	16	3	22 51	19	4
15 51 15	30	17	4	24 9	20	6

Block 3

Sidereal Time (H.M.S.)	10 ♐	11 ♐	12 ♑	Ascen ♑	2 ♓	3 ♉
15 51 15	0	17	4	24 15	26	7
15 55 25	1	18	5	25 41	28	8
15 59 36	2	19	6	27 10	♈	9
16 3 48	3	20	7	28 41	2	10
16 8 0	4	21	8	0 ♒ 14	4	12
16 12 13	5	22	9	1 50	5	13
16 16 26	6	23	10	3 30	7	14
16 20 40	7	24	11	5 13	9	15
16 24 55	8	25	12	6 58	11	17
16 29 10	9	26	13	8 46	13	18
16 33 26	10	27	14	10 38	15	19
16 37 42	11	28	15	12 32	17	20
16 41 59	12	29	16	14 31	19	22
16 46 16	13	♒	16	16 33	20	23
16 50 34	14	1	18	18 41	22	24
16 54 52	15	2	19	20 50	24	25
16 59 10	16	3	20	23 10	26	27
17 3 29	17	4	21	25 33	28	28
17 7 49	18	5	23	27 49	♉	♊
17 12 9	19	6	25	0 ♓ 2	2	1
17 16 29	20	7	26	2 37	3	1
17 20 49	21	8	28	5 10	5	3
17 25 9	22	9	29	7 39	6	4
17 29 30	23	10	♓	10 6	8	5
17 33 51	24	11	2	12 37	10	6
17 38 12	25	12	3	15 52	11	7
17 42 34	26	13	4	18 38	13	8
17 46 55	27	14	6	21 26	15	9
17 51 17	28	15	7	24 15	16	10
17 55 38	29	16	9	27 5	18	12
18 0 0	30	17	10	0 ♈ 13	19	13

Lower table

Block 4

Sidereal Time (H.M.S.)	10 ♑	11 ♑	12 ♒	Ascen ♈	2 ♉	3 ♊
18 0 0	0	17	11	0 19	9	19
18 4 22	1	18	12	2 52	21	14
18 8 43	2	20	14	5 43	23	15
18 13 5	3	21	15	8 33	24	16
18 17 26	4	22	17	11 22	25	17
18 21 48	5	23	19	14 8	27	18
18 26 9	6	24	20	16 53	28	19
18 30 30	7	25	22	19 36	♊	20
18 34 51	8	26	24	22 14	1	21
18 39 11	9	27	25	24 50	2	22
18 43 31	10	29	27	27 23	4	23
18 47 51	11	♒	28	29 52	5	24
18 52 11	12	1	♈	2 18	7	25
18 56 31	13	2	2	4 39	8	26
19 0 50	14	4	4	6 56	9	27
19 5 8	15	5	6	9 10	11	28
19 9 26	16	6	8	11 20	12	29
19 13 44	17	7	10	13 27	14	♋
19 18 1	18	8	11	15 29	15	1
19 22 18	19	9	13	17 28	17	2
19 26 34	20	11	15	19 22	18	3
19 30 50	21	12	17	21 14	19	4
19 35 5	22	13	19	23 2	21	5
19 39 20	23	15	21	24 47	23	6
19 43 34	24	16	23	26 30	24	7
19 47 47	25	17	25	28 10	25	8
19 52 0	26	18	26	29 46	26	9
19 56 12	27	20	28	1 ♊ 19	28	10
20 0 24	28	21	♈	2 50	29	11
20 4 35	29	22	2	4 19	♋	12
20 8 45	30	23	4	5 45	1	13

Block 5

Sidereal Time (H.M.S.)	10 ♒	11 ♒	12 ♈	Ascen ♊	2 ♊	3 ♋
20 8 45	0	23	4	5 45	26	8
20 12 54	1	25	6	7 9	27	9
20 17 3	2	26	8	8 27	29	10
20 21 11	3	27	9	9 49	♋	11
20 25 19	4	29	11	11 7	1	12
20 29 26	5	♓	13	12 23	2	13
20 33 31	6	1	15	13 37	3	13
20 37 37	7	3	17	14 49	4	14
20 41 41	8	4	19	15 59	5	15
20 45 45	9	5	20	17 8	6	16
20 49 48	10	7	22	18 15	6	17
20 53 51	11	8	24	19 21	7	18
20 57 52	12	10	25	20 25	8	19
21 1 53	13	11	27	21 27	9	20
21 5 53	14	12	♉	22 28	10	20
21 9 53	15	13	2	23 27	11	21
21 13 52	16	15	3	24 25	12	22
21 17 50	17	16	5	25 20	13	23
21 21 47	18	17	7	26 15	14	24
21 25 44	19	18	8	27 8	15	25
21 29 40	20	19	10	28 0	16	26
21 33 35	21	21	11	28 51	17	27
21 37 29	22	22	13	29 40	18	27
21 41 23	23	23	14	0 ♋ 30	18	28
21 45 16	24	24	16	1 17	20	29
21 49 9	25	25	18	2 4	20	♌
21 53 1	26	26	19	2 53	21	1
21 56 52	27	28	21	3 38	22	2
22 0 43	28	♈	22	4 23	23	3
22 4 33	29	1	24	5 8	24	3
22 8 23	30	2	25	5 54	25	4

Block 6

Sidereal Time (H.M.S.)	10 ♓	11 ♈	12 ♉	Ascen ♋	2 ♌	3 ♌
22 8 23	0	3	22	6 54	22	8
22 12 12	1	4	23	7 42	23	9
22 16 24	2	5	25	8 29	24	10
22 20 2	3	7	26	9 16	24	11
22 23 35	4	8	27	10 2	25	12
22 27 22	5	9	29	10 49	26	13
22 31 8	6	11	♊	11 34	27	13
22 34 54	7	12	1	12 18	28	14
22 38 40	8	13	3	13 2	28	15
22 42 25	9	14	3	13 45	29	16
22 46 9	10	16	4	14 32	♍	17
22 49 53	11	17	5	15 15	1	18
22 53 37	12	18	7	15 58	1	18
22 57 20	13	19	8	16 41	3	19
23 1 3	14	20	9	17 24	4	20
23 4 46	15	22	10	18 6	4	21
23 8 28	16	23	11	18 48	5	22
23 12 10	17	24	13	19 30	6	23
23 15 52	18	25	14	20 13	7	24
23 19 34	19	27	15	20 54	7	24
23 23 15	20	28	16	21 36	8	25
23 26 56	21	29	17	22 18	9	26
23 30 37	22	♉	18	23 0	10	27
23 34 18	23	1	18	23 42	11	28
23 37 58	24	2	19	24 23	12	29
23 41 39	25	4	20	25 4	13	♍
23 45 19	26	5	21	25 46	13	1
23 49 0	27	6	22	26 28	14	1
23 52 40	28	7	23	27 9	15	2
23 56 20	29	8	23	27 51	16	3
24 0 0	30	9	24	28 12	14	3

HINDU PLANETARY PERIODS

I. Sun's Period = 6 Years	Y.	M.	D.
☉	0	3	18
☽	0	6	0
♂	0	4	6
☊	0	10	24
♃	0	9	18
♄	0	11	12
☿	0	10	6
☋	0	4	6
♀	1	0	0

II. Moon's Period = 10 Years	Y.	M.	D.
☽	0	10	0
♂	0	7	0
☊	1	6	0
♃	1	4	0
♄	1	7	0
☿	1	5	0
☋	0	7	0
♀	1	8	0
☉	0	6	0

III. Mars' Period = 7 Years	Y.	M.	D.
♂	0	4	27
☊	1	0	18
♃	0	11	6
♄	1	1	9
☿	0	11	27
☋	0	4	27
♀	1	2	0
☉	0	4	6
☽	0	7	0

IV. Dragon's Head Period = 18 Years	Y.	M.	D.
☊	2	8	12
♃	2	4	24
♄	2	10	6
☿	2	6	18
☋	1	0	18
♀	3	0	0
☉	0	10	24
☽	1	6	0
♂	1	0	18

V. Jupiter's Period = 16 Years	Y.	M.	D.
♃	2	1	18
♄	2	6	12
☿	2	3	6
☋	0	11	6
♀	2	8	0
☉	0	9	18
☽	1	4	0
♂	0	11	6
☊	2	4	24

VI. Saturn's Period = 19 Years	Y.	M.	D.
♄	3	0	3
☿	2	8	9
☋	1	1	9
♀	3	2	0
☉	0	11	12
☽	1	7	0
♂	1	1	9
☊	2	10	6
♃	2	6	12

VII. Mercury's Period = 17 Years	Y.	M.	D.
☿	2	4	27
☋	0	11	27
♀	2	10	0
☉	0	10	6
☽	1	5	0
♂	0	11	27
☊	2	6	18
♃	2	3	6
♄	2	8	9

VIII. Dragon's Tail Period = 7 Years	Y.	M.	D.
☋	0	4	27
♀	1	2	0
☉	0	4	6
☽	0	7	0
♂	0	4	27
☊	1	0	18
♃	0	11	6
♄	1	1	9
☿	0	11	27

IX. Venus' Period = 20 Years	Y.	M.	D.
♀	3	4	0
☉	1	0	0
☽	1	8	0
♂	1	2	0
☊	3	0	0
♃	2	8	0
♄	3	2	0
☿	2	10	0
☋	1	2	0

SUPPLEMENT TO REVISED EDITION

THE PROGRESSIVE HOROSCOPE

UNDER this title it is the author's intention to add to the information already given in Chapter III on the system of Secondary Directions. It really does not matter whether we call these directions Secondary, Chaldean, Luni-Solar, or by any other name, providing we understand those directions which are formed by the Sun, Moon, and Planets among themselves, and to the radical or birth positions of the various bodies, by their motions in the heavens after birth. It is essential, however, that these directions should be properly calculated, and this is what may be safely claimed has never before been done in any of the published expositions of the system.

In order to support this statement, reference must be made to the specimen horoscope given on page 51 of this work. This figure contains the radical positions of the planets at the moment of birth.

Now, directions of the Sun and Moon to these positions will have the effect of bringing them into action for good or ill, according to the nature of the aspect formed to them by direction, as taught in the " Primary Considerations " on page 159. The nature of the event will be in harmony with the nature of the planet to which direction is made, and the sphere of life affected will be controlled by the House in which that planet may be.

But when we come to consider the practice of directing the Sun and Moon to the places of the planets in their progress after birth, it will be necessary to take into account the natural motion of the heavens during the interval that has elapsed since the moment of birth up to the moment when the direction is completed. This has not received due consideration in any work which has made " Progressive " or Secondary directions the subject of study. In fact, the places of the slower moving bodies, such as Pluto, Neptune, Uranus, and Saturn, as well as others when retrograde, are usually accounted to be the same both in the Radix and the Progress. Thus, if Neptune at birth were in Virgo 23° 27′ just before the cusp of the ninth house as in the figure on page 51, the direction of the Moon to the conjunction with Neptune ninth day after birth (corresponding to the tenth year of life) would be the same as the conjunction to its progressed place, and in practice there would be nothing to distinguish the effects of Moon conjunction Neptune R. and Moon conjunction Neptune P., since both are in Virgo, just before the ninth cusp. Similarly in the case of Moon to the aspect of Uranus, both the radical and progressed positions of that planet being in Taurus on the cusp of the fifth house, the effects are not distinguishable.

But in point of fact this is not the case. The positions are not the same, and the effects are different. The means of distinction is supplied by the proper method of calculating the progressed horoscope. The method is as follows:—

TO CALCULATE THE PROGRESSED HOROSCOPE

1. Count the number of days after birth corresponding to the number of years completed.

2. To the Sidereal Time at noon on that day apply the hour of birth, as instructed on page 47. This will give the Right Ascension of the Mid-heaven in the progressed horoscope, and by the Tables of Houses the horoscope can be erected.

3. The planets' places for the hour of birth on the day of the progress must be set in this figure, and it will then be found that a true astronomical figure, representing the places of the planets in regard to the place of birth a certain exact number of days after birth, is obtained.

All the planets (except such as are retrograde) will have increased their longitudes by their own proper motions in their orbits. But it will also be seen that nearly all the planets have changed their Houses since their last conjunction with the Moon. They have therefore changed their significance, at all events in regard to their progressed positions.

EXAMPLE

In the specimen horoscope, page 51, we may inquire concerning the directions of the 5th and 32nd years of life. Following the rule:—

1. Four days complete reaches to the 14th April 1940 at 1 a.m. G.M.T.

2. This is equivalent 13th at 13 hours past noon. Therefore—

	H.	M.	S.
To the Sidereal Time at Noon ..	1	26	5
Add	13	0	0
Correction for 13 hours ..	0	2	10
Progressed Right Ascension of M.C. ..	14	28	15
Deduct for West Longitude 2° ..		8	0
Right Ascension of Progressed Mid-heaven ..	14	20	15

With this R.A. we enter the Tables of Houses for latitude 52° 28′ N., and under the sign of the 10th house we find 7° 30′ of the sign Scorpio. Under the sign of the Ascendant we find 0° 38′ of the sign Capricorn. Thus we have the progressed Mid-heaven and the progressed Ascendant.

3. The planets' places are then placed into the map for 1 a.m. on the morning of April 14th 1940, and the figure for the progress is completed.

Now at the outset it will be seen that the Mid-heaven is separating from a sesquisquare of the radical position of Saturn and that the progressed Ascendant is separating from a sesquisquare of the radical Uranus and applying to a quincunx of the radical Pluto. The Moon by progression is passing through the seventh house of the map and the sign Cancer. Saturn is in the fourth house of the map and Uranus is near the fifth cusp. This combination would react upon the mental/emotional side of the child's nature in so far as a child of four years could respond to such vibrations, and could signify the experiencing by the mother, Saturn in the fourth house ruling the mother, of conditions of a worrying nature in connection with home and family affairs and in addition it could have shown a recent addition to the family in the shape of a brother or sister, Uranus being on the cusp of the fifth house ruling children, and Pluto being in the sign Leo which also rules children.

Now let us take the indications for the 32nd year of life. Thirty-one days after birth measures to the 11th May 1940 when the calculation is as follows:—

	H.	M.	S.
Sidereal Time at Noon on 10th..	3	12	32
Add time elapsed to hour of birth	13	0	0
Correction for 13 hours at 10 seconds per hour	0	2	10
	16	14	42
Deduct for 2° West Longitude ..		8	0
Right Ascension of Progressed Mid-heaven ..	16	6	42

This R.A. gives the Mid-heaven between the 3rd and 4th degrees of Sagittarius and the Ascendant approximately 1° of Aquarius. The progressed Mercury is found in the 8th degree of Taurus, having moved from near the cusp of the third house (its birth position) to about a third way through the fourth house. The progressed Venus is in the 3rd degree of Cancer, having moved from near the cusp of the sixth house at birth, to part way through the seventh house, whilst Mars in 26° of Gemini has moved through Gemini until just past the Descendant.

The progressed M.C. is applying to a sesquisquare of the radical Sun and a semi-square to the radical Moon's North Node showing an experiencing of troubles and difficulties in connection with vocational interests and warning against a possible loss of favour or support from those who are in higher positions connected with the actual work that is being done and with the social or public activities which are being carried out. The progressed Ascendant, just separating from the opposition of the radical Pluto would signify a degree of financial difficulty and warn against the taking of financial or speculative risks. Mercury would be in sesquisquare to the radical Neptune denoting a danger of encountering some form of intrigue or trickery and warning against an abuse of personal confidence whilst it would signify that the ensuing year would be unfavourable for long distance travel, for emigration or for anything of an overseas and foreign character. Venus makes no aspect by progression and therefore does not exercise any specific influence during the year and the same signification applies to Mars which also does not form any aspect by progression. Therefore the main significations for the 32nd year of life, covering the year as a whole would be taken from the progressed Aspects made by the Mid-heaven, Ascendant and Mercury.

It will therefore be seen that the influence of a lunar or solar direction to the progressed planets will fall in a different sphere of the native's life every time the same aspect is formed, while at the same time the lunar and solar directions to the radical places will have the effects due to their radical positions, as determined by their sign and House. Hence, although the major planets (and also the minor ones when retrograde) do not appreciably alter their longitudes in the course of a lunar revolution, the diurnal progress of the heavens will bring them successively from one House to the next, conversely; that is to say, from the ninth to the eighth, and from the eighth to the seventh, so that they will have successively different influences, and will affect different spheres of the life.

By the ordinary method of the fixed horoscope, the major planets which produce the greatest effects in the life will continue in the same House all through the life—Neptune, near the cusp of the ninth house, Saturn in the fourth house, Uranus on the fifth cusp, Jupiter in the third; effects will happen at every successive good or evil aspect to these planets, every five years bringing up the same influence of the same planet for good, and every seven years bringing up the same influence of the same planet for evil. This is not the case in point of fact, for the influence is gradually changing from one House to another. The Moon does not make a clean sweep of the possible influences of the major planets in a twenty-eight year cycle (28 days), and then return to the same sequence of events. It certainly returns to the same sequence of aspects to these major planets, but as they have all changed their houses by the progress the effects are altogether different.

The aspects formed by the progressed Ascendant and the progressed M.C. to the planets in the Radix and the Progress are to be accounted primary directions, and their effects are of the greatest importance.

Also planets coming to the cusps of Houses by the same Progress are of remarkable significance, according to the nature of the aspects they thus form in Mundo (see page 153, *Mundane Directions*).

The foregoing exposition of the progressed horoscope will supplement and modify the statement of the system already made in this book in regard to Secondary Directions contained in Chapter III. It will not be necessary to erect a series of figures for the successive years of life, but it will suffice for ordinary practice if the Mid-heaven and Ascendant in the Progress are set out in the scale of Primary Directions referred to on page 154. By reference to the Tables of Houses for the latitude of the birthplace, it will at once be seen in what houses the progressed positions of the planets will fall.

The test of this system is made by the directions to the progressed M.C. and Ascendant; for if there were no truth in it, directions to these points would have no influence at all, neither would the transits of the planets over these points be in any way significant, whereas the effects are of the most appreciable nature and altogether convincing.

THE LUNAR EQUIVALENT

The Lunar Equivalent is an extension of the progressed horoscope, in terms of the natural motion of the heavens as seen from the place of birth. We have already shown that each complete day after birth marks a year of life, and that during the revolution of the earth on its axis each day the Sun gains one degree (roughly), throwing the Mid-heaven forward at the same rate, and bringing the Ascendant by oblique ascension to the horizon at a variable rate, as shown by the Tables of Houses.

But there is yet another aspect of this subject which has not hitherto been explained, and which is of considerable importance. It is the Lunar Equivalent, constituting a change in the progressed Mid-heaven and progressed Ascendant corresponding to lunar motion. As one day equals one year, two hours will equal one month, and four minutes will equal one day. Taking any *progressed* horoscope, set for the hour of birth, we have a figure which represents an exact number of solar revolutions round the earth by apparent diurnal motion in the heavens. Thus in the case already cited, at thirty-one days after birth the Mid-heaven is in R.A. 16 hours 6 minutes 42 seconds. At thirty-two years complete it will be in R.A. 16 hours 10 minutes 39 seconds. But the Sun and Mid-heaven do not make one degree of the Zodiac *per saltum*, but gradually, from hour to hour, as the Earth revolves upon its axis while the Sun is moving forward in the Zodiac.

		H.	M.	S.
Consequently, at 31 years 1 month the Mid-heaven will be in R.A.		16	6	42
Plus		2	0	0
Increment for 2 hours				20
R.A. of M.C. for 31 years 1 month		18	7	2

For each successive month a further two hours and the increment for equation will be added to the progressed Mid-heaven, while the Moon and planets are moving forward in the Zodiac. Consequently, at the end of one complete revolution of the Sun round the Earth, the Mid-heaven will have gained twenty-four hours, plus the equation for twenty-four hours (as determined by the Sun's motion in the Zodiac), amounting to about four minutes, which will give the progressed Mid-heaven for the next birthday anniversary, as experiment will show. At the end of this time the Moon will have progressed 13 degrees 22 minutes, that being its diurnal motion for one day between the 11th and 12th May, 1940.

By this method a further series of positions will be obtained for the progressed planets, and the Moon will come into aspect with these planets at different points in their diurnal revolution round the Earth, these points falling in different Houses.

ILLUSTRATION

If we calculate the time of the Moon to the conjunction with Saturn, we shall find that it meets it at 2.50 p.m. on the 26th day after birth, *viz.*, on 6th May, 1940. Thus:—

Saturn's longitude at noon	Taurus	5°	53′	
Moon's longitude at noon	„	4°	27′	
	Difference	1°	26′, log. 1.2239	
Moon's motion in 24 hours	12° 16′			
Saturn's motion in 24 hours	7′			
	12° 9′		log. 0.2956	
Time p.m. of the Conjunction 2 hours 50 minutes			log. 0.9283	

This time is 13 hours 50 minutes after the hour of birth, corresponding to the end of the seventh month after the thirty-first birthday.

								H.	M.	S.
To the R.A. of progressed Mid-heaven	..	..	..	..	16	6	42
Add time elapsed	..	..	..	..	..	..	..	13	50	0
Correction..	..	..	..	..	..	..	..		2	18
								29	59	0
Deduct, as over 24 hours	..	..	..	..	..	..	24	0	0
Lunar Equivalent in R.A. of Mid-heaven	..	..	..	..	5	59	0

Turning to the Tables of the Houses for latitude 52° 28′ N., we shall find that with this Mid-heaven the conjunction will fall in the eighth house. This enables us to add point to the particular influences at work from the conjunction of the Moon with Saturn. Similarly with all other cases. Therefore in preparing the table of lunar aspects as on page 158, it will be advisable to make a separate column of the progressed Mid-heaven, and by reference to the Tables of Houses we can then at once see where the aspect actually falls in the heavens at the time of its exact formation.

THE DIURNAL HOROSCOPE

This horoscope is set for the time of birth on every successive day of the year, and gives many valuable keys for exact prediction. It is based upon the apparent motion of the Sun round the Earth from day to day, each day being completed when the Sun returns to the same distance from the meridian as it held at birth. And since the Sidereal Time is controlled by the Sun's motion in its apparent orbit, it follows that to erect a figure for each successive day of the year at the hour of the birth will be equivalent to taking a diurnal revolution in right ascension.

By means of this horoscope we are often able to fix the *exact date* of an event which is only defined by the methods hitherto considered as likely to happen within a given month.

By means of this diurnal horoscope, knowing of the sickness of Queen Victoria, the exact date of the demise was accurately predicted some time before the event. Also the date of King Edward's decumbiture on the eve of his coronation.

It will simplify explanation if the native is considered to be re-born every day at the same moment of time as at birth, and the horoscope set for this time will be the diurnal horoscope ruling that day of the life.

As may be surmised from the nature of this horoscope, the ephemeral positions of the planets play an important part in the nature of the events predicted from this source.

Observe, therefore, the following rules:—

1. Those days on which the malefic planets—Neptune, Uranus, Saturn, and Mars—are in transit over the meridian or ascendant of the diurnal horoscope are evil in their import; and also those on which the Sun, Moon, and Mercury, when in evil aspect to other bodies, pass these points of the diurnal horoscope.

2. Those days on which the radical places of the malefics (*i.e.*, their places at birth), pass the angles of the diurnal horoscope, are evil, and also the Sun, Moon, and Mercury when radically afflicted.

3. But the transits of Jupiter and Venus, when not afflicted, or the Sun, Moon, and Mercury when well aspected (either in the ephemeris or the radix), are uniformly good.

4. The daily aspects formed by the Moon must be taken in regard to the Houses occupied by the planets aspected. Thus, if the Moon forms a conjunction with Neptune in the second House of the diurnal horoscope, it will indicate danger of being defrauded of money on that day. At the same time the Moon may have a good aspect of Jupiter in the eleventh House, and the advice of a friend will be a corrective.

5. The chief effects are due to the transits over the angles of the diurnal horoscope. Next, the conjunctions that are formed by the major planets with the Sun, next to the mutual aspects and conjunctions of the planets, and lastly to the aspects formed by the Moon to the planets in the ephemeris.

6. The place of the new Moon in the diurnal horoscope is important, as it shows in what sphere of the life *changes* may take place during the month, good or bad according to the aspects to the luminaries.

The basis of all these considerations must always be those directions which are in force at the time, for the diurnal horoscope acts in terms of the prevailing influences, bringing them into operation at those dates when the Diurnal indications are in harmony with the directions.

Note on the Planetary Periods

In review of the information given on page 171, it has been possible to further examine the mean periods of the planets, and the following notes will doubtless be of service to the student.

Taking the mean motion of each planet in its orbit, and applying it to the Sun's mean motion for an equal period, we are able to obtain the mean synodical periods of the various bodies or the times in which they will form their conjunctions with the Sun on the same day of the year. Instead of the periods given on page 171, the following are offered as more approximate to the truth:—

Neptune, 164 years 280 days, mean annual motion 2° 10′ 54″.

Uranus, 84 years gives an advance in longitude of 40′ only.

Saturn, 59 years gives an advance of 1° 53′.

Jupiter, has a period of exactly 83 years.

Mars, 79 years gives an advance of 1° 34′.

Venus, 8 years gives a mean advance of 1° 32′, but inconstant.

Mercury, 79 years gives a mean advance of 1° 27′, but irregular.

To make use of these periods, the following general paradigm may be followed:—

Required the longitude of Uranus for the 15th October 1672 (New Style).
Given Ephemeris for 1902
Subtract 1672

Difference 230 divided by 84 gives 2 periods, plus 62 years.
1902 minus 62 years gives 1840, and 2 periods multiplied by 40′ gives 1.20.
From the longitude of Uranus of the 15th October 1840, Pisces   17.09
Subtract   1.20

Longitude of Uranus on the 15th October, 1672 (N.S.) Pisces   15.49

Required the longitude of Mars for 17th January 1905
Given the ephemeris for 1801

$$79 \text{ years})\ 104\ (1 \text{ period}$$
$$\underline{79}$$
$$25$$
Epoch 1801

Mars' longitude 17th January 1826 is Scorpio 0·21
To which add for 1 period 1·34

Mars' longitude 17th January 1905 will be Scorpio 1°55'

Any number of periods can be thus dealt with, by taking any epoch, subtracting it from the year required if the latter be after the epoch, or taking the required year from the epoch if the former be before the epoch; then dividing the period of the planet into the remainder, we shall have a certain number of periods and odd years. The periods will be multiplied by the mean advance of the planet in one period, and the years when applied to the epoch will give the year in which the longitude of the planet is to be sought on the required date. To this is applied the increment for the mean advance in the given periods, and the approximate longitude of the planet is obtained for the required date.

Note.—To convert Old Style into New Style, for the purpose of this calculation, *add* to the Old Style the following number of days:—

For the 20th Century, 13 days	For the 10th Century, 5 days
„ 19th „ 12 „	„ 9th „ 4 „
„ 18th „ 11 „	„ 8th „ 4 „
„ 17th „ 11 „	„ 7th „ 3 „
„ 16th „ 10 „	„ 6th „ 2 „
„ 15th „ 9 „	„ 5th „ 1 „
„ 14th „ 8 „	„ 4th „ 1 „
„ 13th „ 7 „	„ 3rd „ 0 „
„ 12th „ 7 „	„ 2nd subtract 1 „
„ 11th „ 6	„ 1st „ 1 „